POPULAR RELIGION, ELITES AND REFORM: HOOK-SWINGING AND ITS PROHIBITION IN COLONIAL INDIA, 1800-1894

SOME ADMINISTRATVE DIVISIONS IN INDIA - 1857

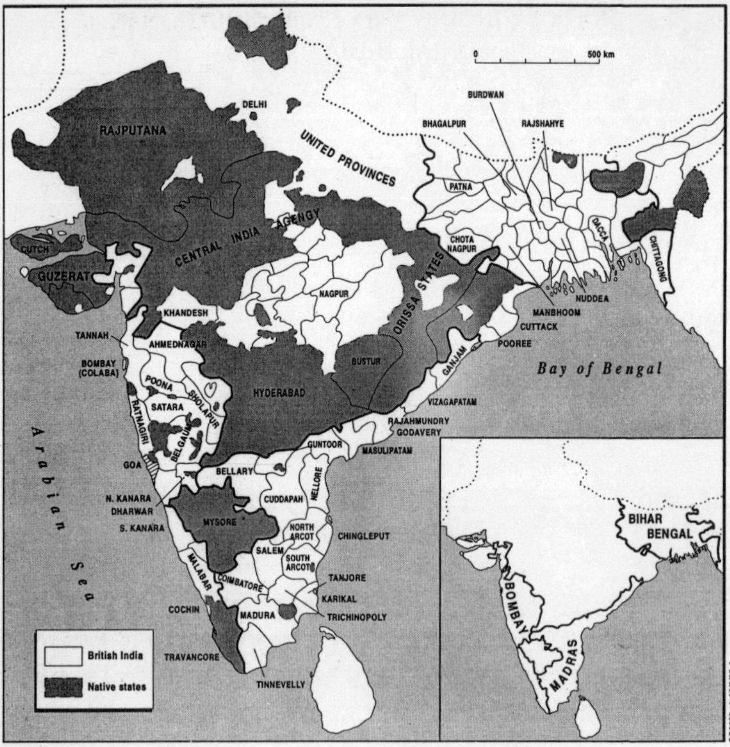

POPULAR RELIGION, ELITES AND REFORM: HOOK-SWINGING AND ITS PROHIBITION IN COLONIAL INDIA, 1800-1894

Geoffrey A. Oddie

MANOHAR
1995

ISBN 81-7304-101-6

First Published 1995

Published by
Ajay Kumar Jain
Manohar Publishers & Distributors
2/6, Ansari Road, Daryaganj
New Delhi - 110002

Lasertypeset by
A J Software Publishing Co. Pvt. Ltd.
305, Durga Chambers,
1333, D.B. Gupta Road,
Karol Bagh, New Delhi - 110005

Printed at
Rajkamal Electric Press
G.T. Karnal Road
Delhi

Preface

Since this manuscript was sent to press the debate over "European knowledge" of India has if anything gained momentum and continues to rage at conferences and in learned books and journals.

It might be noted that there are some scholars who appear to question the idea that the past ever existed as an independent objective reality separate and apart from the commentator. Hence in their view it is pointless for historians ever to attempt to "rediscover" what is for these critics a "non-existent past". It will be obvious that this author is still so "traditional" and "hidebound" as not to share this undoubted "truth". He remains the pathetic victim of illusion—a misguided exponent of the outmoded belief that it is still worthwhile trying to discover *something* about an objective past and about how "others" thought and felt and why they behaved in the way they did.

There are other scholars who may not question the possibility of knowing something of the past, but who virtually dismiss in one fell swoop the possibility that Europeans could know much or even something of the Indian "other". However, even though many accounts of hook-swinging in particular appear in European sources (and in the Portuguese and British colonial context) the author is equally stubborn and naive in adhering to a long held conviction that these sources cannot be dismissed out of hand—that they are not all equally worthless as sources of knowledge of "the other" and that they were often compiled by people with very different agendas and who had very different points of view. Indeed he (the author) has even gone so far as to argue elsewhere (*South Asia,* Vol.17, No. 2 December 1994) that missionary interests and objectives were, for example, not necessarily the same as those of administrators and that even the missionaries as a group differed among themselves. And what may also appear surprising is the author's basic view that European forms of representation are not only varied but need to be assessed critically so as to discover whether one European account is likely to be *more accurate* than another.

Then there is the inconvenience of Indian accounts of social and religious practice. Perhaps we could have adopted the view that anyone who agreed with "European" descriptions of the practice was already "colonized" in mind and spirit and that (in spite of theories of autonomy or "agency") the better educated Indian commentators were little more than clones, empty cymbals who *always and without exception* reverberated with the same noise as their colonial masters! But then what do we do with the comments of those who swung, some of the poor, such as those interviewed in Trichinopoly in 1894? The author should perhaps feel further remorse for not going along with the obvious answer that you can never hear the voice of the poor or glimpse anything of their world when it is mediated through the reports and words of others.

Lastly, there is another slight problem about European sources. How far can they be regarded as a distinct form of "*knowledge*" separate from Indian sources of information? Once again the author can be accused of flying in the face of obvious "truth" when he suggests that European accounts were not always purely European, and that in many cases involving descriptions and estimates of the extent of hook-swinging, European district officers, missionaries and others were influenced by Indian informers and were basing their reports on Indian knowledge of the ritual. (See a further reference to this point on p. 9).

But perhaps, after all, there are few scholars quite as dismissive of European accounts as the author implies and we have taken up too much space in tilting at paper tigers.

Another development which has taken place since the manuscript was sent to press is that the author has obtained further evidence that hook-swinging, or modified forms of the ritual, is still performed in different parts of India. He has met several people, including two French anthropologists, Gilles Tarabout of École Française D'Extrême Orient, Paris, and Marine Carrin Tambs-Lyche of the Centre d' Anthropologie, Toulouse, who have attended hook-swinging festivals. Tambs-Lyche was present during a performance of the rite among the Santals and Tarabout has written an account of his visit to a festival in Tamilnadu near the border with Kerala where a Malayali version of hook-swinging, known in Malayalam as *tūkkaṃ*, took place. Tarabout's account is especially significant as it also confirms the argument that hook-swinging did not always involve the celebrant swinging "round" or in "rotation". Tarabout points out that "the word [*tūkkaṃ*] means 'suspension', but also 'hanging, weighing'. These last two meanings are confirmed by a number of derivatives: *tūkkakkōl* ('tukkam rod') denotes a pair of scales; *tūkkumaraṃ* ('hanging tree'), is a gallows: *tūkkaccāṭu* is both a 'tukkam platform' (...) and a 'gibbet'." (See Gilles Tarabout, "Sacrifier et donner à voir en pays Malabar," *Publications de L'École Française D'Extrême - Orient*, Volume CXLVII, Paris 1986, p. 262).

Finally, a word about the term "popular religion" which appears in the title. It is not intended to suggest that the book is about the religion of the masses as *opposed* to the religion of the brahmans or dominant classes in the Hindu population. Rather the term is used to describe "a world view" including presuppositions, beliefs and practice which these two categories of people shared in common. Here one might mention beliefs in a divine hierarchy, pollution and purity, the efficacy of pilgrimage and other forms of ritual activity which some of the upper as well as lower caste Hindus felt were necessary forms of action or propitiation. Popular religion was therefore "popular" in the sense that it was not only widespread, especially among the lower orders, but also encompassed forms of thought and practice, such as hook-swinging, which influenced and "carried weight", with Hindus higher up the social scale.

I wish to express my gratitude to the University of Sydney for financial assistance in facilitating research and travel overseas, and also to Oxford University Press, Delhi, for permission to reproduce material which appears in chapter five. On a more personal level I would like to thank especially Virginia Macleod, my untiring and ever helpful research assistant, Devleena Ghose for the translation of Bengali texts, Jaya Thuraisingham and Jill Collier for typing and many others for their encouragement, advice and assistance. These include Rosemary Keen, former archivist of the Church Missionary Society, London, Richard Bingle of the India Office Library and Records, Ian Raeside, Polly O'Hanlon, Tony Disney (for introducing me to the literature on the American Indian sun dance rituals) and V.R. Mitragotri of Panaji, Goa. Finally, I would like to express my very special thanks to Nola, my wife, for her unselfishness, untiring patience and support and for the many ways in which she has helped me in preparing the manuscript for publication.

February 1995 Geoffrey A. Oddie

Contents

Introduction

Acts of penance, self-discipline and mortification are aspects of religious practice apparent in all the major religions of the world. Penitents within the Christian tradition have gone to extraordinary lengths to achieve their purpose through self-inflicted punishments such as wearing hair-shirts. scourging, and crawling long distances on hands and knees. In Islam, Shia Muslims may be seen during the month of Muharram commemorating the martyrdom of Husayn, whipping their bodies with cords until the blood flows, and in Jainism, extreme acts of self-mortification leading to debilitation and death have long been a feature of their ascetic tradition.[1]

As is well known, Hindus have also practised 'austerities' and severe forms of bodily punishment. One of these forms was hook-swinging — a custom that was quite common among the lower classes in India in the nineteenth century. The ritual can be very briefly described as a practice involving suspension of the body on hooks and some kind of movement which may increase pain or stress, such as the act of being swung in rotation, bounced or simply lifted or lowered several times in succession.

One of the aims of this study is to analyse the custom as it was practised in India in the nineteenth century. However, any attempt to understand the process in the nineteenth century involves some discussion of the rite's evolution, and of the trends and developments in an earlier period as well.

Evans-Pritchard and others have questioned the anthropologist's earlier enthusiasm for explaining origins.[2] They point, quite correctly, to the futility of speculation about something for which there is no evidence. But while this criticism might well apply to any discussion of the origin of hook-swinging, about which there is no evidence, attempting to discuss origins is not the same thing as considering aspects of the ritual's subsequent development, traces of which one can reasonably argue were still apparent in nineteenth century practice.

It is one of the arguments of this book that, in order to understand the custom as it was practised in the nineteenth century (and prior to attempts at suppression by colonial authorities), it is essential to try to unravel something of its pre-nineteenth century past and to see how it fits in with India's overall cultural and religious evolution. In this connection I have argued that the rite as practised in Bengal, or in areas under Bengali influence, was rooted in a somewhat different tradition from hook-swinging elsewhere: that in the former, it was most closely connected with ideas about the merits of pain and suffering and, in the latter, with notions about the efficacy of blood sacrifice.

The second part of the book is concerned primarily with the development of European and Western-educated Indian attitudes towards the custom. The growth of European and missionary criticism, some pressure (not always consistent) from the India Office in London and, even more importantly, the growth of widespread Western-educated Indian opinion strongly opposed to the practice were factors which prompted official enquiries and local government attempts to suppress the practice in British India from the 1850s onwards. It is suggested that the important part played by the increasingly articulate Western-educated elites in this process is reflected especially in the Bengal and Madras Presidencies, where the most effective measures against hook-swinging were adopted after the rebellion of 1857. This was in spite of the Queen's Proclamation and promise of 'religious neutrality', and in spite of general anxiety among Europeans that interference in socio-religious customs would increase discontent and the possibility of further uprisings against British rule.

Before discussing the custom as it appeared in nineteenth century British India, something might be said about its continued practice to the present day among Indians in Sri Lanka, and about possible parallels with the ritual in societies elsewhere.

Outside India, the rite is still permitted and practised by Hindus and others at Kataragama — a remote site in south-eastern Sri Lanka. Every year thousands of pilgrims flock to the site of Skanda, or Subramanyam (the second son of Siva) also identified with the Tamil god, Murukan, and perform various acts of penance or self-torture, usually in fulfilment of vows made on some other occasion. According to one recent account:

> . . . the god is thought to be pleased by acts which humiliate or

> mortify the self; Hindus may be seen rolling about the shrine on the ground, carrying the *kāvaṭi*,[3] with hundreds of tiny arrows pierced through their flesh, or hanging from gantries by hooks passed through their shoulders and thighs.[4]

In another account of the festival published in 1966 Paul Wirz described the swinging as follows:

> The most intensive self-torture that I ever saw consisted . . . of the penitent letting himself be hanged by eight hooks on a tall scaffold. It was made of iron poles, fixed in the shape of two triangles, one placed on top of the other so as to form the diagram of Skanda. Four hooks were driven into the thigh, two into the buttocks and two further into the back. The scaffold itself was fixed on a small wagon, on which the hanging penitent was carted from temple to temple.[5]

The hook-swinging at Kataragama was until recently confined to Tamils. However, according to Gananath Obeyesekere, who has done considerable field work in the area, it is now practised by Buddhists who have come increasingly to argue that Skanda is a Buddhist and not a Hindu deity.[6] Obeyesekere has not only discussed the general trend among Buddhists to practise what were formerly regarded as Hindu rituals but, in a monograph published in 1981, incorporates details of interviews with two 'hook-hangers' — one of them a Buddhist woman who had hung on hooks on four separate occasions.[7]

Outside India and apart from those examples of hook-swinging derived from India and introduced by Indian migrant communities,[8] the closest parallel to the ritual was probably the practice of self-torture in tribal sun dance ceremonies among the North American Indians in the nineteenth century. Greater public awareness of these ceremonies, as they existed among the Sioux, was created by the release in 1970 of the film *A Man Called Horse*. The film's depiction of the rituals, including the hero's ordeal in being raised, suspended and spun on hooks, was partly based on the artist George Catlin's illustrated account published in 1844.[9] Although Catlin's commentary and illustrations were, at the time, dismissed as being 'fantastic' and a product of that gentlemen's 'fertile' imagination, subsequent research has validated many of the details of his account and has also revealed that sun dance ceremonies, including acts of self-torture, were practised by nearly a score of Plains Indian tribes in the nineteenth century.[10] Not all of those forms of torture involved suspension on hooks. However, in Catlin's account the young men were suspended by 'splints passed through their flesh' and were then spun around 'faster and faster' until they fainted.[11]

Catlin's testimony and subsequent studies have not only shown that American Indian tribes practised self-torture through suspension on hooks, but have also revealed other parallels with the Indian custom. For example, the rite was performed in the context of major religious ceremonies and was in some instances undertaken as a result of a vow to the deity in a period of personal crisis or distress;[12] and, as in India, the vow and subsequent ritual appear to have been based on the assumption that the god or 'great spirit' could be influenced or manipulated and would be pleased with acts of self-mortification (Figure 2).

However, despite these and possibly other parallels between the Indian Hindu and the North American Indian practice, there were also differences. In India the celebrant was invariably suspended, whereas American Indians were not infrequently 'tethered' to a pole which they faced, leaning backwards and 'dancing' until the hooks came out. In some parts of India, the ritual was enacted partly or entirely for the benefit of the village or wider community; whereas in the American case the role of the individual is in dispute, some scholars arguing that the torture was entirely unconnected with the performance of ceremonies for the welfare or prosperity of the community as a whole.[13] Also different were the classes involved. While in India it was most frequently the people drawn from among the marginal classes who performed the ritual, the more powerful and important people, such as chiefs or potential leaders of tribal society, were more conspicuous in performing the rite in America. Furthermore, in India hook-swinging was, especially when associated with force or compulsion, a socially divisive issue, whereas in America the self-torture appears to have had no such effect.

The earliest known eyewitness account of hook-swinging in India was by a Portuguese traveller, Duarte Barbosa, in the early sixteenth century. Describing the marriage customs among the people in the interior of the Malabar coast (possibly present-day Karnataka), he wrote:

Figure 1: *One of the earliest sketches of hook-swinging*: Thomas Bowrey's illustration of 'a barbarous penalty', which appears to show a woman showering petals on the crowd below.

Source: Thomas Bowrey, *A Geographical Account of the Countries Round the Bay of Bengal*, 1669-1679 (first published 1905), Cambridge, p. 12.

> There are amongst them young girls who desire to marry some man for whom they have a liking, and one of these will promise her idol to do it a great service if she should marry such a one whom she wishes for. And if she marries that one, she then says to him, I have to make a feast for such a god, and I have to offer my blood before I deliver myself to you. And so they appoint a day for celebrating that feast. And she takes a large waggon with oxen, and they fix it in a very high crane, such as those with which they draw water, and they fasten it to an iron chain with two iron hooks, and she comes out of her house with great honour, accompanied by all her relations and friends, men and women, with much singing and playing of instruments, and many dancers and jesters; and she comes wrapped very tightly round the waist with her white stuffs, covered from the waist to the knees, the rest bare, and at the door of her house, where the car stands, they lower the crane, and stick the two hooks into her loins between the skin and the flesh, and put into her left hand a small round shield, and a little bag with lemons and oranges. They then raise the crane with great shouting and sound of instruments, firing guns, and making

Figure 2. *Catlin's illustration of the sun dance torture ceremony among Sioux Indians in 1844.* Votaries were hung by rawhide thongs tied to skewers run through the flesh, and then spun.

Source: George Catlin, *Letters and Notes on the North American Indians* (first published 1844), New York, 1975.

> other festal demonstrations: and in this manner the car begins its march on the way to the house of the idol to which the promise was made; and she goes suspended by those hooks fastened into her flesh, and the blood runs down her legs. And she continues to sing and shout for joy, and to strike upon the shield, and to throw oranges and lemons to her husband and to her relations, who go with her in this manner to the door of the said house of prayer, where they take her down, and cure her, and deliver her to her husband; and she gives at that place great alms to the Brahmans and offerings to the idols, and a great feast to as many as accompanied her.[14]

This account was followed by the publication of an increasing number of descriptions of the practice by other European observers — adventurers, traders, missionaries and the like who travelled or lived in India from the early sixteenth to the end of the eighteenth century. Compared with the nineteenth century European reports and commentaries, which were almost uniformly hostile, they reflect a more varied response.

Some writers described the custom in a relatively detached and objective manner, saying nothing about how they felt. Among these were the Portuguese travellers, Gaspero Balbi and Pietro Della Valle, who witnessed hook-swinging exhibitions in 1582 and 1623 respectively.[15] The Frenchman, Sonnerat, who described the rite as practised on the Malabar coast in the eighteenth century, also refrained from personal comment.[16]

Others, however, made little attempt to hide their feelings, whether these were of surprise or amusement or, like later observers, shock and outrage at what they witnessed.

The French Protestant traveller, Tavernier, was surprised, almost impressed, with the way in which healing took place after the body had been cut and pierced with hooks. Describing the custom whereby a great number of 'poor people' hung themselves upon hooks at Malda in Bengal he remarked:

> It is a surprising thing not to see a drop of blood come from this cut flesh, and not to see a sign of it even on the hook, and in two days they are entirely cured by the drugs which the Brahmans give them.[17]

Others were more inclined to view the ceremony as a 'curiosity' or (like some Indian spectators of the nineteenth century) as a source of entertainment. Duarte Barbosa who, as we have seen, was one of the first Europeans to witness the spectacle, seems to have regarded it as a 'marvel' and Edward Moor, who drew attention to the prevalence of the practice among the Marathas in Eastern India in 1794, found it 'very singular', 'curious' and even amusing:

> If any records of these circumstances are kept in the swinging villages, with the causes of swinging, they would, doubtless, make a curious figure in a European dress; for we have heard of a number of causes assigned for the ceremony, that would furnish almost as diverting an essay as the well-known story of the lover's leap, if worked up by so humorous a hand.[18]

Yet alongside these observations were others, written at least as early as the seventeenth century, which reflected very different feelings. These were reactions of moral concern and even repugnance — a type of response which was much in evidence among British observers, and which, strengthened by the Evangelical revival, came to dominate British attitudes towards the practice in the nineteenth century. The English free trade adventurers, Thomas Bowrey and Alexander Hamilton, for example, both believed that hook-swinging was the result of priestly machinations.[19] For Bowrey, it was 'a Sort of Cruel Penants [Figure 1] and for Hamilton, it was not only a 'trick that the priests yearly put upon the people', but also 'a farce'. Even the comparatively broad minded Alexander Dow, who, when writing in his *History of Hindustan*, published in 1768, claimed that travellers had been 'unfair' in their comments on the Hindu system of religion and philosophy, was less sympathetic when it came to describing the antics of the 'vulgar', including swinging, which he characterised as a 'ridiculous' custom.[20] This was indeed a severe stricture coming from someone who, like so many of his contemporaries in the eighteenth century, placed a high value on 'reason' and 'rationality'. Furthermore, it was the same type of criticism which reappeared in Evangelical and Indian comments on the practice in the nineteenth century — criticism which described the ritual as 'absurd' or not worthy of rational human beings.

Finally, what of the sources available for the nineteenth century? Though European attitudes towards hook-swinging in the nineteenth century were even more uniformly hostile than those of previous periods, the British made much greater and more sustained attempts to understand the extent and nature of the custom during that period — even if it was only in order to eliminate the practice. There were five official enquiries which produced a considerable amount of evidence — two of them being conducted through British officers in Bengal, two in Madras and one in Bombay. In addition to these reports and other official material that was based on information partly supplied by Indian subordinates and prominent leaders in Hindu society, there was a considerable amount of Protestant missionary comment. This includes some detailed eyewitness accounts, the historical value of which varies considerably, depending on such factors as the missionary's familiarity with the local language and customs in general and the extent to which observers made enquiries and attempted to check the accuracy of whatever they saw and heard.

Press reports and comments in English and the vernacular are an additional and valuable source of information. This is especially so with regard to trends and developments in 'public' opinion, including the controversies and changing views of the increasingly articulate Western-educated elites.

These and other materials were largely a product of the British and the dominant classes within Indian society. They, therefore, provide the historian with an excellent understanding of what the elites and dominant classes reported and thought about the ritual. But what of the views and feelings of the swingers themselves, most of whom came from the depressed or subordinate classes and were illiterate?

Reports of statements and comments, usually in response to questions put to them, are scattered through much of the material and can be found in government and missionary records and also in press reports of incidents in various parts of the country. Some of the more revealing documents in this connection are the sworn depositions of swingers and relatives of those involved in swinging in Trichinopoly in 1894.[21] Furthermore, even if unable to write, 'the celebrant', relatives and allies were not necessarily incapable of organising petitions to the Government. Some of these were, for example, sent to the authorities in Madras after the attempted suppression of the practice in the 1850s. Comment on comparatively recent though isolated instances of hook-swinging in India,[22] and a report by the anthropologist Gananath Obeyesekere on interviews with hook-swingers at Kataragama[23] have also provided valuable insights, not only into the psychology and attitude of the participants, but also into questions of trance-like states and the sensations and feelings of the people performing the ritual.

Last, but not least, is a mass of evidence about what swingers actually did — how they appeared and behaved, before, during and after the swinging exhibition. Here the historian is involved in 'reading the signs', and in drawing inferences from the context and details of what was happening in order to understand the attitude the possible motivation of the swingers involved. Especially significant are the accounts of the extent to which swingers were prepared by rituals before they swung, how they were dressed and what they took with them, how they behaved while being swung or suspended, the reaction of spectators, and how the performers appeared and acted on being lowered and released.

Not unrelated to this information are illustrations and photographs which provide visual evidence of the swinger's appearance and behaviour as well as of other details connected with swinging. Among the illustrations were paintings by Tamil and European artists, and drawings, including lithographs — some of the latter probably based on photographs which gradually came into vogue after the invention of photography in 1839. As will be seen from the reproductions included in the text, this material is a valuable additional source of information. It not only throws further light on what swingers looked like, how they acted and the variety of ways of swinging, but also provides the reader with a better understanding of the ambience and general context in which the ritual was performed — information which was often omitted from written descriptions of the practice.

NOTES

1. See, for example, S. Settar, *Inviting Death. Historical Experiments on Sepulchral Hill*, Dharwad, 1986.
2. E. E. Evans-Pritchard, *Theories of Primitive Religion*, Oxford University Press (paperback), 1965, pp. 101-2.
3. The *kavati* is an arch decorated with peacock feathers which the devotee places over the shoulder and carries while dancing. It represents the 'peacock vehicle' of the god. It is, therefore, the vehicle in which the god resides and which has rested on the shoulders of the

devotee. [G. Obeyesekere, 'The Firewalkers of Kataragama: The Rise of Bhakti Religiosity in Buddhist Sri Lanka', *JAS*, Vol. XXVII, No. 3, May 1978, p. 464.]

4. B. Pfaffenberger, 'The Kataragama Pilgrimage: Hindu-Buddhist Interaction and Its Significance in Sri Lanka's Polyethnic Social System', *JAS*, Vol. XXXVIII, No. 2, Feb. 1979, p. 266.
5. P. Wirz, *Kataragama: The Holiest Place in Ceylon*, trans. from the German by Doris Berta Pralle, Colombo, 1972, p. 44.
6. Obeyesekere, 'The Firewalkers. . ., p. 457.
7. G. Obeyesekere, *Medusa's Hair. An Essay on Personal Symbols and Religious Experience*, Chicago and London, 1981.
8. On the origin of the Kataragama festival, see, Obeyesekere, 'The Firewalkers ...', p. 459.
9. George Catlin, *Letters and Notes on the North American Indians*, edited with an introduction by Michael Macdonald Mooney in one volume, New York, 1975.
10. J.C. Ewers, 'Self-torture in the Blood Indian Sun Dance', *JWAS*, Vol. 38, No. 5, May 15, 1948, pp. 66-173.
11. Catlin, pp. 194-200; 'The common mode' was, according to Spier, 'tethering or suspending dancers' from the centre pole. See, L. Spier, 'The Sun Dance of the Plains Indians: Its Development and Diffusion', *Anthropological Papers of the American Museum of Natural History*, Vol. XVI, 1921, p. 474.
12. Spier, p. 461; Ewers, pp. 167-8; Clark Wissler, 'The Sun Dance of the Blackfoot Indians', *APAMNH*, Vol. XVI, Part II, 1918, p. 263.
13. Ewers, p.172.
14. Duarte Barbosa, *A Description of the Coasts of East Africa and Malabar in the Beginning of the Sixteenth Century*, trans. by the Hon. H.E.J. Stanley, Hakluyt Society, Vol. XXXV, London, 1866, pp. 95-6.
15. 'Gaspero Balbi's Voyage to Pegu', in J. Pinkerton, *A General Collection of the Best and Most Interesting Voyages and Travels in all Parts of the World* (17 Vols.), Vol. IX, London, 1811, p. 398; and *The Travels of Pietro Della Valle in India*, Hakluyt Society, Series II, Vol.II, London, 1892, p. 259.
16. As quoted in E. Thurston, *Ethnographic Notes in Southern India*, Madras, 1906, p. 490.
17. W. Crooke (ed.), *Travels in India by Jean-Baptiste Tavernier* (first Indian edn.), Delhi, 1977, Vol. II, pp. 198-9.
18. Edward Moor, *A Narrative of the Operations of Captain Little's Detachment*. . . London, 1794, pp. 412-13.
19. Thomas Bowrey, *A Geographical Account of Countries round the Bay of Bengal 1669 to 1679*, Hakluyt Society, Series II, No. XII, Cambridge, 1905, pp. 197-9; 'Hamilton's Account of the East Indies', in *Pinkerton*, Vol. VIII, pp. 360-1.

20. P.J. Marshall (ed.), *The British Discovery of Hinduism in the Eighteenth Century*, Cambridge, 1970, pp. 108, 118-19.
21. IOR P/4621 MJP, 24/9/1894.
22. D.D. Kosambi, 'Living Prehistory in India', *SA*, Feb. 1967, pp. 109-14.
23. *Medusa's Hair*, pp. 124-49.

CHAPTER I

General Features and Regional Variations

One typical nineteenth century account of hook-swinging and of the apparatus used was penned by Dr Alexander Duff in 1840 — ten years after his arrival in Calcutta. Describing the swinging at the annual *charak puja*, he wrote:

> An upright pole, twenty or thirty feet in height, is planted in the ground. Across the top of it, moving freely on a pin or pivot, is placed horizontally another long pole. From one end of this traverse beam is a rope suspended, with two hooks affixed to it. To the other extremity is fastened another rope, which hangs loosely towards the ground. The devotee comes forward, and prostrates himself in the dust. The hooks are then run through the fleshy parts of his back, near the shoulders. A party, holding the rope at the other side, immediately begins to run round with considerable velocity.[1]

By this means, according to Duff, 'the wretched dupe of superstition' was hoisted aloft into the air and 'violently' whirled round and round until the swinging was stopped and the man lowered and released (Figure 3).

All other available accounts referring specifically to the apparatus used in hook-swinging mention the upright pole and the horizontal cross-beam with ropes and hooks at one end and ropes at the other. But it is also apparent from these descriptions that there were important variations in detail — especially in the way in which the ritual was performed in southern and western India.

While in Bengal the swinging was round a pole fixed in the ground, in some other parts of the sub-continent, where temple culture was more pervasive, the swinging was conducted from or around a pole fixed on a platform on the back of a temple cart. The

Figure 3. *Swinging at charak puja, Calcutta* — an illustration in Regional Heber, *Narrative of a Journey through the Upper Provinces of India*, Vol. 1, 3rd edn, London, 1828. Note the use of the *cummerbund* or waistband, which was a common feature of swinging in Lower Bengal.

whole apparatus could be moved and the devotee was kept suspended in the air while the cart was dragged along, bumping its way around the temple (Figures 4 and 5).

This second method of swinging was described by the Rev. Noyes, an American missionary stationed at Kambam in the Madura district of the Madras Presidency. In his account of hook-swinging at a festival he attended in 1868, he remarked that the machine consisted of

> . . . a four-wheeled platform car, in the centre of which is an upright post, 20 or 30 feet high, and upon the top of it a traverse beam, 40 feet long, fitted to work like a well-sweep, and also to be swung around in a circle. Upon one end of this beam, the hooks already inserted in the man's back are fastened by strong ropes. Long ropes are also attached to the other end, by means of which several men manage its motions. The victim is first swung around

in a circle, and then raised high in the air, while the multitudes below fill the air with their shouting. In going up he favours himself by catching hold of the rope with his hands, but pretty soon lets go, and is suspended by the hooks inserted in his back, being bent almost double, his head and feet hanging, and the muscles of his back being pulled out to their utmost tension. While he is hanging in this position, the car is drawn by hundreds of men, over rough ground, around the temple, the man being shaken and tossed from side to side by the motion of the car. It was a full hour, by my watch, that I saw the man thus suspended.[2]

In these and most other accounts of swinging, the ritual involved was what one writer has called 'suspension on hooks and *rotation*'. However, there are well-recorded instances where the swinger was never swung in a circle and where the ritual might best be described as 'hook-hanging'.

Information on this point is derived from a number of very detailed eyewitness reports of the practice in south India.

Figure 4. *Swinging from a car before Paidamma, the tutelary goddess of Peddana, near Masulipatam, December 26, 1844.*

Source: The Church Missionary Gleaner, 1850-51, p. 19.

Figure 5. *Sketch of the car used in the swinging at Sholavandan, near Madura, in 1891.*

> This car was made of timbers, was about fifteen feet square and was supported by four wheels. Projecting from the centre of the car was a large timber, the top of which rose up about twenty feet high from the ground. The top of this timber acted as a pivot for a pole about sixty feet long. This pole was spliced in the middle and where spliced rested on the point of the timber.

Source: IOR P/4247, Van Allen to Second-class Magistrate, Madura Taluk (6/2/1892).

The Rev. J.E. Sharkey (CMS), who visited the festival at Weyoor in Masulipatam district on two separate occasions, made it quite clear that the process there did not include rotation of the body.[3] He described in detail the sequence and different phases in the ritual — the insertion of the hooks, the raising of the beam, the suspension of the man in the air as the temple cart was drawn around and the final act whereby the beam was lowered and the man released. He also notes that the man who swung was followed by three more who went through the same preparation, 'but with this difference', that 'each was raised and lowered and set free — all in two seconds'. What is conspicuous in these accounts is the absence of any mention of the men being swung around. Indeed, final confirmation of the fact that there was no rotation of the body involved in the ritual at Weyoor came some time later when Sharkey, reporting on a hook-swinging exhibition at Rajahmundry, noted that, '*unlike the swinging at Weyoor*',[4] the swinger at Rajahmundry was 'swung round the perpendicular pole of the machine'.[5]

Further evidence of the absence of rotation in some hook-swinging rituals in the south is derived from two other detailed accounts — one by a doctor who described with particular care hook-swinging in Madura in January 1892,[6] and the other, a lengthy article entitled 'The Hook-Swinging Ceremony as I Saw It' by the Rev. J. Knowles (LMS) after a visit to a festival at Kollangodu in Travancore in about 1897.[7]

These descriptions again make no mention of the individual being swung in a rotary fashion. Furthermore, Knowles also supplied photographs of the apparatus. These emphasise his point that the machine was something like a 'giant see-saw' and that the fundamental movement involved was not one of rotation, but of raising and lowering the man or woman at the end of the plank. One photograph in particular makes it clear that the cross-piece which was 'placed through the hole in the piece of timber on the top of the upright frame', could not have been used to rotate the swinger without splitting the wood and destroying the frame which was designed to keep the cross-beam in place.

The drawing of a distinction between swinging involving rotation of the body and swinging that was essentially 'hook-hanging' is especially necessary in view of the fact that two scholars, Powell and Irwin, have constructed theories of the origin of hook-swinging based on the assumption that one of its essential characteristics was 'rotation'. Powell argues that the rotary movement was derived from a time when human victims were spun round during the *Meriah* sacrifice,[8] while Irwin argues that hook-swinging is 'a common misnomer for the solar rite properly called *cakra puja*, literally "the wheel form of (sun) worship"'.[9] In defence of this latter view Irwin cites the Chinese Buddhist traveller Hsúan-Tsang who noted that, when the sun is setting, ascetics climb the pole, and 'clinging on to the pillar with one hand and one foot they wonderfully hold themselves stretched out with one foot and one arm; and so they keep themselves stretched out in the air with their eyes fixed on the sun, and their heads turning with it to the right as it sets'.[10]

Quite apart from the fact that neither of these scholars has established a direct connection between the rotation they describe and hook-swinging at a later period, the theories, as already mentioned, assume that rotation was an essential feature of the process. It has already been shown that there were forms of the ritual that did not involve rotation of the body. Furthermore, where rotation was common or the usual practice (as in Bengal) this can be quite simply explained as one form of movement which was likely to increase pain and stress (mortification of the body) and which was therefore all the more acceptable to the deity. That rotation was not an essential part of the custom is further borne out by the words used to describe the practice in Marathi and Tamil. Powell, Irwin, and possibly other scholars may have been unduly influenced by the fact that the Sanskrit, Hindi and Bengali terms associate hook-swinging with the wheel. Powell for example, notes that the Hindusṭani *charak* means 'wheel' or something that revolves, and that the literal translation of *charak puja* would perhaps be the 'wheel form of worship', or 'revolving ceremony'.[11]

However, swinging in western and southern India did not take place at the *charak puja* and the terms used for hook-swinging in some of the other languages were quite unconnected with the idea of a wheel. For example, there were several different terms for the ritual in Marathi. One of these was *gul tozena*[12] or *gul tosena*, which according to Dr Ian Raeside is obviously *gaḷ ṭocaṇeṃ*, 'to pierce the hook'.[13] According to the Indian Deputy Magistrate of Ahmednagar, who referred to other Marathi terms, 'the ceremony is called in native language Bagad and is of two kinds, the one is distinguished by the name Bhin Bagad or swinging on the ground, and the other by that of Gadi Bagad or swinging in a cart'.[14] *Bagad* can also be spelled *baghat* and probably means 'a frame'.[15] Furthermore, the word for hook-swinging in Tamil was transliterated variously as *cheddle*, *chedul* or *cheddal* and has the literal or direct meaning of 'needle'. The crucial point, at least in the case of the Marathi and Tamil terms, is that they do not suggest the idea of rotation and cannot be used as evidence that rotation was an essential and necessary part of the ritual. As we have seen, the terms used for the process vary. Some of them imply the idea of a wheel or rotation, others do not.

Irrespective of the question of rotation there are other mechanical aspects of the ritual which varied and which require further explanation — especially as they relate to issues about the intention, character and effects of the practice.

Of the two main forms of swinging, from a pole set in the ground, or from a gantry constructed on the back of a temple cart, the former was the most developed in its variations; and this, as we shall argue, was not unconnected with the trend, apparent especially in Calcutta, of encouraging hook-swinging as a public spectacle (Figure 6). One of these variations is illustrated in Figure 7, which is Atkinson's painting of what was known as *ghat charak.* The difference between this and the more usual form of swinging from a post sunk in the ground was that there were *two* beams instead of *one* placed across the top — thus enabling three or even four persons to swing at once.[16] This, however, was not the end of ingenuity. An even larger and more complex structure was the *radha chakra,* which was described in an article in the *Calcutta Christian Observer* published in 1837:

> On the top of the high post is placed a board protruding all over with sharp nails, over which a man stretches himself at full length. Below this, fixed in an horizontal position to the same post, is an immense wheel with *eight* spokes, at the end of each of which a man is suspended by iron hooks. Again, under this, there is a smaller wheel with four spokes, to which a corresponding number of persons are fastened; and the whole of this machine. . . is made to whirl with inconceivable rapidity.[17]

Lastly, there were also variations in the way in which the hooks, *usually* two in number, were used. They were made of iron or steel and were described by various European observers from time to time (Figure 8). For example, commenting on the hooks used in the ritual in Madras in the 1830s, the traveller Basil Hall remarked that they 'might be about the size of a small shark-hook, but without any barb; the thickness being rather less than a man's little finger'.[18] After the back had been prepared by 'thumping' to produce a slight swelling, by rubbing with oil, or in some other way, hooks were inserted in the manner illustrated in Figure 9. According to F. Van Allen, MD, the mission doctor who observed and described the operation as it was performed at Sholavandan in 1891, 'the two hooks were inserted into the skin and subcutaneous tissues, one on each side of the backbone and brought together back to back'.[19] In this, and in many other instances, the whole weight of the body was dependent on the hooks and the swinger or celebrant swung without any other support.[20] Once again, however, it appears that the practice varied and that in

Figure 6. *Variations on a theme — a sketch of swinging at the charak puja,* Calcutta, in 1823 by Fanny Parks (1794-1875). She was an enthusiastic sketcher and author of *Wanderings of a Pilgrim in Search of the Picturesque during Four and twenty Years in the East,* London, 1850. Referring to the illustration, she wrote:

> Sentries from the Calcutta militia were stationed round the swings to keep off the crowd. The men on the mound at the foot of the second swing run round with the bamboo frame which is connected with the pole, at the summit of which are the cross bamboos. As they proceed, the four men above swing merrily on their hooks, scattering flowers and sweetmeats on the people, and repeating verses and portions of the shastras.

Source: *Wanderings of a Pilgrim*, p. 28.

Figure 7. *A European artist's impression of hook-swinging in Calcutta in 1831.* Painted by James Atkinson, formerly of the Bengal Medical Service, the picture shows how two beams could be placed across the post instead of one, thus enabling several persons to swing at once. While three men are swinging with hooks in their backs a fourth (on the left) stands ready to take his turn. The painting illustrates parts of a stanza in Atkinson's *The City of Palaces; A Fragment and other Poems,* published in Calcutta in 1824:

Lo! high aloft a frantic zealot swings
The iron in his body deep and fast,
Suspended by the sinewy back, he flings
His arms abroad revolving round the mast;
Dead to all pain: behold him gaily cast,
Oblations o'er the crowd, the fiends below
Whirl him more rapidly, till tired, at last,
The maddened wretch descends, full pleased to shew
The quivering flesh torn up, – the blood devoted flow.

Source: From the original contained in the India Office Library, London.

Figure 8. This is a hook identical with the one which the Rev. Knowles (CMS) took out of the devotee's back during a swinging festival at Kollangodu, Travancore in March, 1897. From a photo by George Newnes.

Source: J. Knowles 'The Hook-Swinging Ceremony as I Saw it,' *The World Wide Magazine*, Vol. III, April-Sept. 1899, p. 589.

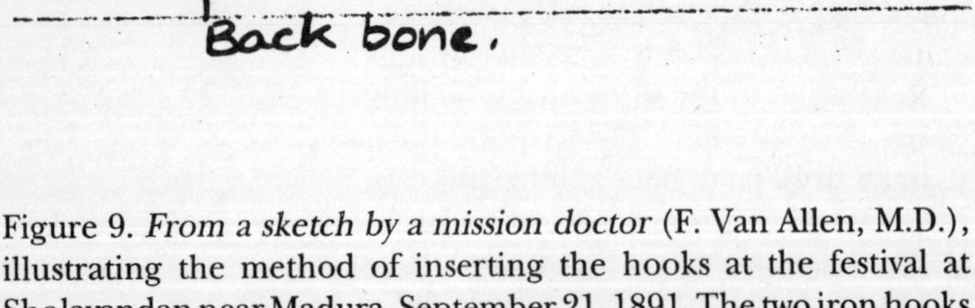

Figure 9. *From a sketch by a mission doctor* (F. Van Allen, M.D.), illustrating the method of inserting the hooks at the festival at Sholavandan near Madura, September 21, 1891. The two iron hooks were inserted 'into the skin and subcutaneous tissues, one on each side of the backbone and brought together back to back'.

Source: IOR P/4247.

the southern part of Bengal, parts of Bombay and elsewhere, the man or woman's body was also supported by a cloth or waistband (Figure 3).

For example, describing the practice in 1859 the Commissioner of the Dacca Division argued that the swinging was not especially dangerous 'for the party swinging is protected by a band passed round his body, which assists in supporting his weight, and would save him from falling to the ground in the event of the hooks tearing the flesh through'.[21] Much the same method was employed in the Burdwan sub-division of Lower Bengal where, according to an official report, 'the skin of the back and shoulders is pulled up from the flesh of the body, and the hook passed through the cuticle'. A strong cloth was then passed 'round the chest and body, and over the loop of the hook'.[22] Yet another variation in the way hooks were employed, but a method which does not appear to have been widely practised, was noted in the Nuddea Division of Lower Bengal. This was the practice, illustrated in Figure 13, of using canes as well as hooks to support the performer's body. The skin was pierced and the canes passed through, the swinger then being suspended by hooks passing through the latter.[23]

If these comprised the technological and mechanical aspects of swinging, where was it practised and how popular was it when surveys were conducted in about the middle of the nineteenth century?

If one looks at a map of Bengal and north-eastern India, it appears that hook-swinging there tended to radiate from Calcutta outwards. According to official reports,[24] the practice, which was usually performed during the *charak puja*, was well established in districts such as Burdwan, Nuddea. Rajshahye, Dacca and Chittagong, but was less prevalent in areas further away from the metropolitan centre. The extent of its popularity in those more distant parts depended at least in some degree on the presence of Bengalis and the extent of Bengali cultural influence.

Responding to official enquiries in 1856, H.D.N. Fergusson, Commissioner of the Patna Division in Bihar noted, for example, that 'the practice alluded to does not prevail among the people of Bihar generally, though occasional cases have occurred near large towns, when many Bengalees happened to be assembled at the time of the Churruck Poojah'.[25] The Commissioner of the Bhagalpur Division, also in Bihar, confessed that he had only recently been appointed, but that from what he had heard in Bhagalpur, hook-swinging was 'not so generally prevalent' in his division 'as in the districts nearer Calcutta'.[26] The Commissioner of the Chota Nagpur Division of Bihar on the south western border of Bengal proper also noted the greater popularity of hook-swinging in areas closer to Bengal. 'In the Gobindopore Sub-division and parts of Maunbhoom bordering on Bengal', he wrote, 'the ceremony has, I think, a much greater hold on the minds of the people than it has in other parts of the division'.[27] Finally, G.F. Cockburn, Commissioner of the Cuttack Division, in the Province of Orissa, wrote that while the practice of swinging at the *charak puja* prevailed 'generally' throughout the districts under his jurisdiction, this was, nevertheless, 'to a far less extent' than in districts in Bengal.[28]

Hook-swinging elsewhere, and outside what might be described as the Bengali zone of cultural influence, was spread very generally from the hills of central India southwards. It was prevalent among the Santals and Gonds of Central India[29] and was also practised throughout the Deccan and southern parts of the subcontinent. The Madras enquiry of 1853 showed that the custom was followed in all the Telugu-speaking and Tamil-speaking districts of the Presidency, though not in Malabar.[30] Missionary and other sources also indicate that the ritual was performed in princely states such as Hyderabad, Mysore, Cochin, Travancore and the French enclave of Karikal on the Coromandel coast.[31] The enquiries conducted in the Bombay Presidency in 1855 revealed that the custom was prevalent in all the districts south of the Narbada river (with the exception of Surat), namely Khandesh, Ahmednagar, Colaba, Poona, Satara, Sholapur, Ratnagiri, Belgaum and Dharwar.[32]

What is especially striking is the absence of the practice in the north and north-west of India — areas which roughly correspond with the older notion of Aryavarta. The Bengal Protestant missionaries who were especially interested in the practice and had contacts in many other parts of india declared in a petition to the Bengal Legislative Council that 'while these practices are common in Bengal. . . in the North-Western Provinces (the original cradle of Hinduism, and the primitive seat of its most ancient institutions), they are confined to the small Bengali communities'.[33] According to magistrates' reports, hook-swinging was unknown in Kaira, Broach, Surat and in most parts of Ahmedabad — the four northern Gujarati-speaking districts of Bombay Presidency.[34] Explaining the situation in Gujarat and in Ahmedabad in particular, J.S. Jardow, the Deputy

Magistrate, wrote as follows:

> . . .from enquiries I have instituted and from my own knowledge during residence in Guzerat since A.D. 1818, the practice of Swinging by the Hook (which operation is commonly known under the appellation of the "Gull") is not at all practised in any part of Guzerat excepting in the City of Baroda [in the Ahmedabad district] belonging to His Highness the Guicowar where there is a temple dedicated to the idol Khundoba and Bheroba the titulary deity of Mahratta, before whose shrine only the deluded pilgrims swing.[35]

Not only does there appear to have been no indigenous Gujarati word for the ritual,[36] but it was apparently unknown in Rajasthan.[37]

From a lingusitic point of view the custom was strongly entrenched among Bengali- and Oriya-speaking people of eastern India, among what were originally Munda- and Dravidian-speaking tribals, among Marathi speakers in western India and among those who spoke the four major Dravidian languages of the south, namely, Telugu, Kanada, Tamil and Malayalam. It was apparently not practised in Assam (among the north-eastern tribal groups)[38] and was not well known among Hindi speakers and some other groups whose languages derived from Sanskrit.

This very general picture of the distribution of the custom in about the middle of the nineteenth century still leaves unanswered questions about variations in the extent of the practice at the micro level and also about variations over time.

In the first place, hook-swinging was not equally popular in all districts or sub-divisions of British India where it was reported to prevail. In 1856, for example, district officers in the Bombay Presidency reported that swinging festivals were conducted in 37 villages in Colaba, 45 in Sholapur and 70 in Ratnagiri,[39] and there was also a considerable variation in the number of ceremonies organised in different districts within the Madras Presidency. According to the Madras reports of 1854, annual swinging festivals were conducted in 10 villages in Trichinopoly, 16 in Madura, 40 in Guntur, 48 in Masulipatam and 78 in Tanjore district.[40] Estimates of the number of swingers involved also varied. In the few cases where these were presented in official reports, they referred to districts in the Bombay Presidency — the estimate for the number of persons swinging annually in Thana being 106, for Poona 1,122 and for Ahmednagar 1,500 people.[41]

But also important were variations in the number of swingers from year to year. The extent and popularity of the practice was changing over time, and the overall situation in India in the mid-nineteenth century was clearly different from what it had been fifty or a hundred years before. In 1854 magistrates in the Madras Presidency were asked specifically to state 'whether the observance of it [hook-swinging] is less frequent and less attractive than formerly'.[42] While it appears from replies that in a few districts the practice was as prevalent as ever, in a majority of cases it was reported that the custom was on the decline. For example, the number of places where the ritual was performed in and around the Madras township had dropped from eight to two, and in Tanjore district from 125 'in former years', to 78 places in 1853.[43] The Magistrate of Masulipatam was even more specific, producing figures on the number of swingers who attended the annual festival at Weyoor over the previous 38-year period. These showed that the number of swingers had dropped from an average of 149 in the first ten years to an average of 37 in the previous eight.[44] District officers in the Bombay and Bengal Presidencies were not asked the same questions but, even so, two heads of divisions in the Lower Provinces, those of Dacca and Chota Nagpur, volunteered information that the ritual was declining in areas under their superintendence.[45]

While, therefore, official reports convey some idea of the extent and popularity of hook-swinging in the middle of the nineteenth century, it is important to recognise that the situation was far from static and that the information available does little more than provide us with a glimpse of a changing picture at a particular point in time. As we have noted, the evidence points to an overall and general decline in the practice — a reduction in the number of those performing the ritual which had begun long before the Presidency governments instituted enquiries with the intention of curbing or suppressing the custom.

The reasons for this decline, prior to government enquiries in the mid-nineteenth century, are not easy to ascertain. One factor may possibly have been economic. The ritual required funding for its continued operation and there are reports from at least two districts that the practice was being abandoned for economic reasons.[46] For example, the Magistrate of Masulipatam, reporting that the number of persons swung had 'generally decreased', explained that this was 'apparently more from the want of funds to encourage and recompense performers, than from the exhibition being less attractive than formerly'.[17] However, there is as yet insufficient evidence about whether these economic problems were a recurrence of endemic local difficulties or were part of a new trend reflecting a more general economic malaise.

Another factor affecting the performance of the ritual was concern about possible injury or death resulting from accidents. Referring to the way in which accidents acted as a deterrent, the magistrate of Colaba in the Bombay Presidency noted, for example, that 'only one fatal result is reported to have occurred about 15 years ago at Mahagaon in the Rajpooree Talooka by the death of the man Swuny, which being construed into a disapproval by the idol of the ceremony has tended to its discontinuance in that village since then'.[48] Accidents were, however, not new, and there is no reason to assume they had become more frequent than they had been in the past. What was new, or at least more effective, was the publicity and reporting of accidents as a result of the development of the English language and vernacular press. For example, the *Dnyanodaya*, the most important Marathi missionary periodical in western India and a Journal read by many Hindus,[49] repeatedly drew attention to accidents and deaths resulting from the practice.[50]

Furthermore, there was an increasing tendency for Europeans to interfere with the practice prior to the official surveys of the 1850s. Municipal authorities were among the first to respond to public pressure. Swinging on *charaks* was prohibited in certain streets and parts of Calcutta in the early nineteenth century,[51] while police intervention reduced the number of places where the ritual could be performed in Madras.[52] The Judge of Khandesh, in the Bombay Presidency, who first witnessed the ceremony in 1854, explained that such a performance would not be tolerated 'for an instant' in the Island of Bombay or in the town of Poona.[53] The custom was also banned in Patna in Bihar and was actively discouraged in the Santal Parganas and in some other parts of the mofussil in Lower Bengal.[54]

These attempts by local authorities to restrict places where the custom could be performed were reinforced by initiatives taken by European residents in a more private capacity. European indigo planters in the Nuddea Division of Lower Bengal did not permit swinging on their estates[55] and missionaries in many different parts of India were in the habit of preaching against the practice in front of *charaks*, or at festivals where hook-swinging was taking place.[56] On at least two of these occasions the missionaries' attempts to stop the practice led to violence and lengthy correspondence in the press.[57]

Last, but not least, the attitude and protests of the Western-educated Indian critics of the custom were, as we shall see, already beginning to have some effect on its patrons and others who began to reconsider their involvement.[58]

While the extent of the custom varied from place to place, there were also differences in both the frequency and dates of hook-swinging festivals in different parts of the country. In Bengal the swinging usually took place annually on about 11 April as part of the *charak puja*.[59] In some instances, however, it was delayed until a few days after, or was repeated at other times, for example, in December, in some of the more remote areas of the mofussil.[60]

In other parts of India, outside of what we have described as the Bengali sphere of influence, the frequency and timing of swinging was still more varied and less predictable. This was partly because it was connected with a very much wider range of deities, many of them of local or restricted influence.

Village festivals or *jatras* at which swinging took place were held in different localities at different times throughout the year.[61] In these circumstances the timing of the swinging depended on the cycle and timing of the local festival which might be held, for example, after the harvest or on some other occasion. In other instances, however, swinging festivals or exhibitions were arranged as separate events whenever sufficient resources were available and the need arose.[62]

Thus, while swinging exhibitions were usually conducted in Bengal and in parts of Bihar and Orissa in April, the timing was sometimes very different in other parts of the country. For example, in Masulipatam district 'generally' swinging took place at those festivals 'held about the full moons, from December to May'.[63] In the Thana district of the Bombay Presidency it was most popular in March/April and in Colaba, in the same Presidency, in April/May.[64] In Madura district in Madras Presidency, it appears to have been especially popular in June/July and in Tanjore district in August.[65]

The performance of the ritual was not necessarily an annual event. In some cases it was conducted only once in every three or four years or even at longer intervals.[66] In other instances, however, it was a more common occurrence, taking place twice or even more frequently throughout the year.[67] When that happened, the more frequent staging of the ritual was, in some cases, a reflection of the difficulties the village people were facing as a result of some type of calamity, such as famine or epidemic disease. The villagers, believing that their tutelary or guardian deity was angry and responsible for these events, conducted hook-swinging in order to placate the spirit, bring rain or prevent further sickness. Referring to the extent to which the rites were periodically performed in North Kanara in the 1860s, for example, the magistrate explained that this seemed to depend 'rather on the presence or absence of epidemic disease than on anything else'.[68]

Corporate calamity was, however, not the only cause for the spontaneous and unscheduled performances of hook-swinging. As we shall note, another reason for the timing and frequency of the practice was individual need — the need for some occasion (apart from annual festivals) when men and women could perform the act for personal or family reasons.

Regional variations

The general impression that one gains from a survey of all available data for the nineteenth century is that the ritual was much more deeply imbedded in the fabric and consciousness of society in areas outside Bengal than it was in Bengal itself. This is not only because, in Bengal and in areas under Bengali influence, the custom was largely restricted to the *charak puja* and the propitiation of one deity at one time of the year, but also because in other parts of India more classes and different sections of the population were involved.

In Lower Bengal the swinging was confined to the very lowest castes and classes in Hindu society. According to Ramkamal Sen, Native Secretary of the Asiatic Society, who presented a paper on the *charak puja* in 1829, the ceremonies were performed by 'the Sudra class only, and generally by the lowest castes and most dissipated characters'.[69] Other writers, such as the author of a series of articles on Hindu festivals in the *Calcutta Christian Observer*, remarked in a similar vein that 'Brahmans, Khettriyas and Vaishyas [the three highest castes of Bengali society] take no share in the festival except as spectators. The celebration of it is confined to Sudras, and even among them, only the very lowest classes take any part in it'.[70] William

Carey, the Baptist missionary, who with Ward and others witnessed the festival on frequent occasions in the neighbourhood of Serampore, was even more explicit, explaining that the swinging was 'only practised by the *hurry*, or lowest cast of Hindoos; who are hunters, bird-catchers, tanners, shoe-makers, etc. and are esteemed execrable by other casts'.[71] Especially conspicuous among those who swung, at least in Calcutta, were members of the *palki*-bearer caste — a widely distributed community whose occupation was carrying *palkis* (palanquins), baskets, water-skins, and other vessels.[72]

The social background of the *charaki* or swingers in other parts of Lower Bengal appears to have been much the same. Replying to the Government of Bengal's request for information in 1859, the Commissioner of the Nuddea Division, for example, stated that the parties who took the most pleasure in swinging were 'the lower Hindoo classes', while the Commissioner of Burdwan also noted the part played by 'Palkee bearers and others'.[73] In Rajshahye and Dacca in the east and in the Patna Division in Bihar in the west, the people who swung were also drawn from the lower classes.[74] The Commissioner of Chota Nagpur noted that those who swung were 'all people of an humble condition in life, and needy in circumstances'.[75] Lastly, in Orissa, where the *charak puja* was also celebrated, the Commissioner of the Cuttack Division noted that 'the more respectable' portion of the community took no part in the practice and that it was 'the lower castes only' who performed the swinging.[76]

In other parts of India outside Bengal and Bengali influence, performers included people of a more varied and higher social status. The ritual was often practised by the lowest castes and classes, but was by no means confined to them. For example, in the Tamil-speaking areas of Madras Presidency the men and women who swung included Kallars and Maravars,[77] some of whom owned land or were important in village administration. According to the author of *Cochin Castes and Tribes*, Nayars (high caste Sudras), Kammalans (carpenters, blacksmiths, etc), and Izhavars (palm cultivators and toddy-tappers) performed the ritual in Cochin state.[78] In Cuddapah, in the Telugu-speaking country, swinging was in vogue among Kapus (well-to-do farmers) and Balijas (cultivators and traders),[79] as well as among those who were described as 'the more ignorant and degraded people of the Sudra castes'.[80] Furthermore, evidence relating to the background of swingers in Bombay Presidency suggests that many of them, perhaps an even higher proportion than in Madras and others parts of the south, were drawn from among the middling or even the higher status communities. In Ahmednagar it was reported that the custom was followed by 'all the castes of the Hindoo community — except Brahman, Goozar-Marwadi and a few other high castes'.[81] Much the same information was provided in official reports on the situation in Colaba,[82] while the Magistrate of Belgaum, in the Bombay-Karnatak, explained that hook-swinging prevailed in his district 'among all Classes and Castes...except Brahmins and Mahomedans', and that it was estimated roughly that it was resorted to 'by rather more than half the population'.[83]

Some indication of the comparative wealth (and probable status) of not a few performers drawn from Belgaum and neighbouring districts is reflected in the level of fees that temple authorities were able to impose on pilgrims wishing to swing at Yellamma's Hill in Belgaum district in the first half of the nineteenth century. In 1834, 175 pilgrims paid Rs18 each for the privilege of swinging before the deity.[84] This was equivalent to at least 125 to 221 days of unskilled labour in the Belgaum district which, in 1853, was worth about 1.3 to 2.3 annas per diem.[85] For a skilled worker, ie. a carpenter, blacksmith or mason, it was equivalent to *at least* 72 days of labour at 4 annas a day.[86]

A comparison of swingers in Lower Bengal with those elsewhere in India not only suggests that a greater proportion of the latter were of higher social status, but that they also included a larger proportion of women.

In Bengal, swinging at the *charak puja* was normally an all-male affair,[87] the instances involving the swinging of women being sufficiently rare, and for William Ward, sufficiently shocking, to prompt him to make special mention of it in his well-known account of the *charak puja* in the early decades of the nineteenth century. Referring to the way in which some *sannyasis* had hooks run through their thighs as well as backs, he commented that in about the year 1800 'five *women* swung in this manner, with hooks through their backs and thighs, at Kidurpoor near Calcutta'.[88]

By way of contrast with this situation, it was not uncommon for women to swing in parts of Madras Presidency, for example, at Weyoor in the Masulipatam district.[89] However, by far the highest proportion of women among those who swung appears to have been in the Bombay Presidency. Those who swung in Ahmednagar district, according to both European and Indian officials, were 'chiefly females'.[90] In Khandesh, the custom was reported to have been followed 'generally by females',[91] and in Belgaum the proportion of women to men was estimated at two to one.[92]

A further difference between hook-swinging in Lower Bengal and other parts of India which emerges through an analysis of government, missionary and other accounts concerns motivation and purpose, issues which will be discussed more fully in a subsequent chapter.

In Bengal all available evidence suggests that the swinging was performed for the benefit of the individual, for relatives, or for the patron or landlord rather than for the benefit of the village community. In other parts of India, however, the ritual also had an important corporate or communal function. Reports from two districts in central India indicate that, among the Gonds, the *bhumka* or priest was swung on behalf of the people[93] and, describing the situation in one part of Bombay Presidency, one of the officials there referred to the practice whereby the priest continued to take the first swing himself.[94] But the swinging of priests or 'victims' on behalf of the village or inter-village community was perhaps even more common in Madras Presidency,[95] where the ritual was performed before guardian deities and where *inams* or special grants encouraged its regular performance.

A final major difference between the rite as performed in Bengal and in some other parts of India, specially Madras Presidency, is connected with notions of propitiation. As we shall argue in some detail in Chapter II, hook-swinging in Bengal and in areas under Bengali influence was strongly affected by the idea that pain and self-torture were pleasing to Siva; whereas in many other parts of the subcontinent swinging rituals seem to have been encouraged more by ancient ideas of blood offerings and human sacrifice, the ritual being more of a symbol or substitute for the offering of life itself.

Regional differences which emerge from a study of hook-swinging (especially differences between the practice in Bengal and elsewhere) should not, however, be permitted to divert attention from the importance of certain common and overriding characteristics.

One of these features was the low status of the great majority of those who performed the rite. In spite of what has been argued above, it is very clear that in western and southern, as-well-as in central India, a large proportion of those who swung were tribals or other poor, marginalised and oppressed people drawn from the lowest ranks of India's population. The reports of the magistrates in Bombay Presidency, *viz.* those of Khandesh, Thana, Poona, Satara, Ratnagiri and Dharwar[96] as well as the evidence of officials and missionaries in Madras Presidency all suggest that the ritual was most widespread among those who might be described as having a depressed class status, and that as a general rule the lower the status the more widespread the practice. Prominent among castes and communities who performed hook-swinging in the Bombay Presidency were the Kunbis (cultivators)[97] and Malis (gardeners)[98] as well as Mahars[99] and Mangs,[100] two major untouchable groups in the region, and also Bhils,[101] a large tribal community in the northwest. In Madras Presidency hook-swinging was performed not only by the aforementioned Kallar, Maravar, Kapu and Balija castes, but more often by lower status groups such as Pallis (or Vanniyans)[102] who were employed chiefly as agricultural labourers; Kuruvans,[103] a partially itinerant community of basket-makers, and untouchables, notably the Pallars[104] and especially Pariahs.[105]

The reason for the prevalence of the custom especially among the depressed classes (including tribals) is partly explained by their powerlessness (linked with their economic and social condition) as well as religious tradition and views of the world.

As will be noted in Chapter III, one important reason for swinging, particularly in Bengal, was compulsion — individuals who were drawn from the lowest ranks of society being pressed into service and compelled to swing for landlords and others who had much to gain from the patronage and perpetuation of hook-swinging exhibitions.

Another important factor was financial inducement. The poor, unemployed and needy adopted the practice as one way of gaining an income. Indeed, there is extensive evidence that many *charakis* in Lower Bengal, and some of those who swung in Madras Presidency, were paid to perform, or offered some other material inducement. In his account of the *charak puja* ceremonies, Ramkamal Sen remarked that the greatest number of people engaged in it 'as a lucrative exhibition',[106] and there are many other accounts of *sannyasis* in Calcutta and in other parts of Lower Bengal being hired for the occasion. Commenting on his visit to an exhibition in Calcutta in April 1838, the Rev. Wybrow (CMS) explained that he and his colleague (the Rev. Sandys) were 'astonished' at the man's endurance. After the swinging was over, the man approached them at their request and 'with great respect' presented his back, 'that I might look at and feel the wounds made by the two hooks'. Wybrow continued:

> His skin seemed to have acquired the toughness consistency of leather & the long series of scars on his back shewing how frequently during the course of years he had submitted to this penance. To my utter surprise when we asked him what could possibly induce him thus to torture himself, he replied that he was a poor man with three children & that he did these things in order to get 'kicher takee a little money' Why rejoined we what amount do you get, for the submission to this ceremony. They give he replied one rupee (2/-) among four of us for swinging.[107]

Referring to hook-swinging in Orissa, the Commissioner of the Cuttack Division noted two categories among those who swung: those who made a vow to swing and those who took part 'for the sake of the pice and crowries'.[108] Furthermore, officials in Bihar who responded to government enquiries in 1859 all stressed the importance of financial inducements.[109] In his report on the situation in Chota Nagpur, for example, the Commissioner remarked:

> I have lately had before me an individual who has on his back the marks of having swung some dozen times in as many years, receiving, he states, each year a Rupee and a cloth as recompense. The persons who swing are all people of an humble condition in life, and needy in circumstances, and the trifling present given them is considered by them sufficient to compensate them for the pain and inconvenience they undergo... I find that year after year the same people swing.[110]

The reports of officials and missionaries from western India, in contrast with those from Lower Bengal, seldom refer to swinging for financial reasons, the emphasis in their reports being on swinging in fulfilment of religious vows. In Madras Presidency the financial considerations were sometimes important, *inams* or government grants for the purpose making it possible for some village authorities to pay individuals to swing on behalf of the community . In the mid-nineteenth century *inams* in support of the ritual existed in many parts of the Presidency, *viz.* Guntur, Nellore, Cuddapah, Rajamundry and Ganjam in Telugu country and Madura, Chingleput and North Arcot in the Tamil-speaking regions.[111]

Rates of pay (whether the money was available through *inams* or from some other source) varied. According to the Magistrate of Masulipatam, *Vettiess* (minor government servants appointed to assist the village headman) or Pariahs of the village were the 'performers', and received between one and four rupees from a general fund subscribed by the villagers or granted for the purpose by some public-spirited individual.[112] At Weyoor, in the same district, it was customary for the village treasury to pay five rupees (or the equivalent of 40 days pay for an unskilled labourer) to any Pariah of the village who was willing to swing on behalf of the community;[113] while in the nearby village of Peddanah the man fulfilling a similar role was paid four rupees.[114]

In some cases the economic and financial rewards of performing the ritual were even greater. According to the Rev. Noyes, an American missionary who was present at a hook-swinging ceremony near Kambam in Madura district in 1865, the man who swung from the back of a platform car was 'presented to the people to receive their offerings, and receives large presents of money and lands — property such as he could not have accumulated by the labor of years'.[115] The Rev. John Chandler, who perhaps even more than Noyes made a study of the custom, also reported that for several months after a similar incident involving the swinging of a young man in the same district in 1891, he received money from the bazaar men and others by showing them the knife and hooks.[116]

As in Bengal, some individuals were paid to swing as proxies for higher caste and wealthier Hindus. In Masulipatam, for example, higher castes paid low caste proxies a sum between one and four rupees[117] (or the equivalent of between eight and 32 days pay for unskilled labourers in the district in 1859),[118] a sum which appears to have been somewhat higher than in Cuddapah where, in 1838, the going rate, according to one account, was no more than eight annas.[119]

Financial rewards for performing the ritual were, however, not the only 'worldly inducements'. Another consideration was enhanced reputation and status, especially within the family, among peers, or in the wider caste or tribal community or in the village. These status considerations are perhaps nowhere more clearly illustrated than in the *Madura Mail*'s account of the swinging ceremony at Sholavandan in Madura district in Madras Presidency in 1894:

> This year, the prize, rather, the privilege of swinging by the hook, has been won by the son of the Kavalgar of Sholavandan. It seems that there is a regular casting of lots among the Kavalgars and their sons, of the four villages — Thenkaral, Sholavandan, Mallipallum and Pettai — that is, it thus turns out that only four families of Kallars who are the Kavalgars of these four villages pretend to have the right to the exercise of this privilege.[120]

In his account of swinging at the *charak puja* in Bengal, Ramkamal Sen observed that those who swung engaged in it, not merely because it was lucrative, but 'from a desire to acquire a character for courage in the opinion of their friends'.[121] Like the American Indian sun dance, swinging was and could be seen as a feat of endurance. Some performers deliberately increased the pain and difficulty by carrying up weights, jerking while in the air, swinging from hooks in the shins, or by asking their helpers to continue the swinging after the usual third round.[122]

Describing 'exhibitionism' at the *charak puja*, William Ward wrote that some of the swingers:

> . . . take the wooden pipe, and smoak while swinging, as though insensible of the least pain. Others take up fruit in their hands, and either eat it or throw it among the crowd. I have heard of a person's having a monkey's collar run into his hinder parts, in which state the man and the monkey whirled round together. On one occasion, in the north of Bengal, a man took a large piece of wood in his mouth, and swung for a considerable time without any cloth round his body to preserve him, should the flesh on his back tear.[123]

This type of bravado, described by numerous witnesses throughout India, was not the only source of the swingers' increased reputation and status. In some cases, status was enhanced, wholly or in part, by the fact that the performer or celebrant was seen as enacting a spiritual drama and, in doing so, becoming possessed,[124] or at least imbued with something of the deity's power.

An attitude of reverence for swingers was not infrequently re-

Figure 10. *A painting of hook-swinging by a Tanjore artist of the mid-nineteenth century.* According to Sonnerat, who observed the practice on the Malabar coast in the eighteenth century, the swinger 'commonly has a sword and shield in his hands, and makes the motion of a man who is fighting'. On some occasions the performer was declared temporarily divine and, when brandishing sword and shield, may well have been representing Kali who fought the demon Darika. The latter was completely defeated, and the former, biting him on the back, drank his blood to gratify her feelings of animosity [see L.K. Anantha Krishna Iyer, *The Cochin Tribes and Castes,* Vol. 1, p. 324, Madras, 1909].

Source: IOR Addoc 679.

Figure 11. '*Devotees swinging from hooks penetrating the tendons of the legs*', Yellamma's Hill, Belgaum, Bombay Presidency, June 1828.

Source: The Missionary Magazine and Chronicle, No. XXXII, January 1839.

flected in what they wore. For example, the Rev. Mateer, who witnessed an exhibition in Travancore, wrote that when about to swing, the swinger's ears, neck and waist were 'adorned with golden ornaments, and a silver belt or chain'.[125] J.E. Sharkey remarked that the swinger's body was 'besmeared with turmeric and his person decked with jewels'.[126] In a swinging incident in Mysore the man was adorned with 'floral garlands'[127] and at Manargudi in Tanjore district he was 'covered with ornaments of bell and flowers'[128] (Figure 12).

Figure 12. *A hook-swinger, ritually dressed in silk breeches and garlanded with flowers.* From a photo taken in a secret location somewhere in Maharashtra in about 1966.

Source: D.D. Kosambi, 'Living Prehistory in India', *Scientific American*, February 1967, p. 111.

It was not only swingers who dressed like deities who were believed to be able to confer special blessings. One of the most common actions of performers while swinging was to shower the people below with flowers or fruit, symbols of blessing and fertility.[129] These objects were picked up or taken as 'very holy things', like the sweet-meats distributed by the *sati* shortly before she mounted her husband's funeral pyre.[130] The Rev. Thomas, a Baptist missionary in Bengal, remarked that 'whatever he [the *charaki*] throws down of fruit or the like, is caught up with great avidity, and counted sacred'.[131] Referring to the same practice of throwing flowers over spectators while swinging in south India, the Rev. Hoole noted that the people 'struggled to catch and preserve them, as though they had been blessings from heaven'.[132] According to Dr Joseph Little (WMMS), the flowers were, on another occasion, 'caught eagerly as relics of infinite value' and according to another account the people eagerly seized them as 'the most valuable treasures'.[133]

There can be no doubt that some individuals performed hook-swinging for financial and/or social reasons and that the custom gave some of them an opportunity to improve their standing among friends, within the family, or in the larger community. However, one of the reasons for this increased reputation or change in status was, as we have argued, due to the fact that the custom was regarded as a sacred ritual — the performer deriving status and sanctity from what he or she was perceived as doing at a spiritual level.

Thus, while it is possible that some swingers may have used the custom for their own particular purposes without any thought for its 'religious' dimension, the usefulness of the custom derived at least in part from the fact that some people regarded it as especially sacred and as an activity which gave them access to blessings or spiritual power. Furthermore, some of those who swung were, quite clearly, not interested in its financial benefits and were prepared to pay what were for them large sums of money in order to perform the rite. Hence, while on the one hand people were paid to swing, the opposite was also true — when in some cases the people themselves paid for the privilege of using the apparatus and of undergoing the ordeal. For example, writing in 1856, the Magistrate of Poona remarked that 'a person desirous to swing in compliance with a promise or vow to his idol for any object he wishes or has obtained, pays a fee to the temple to which the swinging apparatus is attached'.[134] At Weyoor the cost of swinging for one's own private reasons (as distinct from swinging on behalf of the community) from about 1815 to 1853 was Rs 2 per person[135] — an amount equivalent to about 16 days' wages for unskilled workers.[136] During that period something like 5,000 people appear to have paid the fee. In Belgaum, as already noted, the cost of swinging at Yellamma's Hill was Rs 18—an amount of money which, for an unskilled worker, was equivalent to at least four months' pay.

For many of the people who paid fees such as these, as well as the spectators who expected blessings from those engaged in the performances, the ritual was an expression of their deep-seated beliefs about the world in which they lived. The custom was popular especially among the low and depressed class people, not only because it increased their 'worldly' options and opportunities, but also because it made sense theologically; because it reflected a view of the world which was already inhabited by particular kinds of deities who were believed to control natural forces and who could be pleased or mollified by the 'victims' suffering of self-sacrifice. The practice was, in its religious aspect, a resource — something which, if used effectively to please or manipulate supernatural power, could make a difference between life and death, rains and drought, health and sickness or fertility and infertility.

NOTES

1. Alexander Duff, *India and India Missions*, Edinburgh, 1840, pp. 268-9.
2. *MH*, Vol. LXIV, 1868, p. 408.
3. CMS CI 2/0222/3, Journal, 20/2/1848 and CI 2/0222/9 Journal, 15/2/1851.
4. My italics.
5. CMS CI 2/0222/9, Journal, 25/3/1851.
6. IOR P/4247 MJP, 17/5/1892, F. Van Allen to Second-class Magistrate, Madura Taluk, 6/2/1892.
7. J. Knowles, 'The Hook-swinging Ceremony as I Saw It', *WWM*, Vol. III, April-Sep. 1899, pp. 585-91.
8. J.H. Powell, 'Hook-swinging in India', *FL*, Vol. XXV, June 1914, esp. pp. 147-8, 183-8.
9. J.C. Irwin, 'The Sacred Anthill and the Cult of the Primordial Mound', *HR*, Vol. 21, 1982, p. 341 (footnote 4).
10. J.C. Irwin, 'The Ancient Pillar-Cult at Prayaga (Allahabad): Its pre-Asokan Origins', *JRAS*, No. 2, 1983, pp. 253-80.
11. J.H. Powell, p. 148.

12. IOR F/4/1669, Board's Collection; *CCO*, Vol. VII, May 1838, p. 269.
13. Department of Indology, School of Oriental and African Studies. London (letter dated 14/10/1992).
14. IOR Bom. JP, 31/7/1856; See also *Dnyanodaya*, 2/6/1845.
15. Raeside, Letter, 14/10/1992.
16. *CCO*, Vol. VI, April 1837, p. 182.
17. Ibid.
18. *Fragments of Voyages and Travels*, Third series, London, 1833, p.83. For an illustration, see Figure 8, and for other descriptions, *WMMS*, Lynch to Sec., 25/8/1820, *AJ*, Vol. XX, No. 116, p. 161; *Dnyanodaya*, 5/2/1856; *Hindu* 19/5/1893.
19. IOR P/4247, Van Allen to Second-Class Magistrate, 6/2/1892.
20. See, for example, CMS CI 2/0222/3, *Sharkey's* Journal, 21/2/1848; CI 2/0101/5, H.W. Fox, Journal, 27/12/1844, IOR P/406/43 Bom. JP (Ram Naid) and Bom. JP, 31/7/1856 (Dufterdar and Head Accountant Ahmednagar, 30/11/1855); E Hoole, *Madras, Mysore and the South of India; or A Personal Narrative of a Mission to those Countries*, 2nd edn, London, 1844, p. 358; *MH*, Vol. LXIV, 1868, p. 408, and Vol. LXXXVIII, 1892, p. 8.
21. IOR P/188/61, p. 37.
22. Ibid., p. 38.
23. Ibid., p. 35.
24. IOR P/188/61 Fort William, 10/2/1860 (Reports of Commissioners)
25. Ibid., p. 33.
26. Ibid., p. 34.
27. Ibid., p. 40.
28. Ibid., p. 39.
29. *Central Provinces District Gazetteer, Hosangabad District*, Vol. A, Calcutta, 1908, pp. 58-9; V.Ball, *Jungle Life in India; or Journeys and Journals of an Indian Geologist*, London, 1880, pp. 232-3.
30. Sel. Mad.
31. At a quarterly meeting of CMS missionaries held at Masulipatam in May 1862 they complained that the swinging festival was still observed in the Nizam's territories, including localities such as Bendakur, Minaval and Bannigallapad in the immediate neighbourhood of British territory. (CMS Proceedings of the Fourteenth Quarterly Meeting of the Masulipatam Missionary Clergy held at Masulipatam, 18-22 May, 1862. For hook-swinging in Mysore, see *HF*, Vol. I, April 1862, pp. 135-7 and Vol. 3, April 1864, pp. 140-2; for a discussion of the practice in Cochin see L.K. Anantha Krishna Iyer, *The Cochin Tribes and Castes*, Vol. 1, Madras 1909. p. 324; for Travancore see S. Mateer, *The Land of Charity. A Descriptive Account of Travancore and its People*, London, 1871, pp. 185-6, 219-22 and Knowles, pp. 585-91, and for Karikal see IOR P/4409, C.G. Todhunter to Chief Secretary, Government of Madras, 7/9/1893.

32. IOR Bom. JP. 31/7/1856.
33. *CCO* Nov. 1858, pp. 480-1. See also, *Calcutta Christian Advocate*, 7/3/1840, p. 383 and 1846, p. 183.
34. IOR Bom. JP, 31/7/1856.
35. IOR Bom. JP, 31/7/1856, S. Jardow to J.W. Hadow, 28/9/1855.
36. IOR Bom. JP, 17/1/1857.
37. Ibid., 31/7/1857. (Magistrate of Khandesh).
38. IOR P/188/61, p. 41.
39. IOR Bom. JP, 31/7/1856.
40. Sel. Mad.
41. Describing the situation in the Belgaum district, where the ritual was probably more popular than in most other parts of the Presidency, the magistrate wrote: 'it is roughly estimated that it [swinging] is resorted to by rather more than half the population whenever circumstances arise, which call for the exercise of their faith in the efficacy of vows'. (IOR Bom. JP, 31/7/1856).
42. Sel. Mad.
43. Sel. Mad. pp. 3, 8.
44. Sel Mad. p. 15.
45. IOR p/188/61.
46. Sel. Mad. (Nellore, p.12, Masulipatam, p.13).
47. Ibid. p. 15.
48. IOR Bom. JP, 31/7/1856 (see also magistrates Ratnagiri and Poona).
49. Rosalind O'Hanlon, *Caste, Conflict and Ideology. Mahatma Jotirao Phule and low caste protest in nineteenth century Western India*, Cambridge, 1985, pp. 66-7.
50. *Dnyanodaya*, Vol. 2, No. 6, June 1843; 1/2/1845; 1/2/1848; 1/4/1854; 15/2/1854. See also *Bengal Herald*, 16/4/1837; *FI*, 20/4/1837; and *Reformer*, 16/4/1837.
51. Infra. p. 109.
52. Sel. Mad.
53. IOR P/406/43 Bom. JP, 19/9/1855.
54. IOR P/188/61, Reports of Commissioners.
55. Ibid, p. 35.
56. LMS, South India, Telugu, Box 2, Folder 2, jacket c, Howell to Ellis, 4/4/1838; North India, Bengal, Box 5, 1837, Campbell to Ellis, 2/5/1837; CMS CI 2/0101/5 H.W. Fox, Journal 27/12/1844. CI2/0222/3 J.E. Sharkey, Journal, 21/2/1848; *CCO*, Vol. VIII, May 1839, pp. 297-304; Vol. XI, June 1842, pp. 359-66.
57. E. Boaz, *The Mission Pastor: Memorials of the Rev. Thomas Boaz, LLD. Twenty-Four Years Missionary in Calcutta, by his Widow*, London, 1862, pp. 192-3; *CCO*, Vol. VIII, May 1839, pp. 297-304; Vol. XI, June 1842, pp. 359-66.
58. Infra. pp. 120-4.
59. *CCO*, Vol. V, 1836, p. 195.

60. *Bengal Hukaru*, 23/3/1865; IQR. P/188/671, Magistrate of Rajshahye.
61. See, for example, H. Whitehead, *The Village Gods of South India*, London, 1921, p.45.
62. IOR Bom. JP, 31/7/1856 (Magistrate of Poona); Sel. Mad., p. 14; *MH*, Vol. LXIV 1868, pp. 408-9.
63. Sel. Mad., p.14.
64. IOR Bom. JP, 31/7/1856.
65. *MH*, Vol. LXIV, 1868, pp. 408-9; IOR P/3784.
66. IOR Bom. JP, 31/7/1856 (Dharwa, Belgaum, Thana and Colaba); Sel. Mad. (North Arcot, Nellore).
67. IOR Bom. JP, 31/7/1856 (Dharwa); *Gazetteer of the Bombay Presidency, Belgaum*, Bombay 1884, p. 613.
68. IOR MPP 21-30, April 1860, Fisher to Prycroft, 16/4/1860. See also IOR MPP 28-31, May 1859, Subrick to Prycroft, 25/1/1859, and Sel. Mad., p.14.
69. *JAS*, No. 24, December 1833, p. 610.
70. *CCO*, Vol. V, 1836, p. 196. See also J.J. Weitbrecht, *Protestant Missions in Bengal*, (2nd edn), London, 1844, p. 125.
71. Extracts from Carey's diary, *Periodical Accounts*, Vol. 1, p.197.
72. *JAS*, No. 24, December 1833, p. 613. See also, J.H. Powell, p. 172.
73. IOR P/188/61, p. 36.
74. Ibid., pp. 33, 34, 38.
75. Ibid., p. 41.
76. Ibid., p. 39.
77. MH. Vol. 88, 1892. p. 8; IOR P/4409, MJP 21/12/1893, p. 59.
78. L.K. Anantha Krishna Iyer, p. 324.
79. The Kapus or Reddies, who were described as 'the principal landowners of the Deccan', were usually the village magistrates in Cuddapah district. (See J.D.B. Gribble, *Manual of the District of Cuddapah in the Presidency of Madras*, Madras, 1895, p. 34, and *Madras District Gazetteers*, C.F. Brackenbury, *Cuddapah*, Madras 1915, pp. 65-6.)
80. IOR P/4409 MJP, 21/12/1893, p. 65.
81. IOR Bom. JP. 31/7/1856.
82. Ibid.
83. Ibid.
84. *Gazetteer of the Bombay Presidency*, Vol. XXI, *Belgaum*, Bombay, 1884, p. 613.
85. Ibid. p. 298.
86. Ibid., p. 297.
87. See, for example, descriptions by Willam Ward, *A View of the History, Literature and Mythology of the Hindoos*, Vol. III, London 1822, pp. 15-23 and the account in *AJ*, January 1828, pp. 32-5.
88. Ward, p.21.
89. CMS CI 2/0222/9, Journal 15/2/1851.
90. IOL Bom. JP, 31/7/1856.

91. Ibid.
92. Ibid. See also the comment by the author of the Poona District Gazetteer of 1885, who when referring to Jejuri remarked that 'in those days hook-swinging was practised at all the fairs chiefly by women' (*Gazetteer of the Bombay Presidency*, Vol. XVIII, Part III, *Poona*, Bombay 1885, p. 132).
93. *Central Provinces District Gazetteers, Seoni District*, Vol. A, Allahabad 1907, p. 49 and *Betul District*, Vol. A, Allahabad 1907, pp. 56-7.
94. IOL Bom. JP, 31/7/1856 (Colaba).
95. Infra. pp. 61-64.
96. IOR Bom. JP, 31/7/1856.
97. IOR Bom. JP 17/9/1855 (Ratnagiri) and 31/7/1856 (Poona).
98. Ibid. 17/9/1855; *Dnyanodaya*, 2/6/1845.
99. IOR Bom. JP, 31/7/1856 (Khandesh and Ratnagiri).
100. Ibid. (Khandesh).
101. *Dnyanodaya*, June 1843. For further information on castes and tribes in western India see R.E. Enthoven, *Tribes and Castes of Bombay*, 3 vols., Bombay, 1920.
102. Sel. Mad., p. 2.
103. *The Hindu* 19/5/1893; *Census of India*, 1901, Madras, Vol. 15, Part 1, p. 164.
104. Sel. Mad., p. 2.
105. Ibid. IOR P/3784, 27/8/1890; *HF*, Vol. 1 April 1862, p. 135; CMS CI 1/0222/3, Sharkey's Journal 21/2/1848.
106. *JAS*, No. 24, December 1833, p. 610. See also William Ward, p. 20; *AJ.*, 1828, p. 34; *CCA*, Vol. VI, 4/5/1844, Vol. VIII, 16/5/1846.
107. CMS CI 1/M7 1837-9, F.Wybrow to Ass. Sec. CMS, 4/5/1838.
108. IOR P/188/61, p. 39.
109. Ibid (Reports of the Commissioners of Patna, Bhagulpore and Chota Nagpur).
110. Ibid., p. 40.
111. Sel. Mad., p. 16; IOR P/3784, MJP, 10/8/1890. While an analysis of details supplied by the Collector of Rajahmundry show that the *inams* for swinging were not worth much more than Rs. 2 As. 8 per annum, 14 villages were receiving them in the district in 1857 (IOR P/249/61, MPP 27/1/1857.
112. Sel. Mad., p. 16.
113. CMS CI 2/0222/3, Sharkey's Journal, 21/2/1848.
114. CMS CI 2/0101/5, Henry W. Fox, Journal, 27/12/1844.
115. *MH*, Vol. LXIV, 1868, p. 408.
116. W.T. Elmore, *Dravidian Gods in Modern Hinduism*, Madras, 1925, pp. 32-3.
117. Sel Mad., p. 14.
118. S. Srinivasa Raghavaiyangar, *Memorandum of the Progress of the Madras Presidency*, Madras 1893, p. cxcviii.

119. LMS, South India,Telugu, Box 2, F2, Jc, Howell to Ellis, 4/4/1838.
120. *The Hindu*, 11/6/1894.
121. *JAS*, No. 24, December 1833, p. 610.
122. Infra.
123. Ward, p. 21.
124. For references to possession, see especially WMMS, J.Lynch to Sec. 25/8/1820 and *CMG*, 1850-51, pp.16-19.
125. S. Mateer, p. 220.
126. CMS CI 1/0222/3 Sharkey's Journal, 21/2/1848.
127. *HF,* Vol. 3, April 1864, p. 140.
128. WMMS, Little to Sec. 18/5/1844. See also Lynch to Sec. 25/8/1820.
129. Ramkamal Sen refers, for example, to a specific ceremony during the *charak puja* when sannyasis collected and distributed dates and coconuts. According to this account, the barren women who resorted to the place received the fruit 'with joy as an omen of their becoming pregnant through the favour of Siva'. (*JAS*, No. 24, December 1833, p. 610).
130. See, William Carey's account of the immolation of a *sati* which he witnessed in 1798. *Cambridge History of India.* Vol. VI, Delhi 1958, p. 134.
131. *Periodical Accounts*, Vol. 1, 1800, p. 28.
132. Hoole, p. 358.
133. WMMS, Little to Secs., 18/5/1844; Lynch to Sec., 25/8/1820. See also Basil Hall, p. 83.
134. IOR Bom. JP, 31/7/1856.
135. Sel. Mad., p. 15.
136. Raghavaiyangar, p. cxcviii.

CHAPTER II

Controlling the Spirits: Siva and the Saktis

Hook-swinging was seldom if ever conducted before deities such as Vishnu or his incarnations, but rather before gods and goddesses who represent to a much greater extent the more volatile, dangerous and destructive as well as creative aspects of nature. They were perhaps more the objects of apprehension and fear than of trust and adoration and usually required a great deal of pleasing and propitiation.

In Lower Bengal the swinging was, as we have noted, one of the activities performed with the idea of propitiating Siva.[1] In Bombay Presidency the practice was common in connection with Khandoba, who was viewed as an incarnation of Siva or 'Siva's servant'.[2] The god, who was thought to be dangerous as well as benign, was especially popular among the lower classes, who performed hook-swinging at his central shrine at Jejuri, a village on the road between Poona and Satara, and at other places in Bombay Presidency.[3]

Other male deities mentioned in records in connection with hook-swinging in Bombay Presidency were Bhairara, another incarnation of Siva,[4] Jotiba, patron saint of Maratha soldiers,[5] and occasionally Hanuman, the monkey god and faithful servant of Rama, celebrated in the *Ramayana*.[6] Female deities or *saktis* are also referred to in accounts of hook-swinging in the same region. Those before whose shrines the ritual took place included Bhawani,[7] Siva's *sakti*, Yellamma, also regarded as one of the forms of Parvati (Siva's wife),[8] and Durgara and Dayamava.[9] Yellamma ('the mother of all' and probably the same as Ellamma in the Telugu country)[10] was especially well-known and influential in the Bombay-Karnatak, her central shrine in the hills of the Belgaum collectorate being one of the more popular and sacred sites in Bombay Presidency where hook-swinging was conducted on a large scale[11] (Fig. 11). Durgara

(Durga) the goddess of cholera, and Dayamava, the goddess of small-pox, appear to have had a much more localised influence.[12] Nevertheless, for people in Dharwar, for example, their powers were just as frightening as the prospects of disease and death itself and hook-swinging was conducted in order to appease or avert their wrath.

The relationship between the incidence of hook-swinging and the worship (or rather propitiation) of female deities was stronger still in southern India. The Tranquebar missionaries in the eigthteenth century mention hook-swinging in connection with the supreme god, Iyenar, the lord of the ghosts, destroyer of enemies, breaker of droughts and guardian of the fields and villages.[13] However, all available reports on the custom in southern India in the nineteenth century refer to the practice taking place in connection with *saktis*, who may or may not have been identified as Siva's wife.

One of the best known and widely feared of these female spirits was Mariamma, the mother of small-pox and goddess most frequently mentioned in connection with hook-swinging exhibitions.[14] Another goddess who it was felt would be pleased by the performance of the hook-swinging ritual was Ellamma, the original *sakti* and cause of the universe, and deity who was specially popular and influential in Andhra Pradesh.[15] Other south Indian goddesses such as Angaramma, the goddess of cholera and disease in general, and Durga, Kali and Bhadrakali (all various names for the India-wide goddess of demons and the wife of Siva)[16] are also mentioned in connection with the custom in different parts of the south.[17] Furthermore, while in these cases the rite was performed before the deities whose names were known and feared across vast stretches of the country, exhibitions were also enacted before the shrines of little-known *saktis* whose power was restricted, in some instances, to a single village. Such were the deities mentioned in the official memoranda on hook-swinging in North Arcot district, who presided over the fortune of one particular village — the village itself taking its name from the local spirit.[18]

In spite of the multiplicity and variety of all these deities, who prompted or who were in some way connected with hook-swinging exhibitions, some over-riding features are clearly apparent. As suggested above, except on rare occasions, swinging was associated with Siva or with his *saktis*, or with independent and local female deities. Key factors were Siva and the female principle and not Vishnu or any of his benevolent incarnations. Totally absent are reports of swinging in honour of Vishnu or his avatars, such as Rama or Krishna, and linked with this is the striking omission of reports of swinging at shrines of the popular god Vithoba (regarded as a form of Vishnu) in Bombay Presidency.

All of these deities, it was felt, could in some way be influenced, controlled or manipulated and all of them, it was assumed, required some form of pleasing or propitiation. The significant question then was, what would please or placate them the most easily? The history, mythology and structure of the *charak puja* in Bengal, as well as comments by Sen and others, all suggest that the purpose was propitiation, primarily through self-inflicted pain.

Referring to the supposed origins of the *charak puja,* Ramkamal Sen remarked the some of the performers:

> . . . Consider it as an act of piety and religion, in commemoration of the austerities performed by VANA Raja, a king and Daitya [fiend], who by acts of self-torture and denial obtained the special favour of MAHA DEVA [Siva], and who first introduced the festival.[19]

This view, which highlights the importance of austerities and self-torture, was reiterated in another slightly different account of the *charak puja* in Orissa.

According to the Rev. A. Sutton, a British Baptist missionary at Cuttak:

> The Hindoos ascribe the origin of the swinging festival... to the austerities of a certain ancient raja. This individual was desirous of an interview with Seeb [Siva]. He accordingly had recourse to the various modes of self-torture usually practised at this festival, when Seeb made his appearance and gratified all his wishes.[20]

The ideas of the importance of austerity and self-inflicted pain as factors that would influence the deity were clearly reflected in the events that preceded or took place during the festival. According to a report published in the Calcutta *Government Gazette* in about 1827, the participants who adopted the title of *sannyasin* (one who has renounced all worldly attachments and values) prepared themselves for about a week or ten days before the commencement of the chief events:

> At this time individuals, of the lowest orders, enroll themselves in a band, or fraternity, under a common head, as Sanyasis...On entering the troop, each individual assumes the thread which is characteristic of the Brahmanical order, discards all superfluous clothing, wears the sectarial Saiva marks upon his forhead, braids his hair in a particular fashion, and smears his body from head to foot with fine ashes of burnt cow-dung. He also takes a vow to abstain from all slothful and sensual indulgence, such as sleeping on a bed, or eating fish, for the term of the solemnity. Each takes but a single meal daily of rice and pulse, which he cooks for himself after sunset, and, if whilst dressing or eating it, he hears the sound of a drum, or is addressed by any one, he immediately desists, and goes without his dinner; a privation of some moment, as it is part of his duty to sit up during the greater part of the night, singing hymns in praise of Mahadeo.[21]

During the festival *sannyasis* performed one of a number of acts of self-torture. Apart from feats such as hanging upside down over a smoking fire or rolling on branches of rough and prickly plants, these included major events such as the *Jhamp Sanyas* and *Ban Sanyas.* During the *Jhamp Sanyas* or the day which the jumping took place, *sannyasis* cast themselves from specially constructed bamboo platforms (the highest about twenty feet from the ground) onto spikes or knives embedded in mattresses below. The knives or spikes were placed at an angle so that when the person fell the instruments fell flat instead of entering the body. During the *Ban Sanyas*, or mortification of Raja Ban, groups of *sannyasis* went in procession to the Kali temple at Kali Ghat or to the adjoining one dedicated to Siva as Nakuleswara. There, with the help of blacksmiths or other assistants, they endured operations involving the piercing of sides and tongues. Some had nails stuck under their skin from hip to shoulder; some had two long, slender cords passed under the skin on each side and these were then held at either extremity by assistants while the *sannyasin* 'danced' backwards and fowards along the line; some ran sharp rods and canes through the tongue, lips and cheeks while others had pieces of tin or iron stuck into the forehead. The swinging which took place on the last day was a final act of self-torture — a penance which gave its name to the festival.[22]

In Bombay and the south, hook-swinging was also associated, at least to some extent, with the same idea of propitiating the deity through pain and suffering. Some of the festivals at which the ritual was performed were, as in the case of the *charak puja*, occasions during which devotees practised other forms of self-mortification. For example, one of the LMS missionaries describing the swinging festival in honour of Bhadrakali near Kolachal in Travancore in about 1839, wrote that:

> In one direction will be observed the swinging machine, with the victims of superstition being hoisted up by hooks inserted in the backs; other persons will be seen rolling in the dust a considerable distance round the temple, until they are exhausted by the heat and exertion which are required to perform this vow in the hottest month of the year; others, with a thin piece of cane inserted in their sides, dance along with apparent joy, while two persons in front and behind take hold of the cane, and keep step with the poor creature at a quick pace for a considerable distance.[23]

Deities such as Khandoba, Mariamma, Angaramma and Bhadrakali were believed to be pleased, not only with the swinging, but also with other displays of endurance and self-punishment.[24] Some of these forms of self-inflicted torture were similar to those popular at the *charak puja*, such as passing a thread or cane through the skin on the sides of the body (one of the techniques described above), or sticking skewers in various parts of the body, such as the abdomen, sides, back and arms or piercing the tongue. The dragging of carts attached by a rope to hooks inserted in the back, passing a hot wire through the cheek and other 'feats' are also mentioned in other descriptions of swinging festivals in western and southern India.

All of this evidence suggests that the idea of the persuasive power of self-inflicted pain was the predominant rationale behind hook-swinging in Bengal and was an idea not without influence in some other parts of India in the nineteenth century. And yet, as we shall argue, the question of how much pain was actually experienced as a result of the process is somewhat problematic. It was an issue which divided contemporary observers of the practice and which appears to have divided participants as well.

In 1894 two swingers from Trichinopoly, who were interviewed by the sub-magistrate after one of their number had died 'from the effect of injuries caused by the swinging', made statements under oath. Para Andy, who had swung forty or fifty years previously, declared: 'There is intense pain caused by the swinging', and Para Periannan stated: 'Persons swung cannot take up work or anything for one-and-a-half months owing to the pain out of injuries received'.[25]

On the other hand, the man who was suspended for one and a quarter hours during a revival of the festival at Sholavandan near Madura in 1891, when interviewed by officials, said there was 'no pain',[26] and Ram Naid, Deputy Magistrate of Khandesh in Bombay presidency, who interviewed hook-swingers there, was told much the same thing. 'Several persons' who had frequently undergone the penance themselves, assured him that 'except on the first occasion, when they received a certain shock on the hook first being introduced into their back', they had 'always enjoyed the swing rather than suffered from it'.[7] Obeysekere's recent interviews with 'hook-hangers' at Kataragama also suggest that, at least for them, there was very little or no pain. Sirima Hettiaracci, a Buddhist woman who had six iron hooks inserted under her flesh and skin and hung from a tree in the temple courtyard stated:

> I felt a slight pain while I was being pierced with the hooks, but not while I was hanging from the tree. I saw my mother faint — nothing else. I had no thoughts, no sense of any thing, as if I was unconscious.[28]

Furthermore, Tuan Sahid Abdin, who went to Kataragama every year without a break and who performed the ritual 'practically every day during the festival', claimed that he suffered no pain. When the iron hooks pierced his body he said he felt cold 'as if he were in a refrigerator chamber'.[29]

It is important to note that thresholds of pain are different and also that those who claimed to feel pain were already opposed to the practice, while others, who said they felt little or no pain, had greater faith in its benefits. Degrees of pain may also have varied depending on how far the back was prepared for the operation and the care and skill of those inserting the hooks. The hooks were, in fact, usually inserted by 'specialists' with considerable experience, and the manner in which this was done impressed more than one sceptical European observer. Writing in about 1833, for example, the English traveller Basil Hall, who witnessed hook-swinging in Blacktown, Madras, remarked that 'the points of the hooks being extremely sharp, they were inserted without lacerating the parts, and so adroitly, that not a drop of blood flowed from the orifices; in fact, the native, who appeared to suffer no pain, conversed easily with those about him'.[30]

Furthermore, while in many cases the whole weight of the swinger's body was entirely dependent on hooks (the swinger performing without any other means of support) this was not, as noted in Chapter I, the only method of swinging.[31] In many instances the pressure on the hooks, and therefore on the flesh and tendons, was alleviated by a waistband. Finally, even in those cases where the performers were supported only by the muscles and flesh of the middle of the back, they were sometimes provided with a safety rope (Figure 16) which could be held or taken up from time to time to shift the balance of the body and ease the pain.[32]

But perhaps other more important factors which relieved the pain were the habit of deliberately taking drugs or intoxicants, as well as a readiness and capacity to enter into a state of trance.

It was claimed by Ramkamal Sen, when describing the *charak puja* in Bengal, that: 'the ceremony which was called an act of piety' was, among other things, an occasion for drunkenness.[33] These views were echoed in Bengali newspapers such as *The Reformer* and *Hindu Intelligencer.*[34] Reports of hook-swingers being drunk or taking *bhang* or other drugs before swinging were specially common in Bengal where individuals were not infrequently urged to swing with offers of drink, or were paid or even forced to perform the act. According to information supplied by the Commissioner of Rajshahye, the exhibitors were 'commonly' drugged.[35] According to his counterpart in the Nuddea Division, in some cases, the swingers braced themselves up for the task 'by exciting themselves with *bhang*, and ascent the Churruck in a more or less drunken state'.[36] The missionaries of the Calcutta Missionary Conference in a memorial to the Legislative Council in 1858 also stated that hook-swingers were commonly 'stupified with drugs for the occasion'.[37]

There are similar claims or reports from other parts of India, though much less common, of paticipants swinging while under the influence of drugs or liquor.[38] However, it is quite possible that the extent of this practice, especially among those who were not offered liquor as an enticement, was somewhat exaggerated by European and missionary observers who mistook the symptoms of trance and ecstasy for those of drunkenness. Stuart Piggin, in his book *Making*

Evangelical Missionaries, 1789-1858, has pointed to the extent to which British Evangelical missionaries distrusted 'enthusiasm' and eschewed overt and excessive displays of emotion in religious practice.[39] British and possibly other missionary observers such as the American Evangelicals, being unfamiliar with the expression of intense feeling in religious ceremony, may therefore have found it difficult to recognise, let alone understand, such highly charged emotional states as ecstasy and trance as they appeared in non-Christian religions.

One indication of what was possibly a missionary misunderstanding was the case of the man who swung at Sholavandan in September 1891. According to the American missionary, John Chandler, who went to the spot and who wrote a detailed report in the *Missionary Herald,* there could be 'no doubt' that the man was given *arrack* (country liquor) prior to swinging ;[40] and while the mission doctor, who was also present, did not specifically mention drink in his report, he was also of the opinion that there could be 'no doubt' that the swinger had had strong stimulants.[41] The report of Wynne, Acting District Magistrate was, however, somewhat different, and tended to contradict Chandler's claim that the man was under the influence of alcohol. According to Wynne, the man was given some *arrack* after the exhibition, 'but says he had none previously'.[42]

If one accepts the swinger's own version of what was happening, then this suggests that, far from being drunk, he was probably in a state of trance. Some confirmation of this interpretation comes from the mission doctor who explained that the man's attendants were fanning him and urging him to 'a dancing motion' and that 'the man was evidently under strong excitement'.

The extent to which performers were in a trance or 'possessed' is impossible to estimate. However, a number of descriptions, most notably of the behaviour of hook-swingers in southern India, are consistent with this condition, a state of mind or being which again helps to explain why some swingers claimed they felt no pain.

Two missionary commentators refer to a point in the preparatory rituals prior to swinging where the performer was given temporary divinity[43] (Figure 10). In one instance in Madras in 1820 the priest yelled in the man's ear.[44] 'Wishing to know the meaning of this', wrote the Rev. Lynch, 'they informed me by my friend who knew Tamul that it was to put the god in him or on him'. In the second case, the Rev. Noyes of the American Madura Mission noted in 1868:

'The priest performs a ceremony over him [the swinger], uttering munthrams . . . and he pretends to be under the influence of devils, and acts like a mad man'.[45]

Writing to his brother from Masulipatam in about 1845, the Rev. H.W. Fox described in some detail the appearance and behaviour of a man who, having performed rituals preliminary to swinging, was also on that occasion possessed by the spirit:

> He was now rubbed all over, from the crown of his head to his feet, with tumeric — a yellow powder — and had his feet striped with red: a small cloth around his waist, and a small turban on his head formed the whole of his dress, while around the calves of his legs were tied strings of little bells, which rattled as he moved. He came along dancing and leaping, flinging his arms and legs about like a maniac, sometimes bellowing, sometimes screeching, sometimes shouting in praise of the goddess . . . The crowd of spectators were highly delighted, and called out, 'See the power of the Ammavaru!' 'Great is our goddess!' with other like expressions; and telling us that now he was possessed by, and actually represented, the goddess.[46]

It is unlikely that these and other hook-swingers who were in a trance or a semi-hypnotic state of ecstasy and excitement experienced normal levels of pain. Obeyesekere, who cites the results of laboratory experiments at Stanford on the effects of hypnosis in the relief of pain,[47] suggests that the states of trance or self-hypnosis, such as one finds among hook-hangers at Kataragama, was a significant factor in lowering the levels of pain among men and women who practised the ritual there in the 1970s.[48]

Thus there is an apparent contradiction in the hook-swinging custom. On the one hand one of its main purposes appears to have been to please or placate the deity through self-imposed suffering or pain, and the greater the pain, the more effective the ritual. On the other hand there were several factors involved (including the deliberate use of drugs or intoxicants) which reduced the pain and which therefore were likely to make the ritual less effective as a method of influencing or manipulating the supernatural.

One possibility is that those who went through the ordeal for the first time were not to know that it was not as painful or traumatic as they thought. Secondly, even for those who repeated the performance (a not uncommon occurrence), there was always a risk that there could be pain on the next occasion — a possibility that could not be dismissed in view of the fact that *some* hook-swingers did experience intense pain during the performance.

****

A second influential assumption underlying hook-swinging was not so much the idea of appeasement by pain, but the notion that the gods and goddesses could be appeased by human and bloody sacrifice. Thus, while a view of hook-swinging as pain and penance was dominant in Bengal and in those areas under Bengali influence, ideas of the custom as a blood offering or a substitute for bloody sacrifice tended to predominate elsewhere.

The difference between the two ideas of propitiation associated with the custom was clearly reflected in a Telugu myth of origin which, unlike the Bengali and Oriya accounts, suggests that hook-swinging was not the original form of devotion which pleased the deity, but a *substitute* for human sacrifice.

According to the District Magistrate who recorded the story at Cuddapah in Telugu country in the late nineteenth century, it ran as follows:

> There were two sages called Vasishta and Vishwamitra. They fell out with one another and the latter cursed the former, in consequence of which Vasishta's sons became Pariahs and began to offer human sacrifices to deities in performing their vows. Vasishta became very uneasy at the fate of his sons, and asked Vishwamitra to point out some means by which they could find salvation. Then Vishwamitra proposed the process of hook-swinging, and said that it answered as well as human sacrifice, as it involved human torture.[49]

There is very general consensus that human sacrifice was once widespread in India and, reflected in this practice, was the idea that the spilling of human blood was especially efficacious.[50] While it cannot be argued that the story proves that swinging *in general* had its origin in a form of human sacrifice (an argument which has been put forward by Powell in his study of tribal practices in Chota Nagpur), it certainly suggests a connection between hook-swinging and human sacrifice, *in some cases,* in areas outside Bengal. Further confirmation of this are accounts of the custom in Mysore. According to Ramakrishna Rao, a palace official, who is cited in Whitehead's *Village Gods of South India,* the worship of village deities in Mysore city included the symbolic re-enactment of a human sacrifice which was linked with and followed by a hook-swinging exhibition.[51]

The link between hook-swinging and the offering of human life is also dramatically illustrated by a seventeenth century Portuguese account of swinging at the great festival of Lord Jaganatha at Puri in Orissa. In his account of his travels published in 1643, the friar Sebastiao Henrique wrote:

> One can see the crowd of pilgrims, the rich offerings, the curious processions of the victorious chariots, the demented excitement of the Yoguis and the devotees handcuffed with heavy iron chains who, on reaching the Temple, free themselves of the chains as if by an occult or supernatural power, the high-pitched cries, the savage singing, the sudden flight of the crowd of naked people. And soon afterwards, the following events take place: the moment the big chariot Jaganatha (*Rath*) arrives, the hysteria reaches its zenith and some of the Yoguis and pilgrims in a fit of frenzy, with their lips frothing, throw themselves under the wheels and are crushed; others pierce their back muscles with hooks fixed by means of ropes to a wheel which spins on its axis and they are thus rotated on and on like horses in a merry-go-round, balancing themselves on their way while their blood goes on spilling over the devotees below. This torture continues until they are dead.[52]

Although accounts of this type of suicide while hook-swinging have so far not been discovered for the nineteenth century, there was always the possibility that the flesh might tear, the ropes break or the post give way, dashing the devotee to the ground. Death may not have been so intentional, but it could and did occasionally occur in the latter period as is evident from accidents reported in official papers, the press and elsewhere.

Furthermore, the association between the shedding of blood (human or animal) and hook-swinging was carried over into many festivals in the Madras and Bombay Presidencies and some of the Native States in the nineteenth century. All the deities already mentioned in connection with the ritual, with the exception of

Hanuman, were believed to be blood-drinking and to delight (at the very least) in animal sacrifice.[53] In some cases, animals were killed prior to the swinging so as to ensure the safety and well-being of the person performing the rite.[54] In other cases, however, the way the ceremony developed suggests that the swinger was a symbolic victim sacrificed, either alone or together, with the slaughter of animals. In Mysore in 1862, where three buffaloes were slain and sacrificed to Mari (Mariamma), 'one on account of each man swung', animals appear to have been substituted for men,[55] but on some other occasions the swinging might be interpreted as part of a more general slaughter. Thus, the missionaries who visited the swinging festival at Peddanah, a large village near Masulipatam, were told that the goddess there required offerings of the blood of 'both man and beast'.[56] T.D. Lushington, the magistrate reporting on results of more extensive enquiries in the same district, noted that swinging exhibitions took place at the same time as the slaughter of animals. Referring to his experience of work in Kanara district, he noted that there too swinging was 'combined with a large slaughter of animals', the pole being erected 'in the close vicinity of a high heap of a reeking heads which was constantly receiving additions'.[57]

Personal, family and communal considerations

There is sometimes a distinct difference between the ideas implicit in the mythology, history, content and structure of certain ceremonies and the beliefs of those who participate. It cannot be assumed, for example, that all those who took part in swinging ceremonies were necessarily aware of all that the ritual implied. However, there was undoubtedly a widespread conviction among performers concerned with the supernatural, that the practice would, in some way, please or placate the deity; and that this was all that was necessary to know if one was to deal with problems in the present, or exercise some control over future events.

The decision to swing was usually made weeks, or months or even longer before the swinging took place. If the individual involved was doing it for his or her own particular reasons (as opposed to those who acted as proxies or swung as 'victims' on behalf of the community), then the swinging was invariably the result of a vow — votaries promising to perform the ritual if the deity would grant their request. In that sense, therefore, the purpose of hook-swinging was much the same as that of pilgrimage, fire-walking or some other ritual undertaken as a result of a vow made to the deity at a time of crisis or personal need.

The reasons for performing hook-swinging as distinct, for example, from some other forms of penance or self-mortification are undoubtedly complex and probably depended to some extent on the established tradition of particular regions. As we have seen, in some parts of India, for example in the North West Provinces, there was no tradition of swinging and the class of people who elsewhere tended to perform the ritual, fulfilled their vows by going on pilgrimage or practising other types of penance.[58] Furthermore, as previously argued, the custom was linked with the prevalence and presence of certain types of deities — namely those that required frequent propitiation. Swinging was therefore less likely to occur or to be chosen as an option in those areas where different types of deities and different theologies, such as the *bhakti* tradition, were especially influential.

As in the case of *sati*, the tradition of swinging was probably more common in some families than in others. According to *The Hindu* newspaper, for example, the privilege of swinging at the festival at Sholavandan in south India was restricted to certain families among the Kallar community.[59] While the young men who took it in turns to perform the rite were acting on behalf of the community, it is possible that, in other cases, a consciousness of the family's past involvement in performing the ritual encouraged family members to follow the same pattern when making a vow to undertake some kind of penance.

It might also be noted that not all of those who made a vow to swing chose the custom as a first option. One example of this was a man who swung at Royapattah in Madras in August 1820 who, according to the Rev. Lynch, undertook the penance only as a last resort — and after other attempts at influencing the deity had failed:

> It seems from what I afterwards learned, that some time ago he was attacked by Cholera Morbus, and having made many sacrifices to his god to obtain the cure, without effect, he made a vow that if he did recover, he would undergo the torture of swinging thus gratify reward the idol for restoring him to health.[60]

Finally , there was the strong possiblity that some of those who vowed to swing had particular psychological and emotional needs and were seeking severe forms of chastisement as a result of their personal and family experience. Obeyesekere has argued that the ideology governing abject penances to Kataragama is based on filial piety. 'The son surrenders to the father, who then forgives him, even though he has done wrong'.[61] He also describes in detail the case of a woman who performed hook-hanging. After researching her past history he stated his suspicion that in her case 'Sex and aggression inhibition' resulted, not in hysterical symptoms, but in 'deep characterological problems of self-punishment'[62]—that in that instance she deliberately chose hook-hanging as one of the more difficult and severe forms of self-chastisement.

Whether the author's particular analysis of these cases is correct is not especially relevant for our purpose. What is important is that his work suggests that psychological factors (perhaps including a strong desire to inflict self-punishment) can be used in attempts to explain why some people preferred to make a vow to swing while others chose a somewhat easier or less painful path.

According to a range of Bengali and European observers who commented on hook-swinging in Lower Bengal, those who swung at the *charak puja* with a serious religious intention did so in order to win the special favour of Siva, or as a result of vows made to the deity in order to secure health and prosperity, the birth of a child or some other special boon or favour.[63] In Bombay Presidency, magistrates who responded to the official enquiry of 1855-56 and who commented on the reasons for swinging all emphasised that it was performed 'in fulfilment of vows' made 'in order to obtain a desired object or to avert an actual or impending evil'.[64] Missionary and other accounts also drew attention to the influence of a similar impulse,[65] while in Madras Presidency it also appears that the rite was commonly performed as a result of vows made to the deity on previous occasions.[66] For example, the Rev. E. Hoole, a Methodist missionary who observed hook-swinging near Madras 'for several years successively' in the 1820s, remarked that the ceremonies took place 'in consequence of vows made in time of sickness or danger, or for the obtaining of children or for some other desired object'.[67]

As will be apparent from the discussion above, the specific reasons for making the vow varied. In some cases, it was made for 'temporal' benefits such as employment.[68] In a large number of instances, however, as in the case of the man who swung at Royapattah, swinging was undertaken as a result of a vow made in times of sickness such as when the man or woman concerned was suffering from cholera.[69]

Another extremely influential consideration, especially in the case of women, was the desire for children. According to the Magistrate of Belgaum the ceremony there was 'perhaps most commonly employed by women who have been safely delivered of children after a period of supposed barrenness and who attribute this result to the effect of their vows to perform the penance at some particular Jatra'.[70] Some deities were especially popular for their power in enabling barren women to conceive and deliver children. For example, on his first visit to Weyoor in March 1848 the Rev. J.E. Sharkey was struck by the number of young females prostrating before the temple 'imploring the aid of the goddess for the power to conceive'.[71] On his second visit to the festival three years later, he noted that most of the thirty-three persons who swung were women or girls and that several of the women who swung carried newborn infants in their arms.[72]

Hook-swinging, like firewalking, was performed not only as a method of meeting personal and family needs, but also for the sake of the village or some other social group.

While, as noted in an earlier chapter, swinging for collective reasons is seldom mentioned in material relating to Lower Bengal (except with reference to the Santals of Chota Nagpur) there are more frequent references to this type of swinging elsewhere.

A connection between hook-swinging and the forces of nature (which were of concern not only to individuals but to the whole community), was hinted at in at least one European account of the custom in the eighteenth century. Alexander Hamilton, who witnessed the ceremony at Karwar on the Kanarese coast south of Goa, declared that hook-swinging was performed at 'a feast celebrated to infernal gods, with a divination or conjuration to know the fate of the ensuing crop of corn'.[73] A century later Lushington, commenting on the results of widespread police enquiries in Masulipatam district, stated that 'in case of famine, cholera or other calamity, a swinging exhibition takes place for the purpose of propitiating the deity'.[74] In Weyoor, in the same district, all the village officers attended an annual festival when a Pariah was paid to swing, 'to ensure the favour of the goddess in behalf of the villagers'.[75] The reports of district officers and missionaries from other parts of Madras Presidency also refer to the performance of hook-swinging for corporate reasons — as a ritual sacrifice for the benefit of caste or village communities. Writing in 1893, Toke Jeyaram Nayudu, a retired *sheristadar* in Nellore district, noted that in some cases the practice was followed 'for the propitiation of the village goddess when famine, cholera or other calamity occurs and when men and cattle die in numbers'.[76] Confirming earlier missionary evidence, the district magistrate of Madura remarked:

> . . . the great idea is to put the goddess into a good humour and get her to interfere in cases of outbreak of small-pox, scarcity of rain, etc. The goddess, it is thought, likes to have as much 'tamasha' as possible during these festivals, and as 'hook-swinging' brings together a large crowd of worshippers, the goddess is pleased with the practice and is likely to be angry if the custom be discontinued . . . At the same time, I am informed — and I think there is some truth in it — that on certain occasions during a great famine or of a severe outbreak of cholera swinging is resorted to as a *special* means of invoking the aid of the goddess.[77]

Lastly, there is evidence that the festival was performed for community as well as for individual reasons in Tanjore district as late as the 1890s. A *mirasidar* and resident of Vanathurai in Kumbakonam taluk reported that hook-swinging was performed by 'hired men' in a nearby village 'as a means of propitiating the village goddess'.[78] Furthermore, after further enquiries in and around Negapatam, C. G. Todhunter, Sub-divisional Magistrate of Negapatam (also in Tanjore district), remarked that hook-swinging there was practised mainly by shepherds and fishermen and was regarded as 'a general penance on behalf of the community',[79] as well as having particular efficacy as a vow on the part of individuals. Referring to his attendance at a festival at Patnacheri, in the neighbouring French enclave of Karikal, he wrote:

> The temple at which it [hook-swinging] is performed belongs to a small fishing community, who regard the hook-swinging festival, so far as I could ascertain, as a yearly penance for the offence given to the goddess by the killing of fish.[80]

These reports emanating from southern India can be compared

with similar accounts of hook-swinging rites performed on behalf of tribal communities in the southern districts of the Central Provinces. For example, Vincent Ball, who was working for the Geological Survey of India and who visited the Santals in a remote part of the south-eastern Central Provinces in 1870, commented that, among other requests, they asked him to give them permission to perform the *charak puja*:

> They said that in consequence of the *Bhut*, or evil spirit, not being appeased, their women and children were dying from sickness, and their cattle were being killed by wild beasts. When I replied that I had no authority to give them such permission, they then became most urgent that I should send a petition to the Government...representing the hardships they suffered in consequence of the prohibition, and praying for its repeal.[81]

Furthermore, according to official accounts of religious ceremonies among tribals in the Betul and Seoni Sub-divisions of the Central Provinces, hook-swinging there was performed not only by individuals for personal reasons, but also by the *Bhumka* or village priest, as the practice was 'supposed to exercise an important influence in the direction of securing the success of crops'.[82]

Whether hook-swinging was the result of a vow and conducted for personal and family reasons, or whether it was performed by 'victims' on behalf of the tribe, caste, village or larger unit, the underlying assumptions were the same. The god or (more commonly) the goddess would be pleased by the performance — the ritual, hopefully, having the effect of modifying or changing the deity's behaviour. If the individual was swung on behalf of the community, then this could bring rain, end epidemics or ensure the general prosperity of the community involved. If the individual made a vow to swing, this too could have a marked effect in the restoration of health or fertility or in bringing some other boon.

Some idea of the depth of these convictions is not only reflected in the Santals' fears about what would happen if they gave up swinging at the *charak puja*, but also in petitions to authorities in Madras Presidency as a result of Government attempts to suppress the practice in the second half of the nineteenth century. In 1857 one of the magistrates received petitions from villagers in two different sub-divisions complaining that their families had suffered 'very much' from sickness and mortality 'in consequence of their having ceased to perform these ceremonies' and asking him for permission to resume the practice.[83] A few years later the Magistrate of Kanara, who was meeting with some resistance in his attempts to suppress the practice, remarked:

> The extent to which these rites are periodically performed, seems to depend rather on the presence or absence of epidemic disease, than anything else, and I fear that neither persuasion or advice is likely to induce the people to give them up.[84]

Furthermore, in the 1890s the Government of Madras was approached by a cultivator on behalf of the community, requesting permission to revive the practice in a certain village in Madura District. He claimed that since the ceremony had been stopped the rainfall had been deficient and the crops scanty; cholera had been prevalent; and in families where there were five or six children ten years previously, there were now only two or three.[85]

NOTES

1. *JAS* No. 24, December 1833, pp. 609-10. The more correct name for the festival was, in fact, Sivotsava, or the festival of Siva, *AJ*, January 1828, p. 32.
2. *CCO*, Vol. XV, March 1846, pp. 222-3, Vol. XXIV, June 1855, p. 282; M. Monier Williams, *Religious Thought and Life in India* (1883), Delhi, 1974, p. 266; G. Oppert, *On the Original Inhabitants of Bharatavarsa or India* (1st edn 1893), reprint, New Delhi, 1986, p. 157; *Dnyanodaya*, 15/2/1850: *JRAS*, Vol. 7, London, 1843, pp. 106-8.
3. *Dnyanodaya*, 15/2/1850; *CCO*, June 1855, p. 281.
4. IOR Bom, JP, 31/7/1856 (see magistrates' reports on Satara, Ahmadnagar and Poona), *Dnyanodaya*, June 1843; Oppert, pp. 157-60.
5. IOR Bom. JP, 31/7/1856 (Satara); J. Grant Duff, *A History of the Marathas*, Vol. 1, London, 1912, p. 16.
6. IOR Bom. JP, 31/7/1856 (Ahmadnagar); M. Monier Williams, pp. 220-2; J.A. Dubois, *Hindu Manners, Customs and Ceremonies*, trans. and edited by H.K. Beauchamp, 3rd edn, Oxford 1897, pp. 637-8.
7. IOR Bom. JP, 31/7/1856 (Colaba and Ahmadnagar).
8. Ibid. (Dharwar); LMS W. Beynon to Ellis, 25/7/1837.
9. *Gazetteer of the Bombay Presidency*, Vol, XXII, *Dharwar*, Bombay, 1884, pp. 807-12; IOR Bom. JP, 31/7/1856 (Dharwar).

10. See especially Elmore, p. 24 and LMS Beynon to Ellis, 26/7/1837.
11. IOR Board's Collection F/4/2691; *Gazetteer of the Bombay Presidency*, Vol. XXI, Belgaum, pp. 612-3.
12. *Gazetteer of the Bombay Presidency*, Vol. XXII, *Dharwar*, pp. 807-12; IOR Bom. JP, 31/7/1856 (Dharwar).
13. B. Ziegenbalg, *Genealogy of the South-Indian Gods* (trans. by G.T. Metzgèr), Madras, 1869, p. 138. One of the best nineteenth century descriptions of Iyenar and the more important *shaktis* is in Oppert, pp. 464-513.
14. Oppert, pp. 471, 480-2; Ziegenbalg, p. 138; IOR P/4409 MJP, 30/6/1893, pp. 59, 72, 145; CMS CI 2/091/15, Elouis to Secs., 29/7/138; *WMN*, 1852, p. 139; *HF*, Vol.3, April 1864, p. 141; *MH*, Vol. 88, 1892, p.8; Elmore, p. 490; Dubois, p.598; E. Thurston, *Ethnographic Notes*, p. 490; M.Phillips, *The Evolution of Hinduism*, Madras, 1903, p. 123.
15. Elmore, p. 102; Oppert, pp. 464-71.
16. Oppert, pp. 495-504; Whitehead, pp. 71, 86.
17. Oppert, p. 471; Sel. Mad., p. 16; IOR P/4409 MJP, 30/6/1893, pp. 61-2; Thurston, *Ethnographic Notes*, p. 494; Mateer, *Land of Charity*, p. 221; *WWM*, Vol. 3, April-Sept. 1899, p. 586.
18. Sel. Mad., p.6.
19. *JAS*, No. 24, December 1833, p. 610.
20. A. Sutton, *Orissa and its Evangelization*, Derby, 1850, p.80.
21. *AJ*, 1828, p.32.
22. For some of the more noteworthy accounts of the *charak puja* during the first half of the nineteenth century, see Ramkamal Sen's account in *JAS*, No. 24, December 1833, pp. 609-13; *AJ*, 1828, pp. 32-5; Ward, pp. 15-23 and *CCO*, Vol. 5, 1836, pp. 195-8.
23. Mateer. pp. 219-21.
24. *Dnyanodaya*, 15/3/1845, 5/1/1846; Dubois, p. 599; IOR P/4409, MJP 21/12/1893; Oppert, p. 485; Elmore, pp. 18-19; *Madras District Gaztteers*, F.R. Hemingway, *Trichinopoly*, Madras, 1906, p. 318.
25. IOR P/4621 MJP, 24/9/1894, Inspector-General of Police to Chief Sec. of Government, 8 September 1894.
26. IOR P/4247, S.H. Wynne Acting Dt Magistrate to Government of Madras, 24/2/1892.
27. IOR P/406/43 Bom. JP, 19/9/1885.
28. Obeyesekere, *Medusa's Hair*, p. 130.
29. Ibid., p. 146
30. Basil Hall, p. 83.
31. Supra, pp. 19-23.
32. See, for example, WMMS, Lynch to Sec., 25/8/1820; CMS CI 2/091/15, Elouis, 29/7/1838 and CI 2/0101/5, Fox, Journal, 26/12/1844; Hoole, p. 358; *MH*, Vol. LXIV, 1868, p. 408 and Vol. LXXXVIII, 1892, p. 10.
33. *JAS*, No. 24, December 1833, p. 610.

34. *Reformer*, 7/4/1833, 24/3/1834; *Hindu Intelligencer*, 20/4/1857.
35. IOR P/188/61, p.34.
36. Ibid. See also report of the Commissioner of Burdwan, 7/7/1859.
37. *CCO*, November 1858, p. 480.
38. Bom. JP Magistrate of Belgaum, 25/1/1856, 31/7/1856; Oppert, p. 481; Mateer, p. 220.
39. S. Piggin, *Making of Evangelical Missionaries, 1789-1858. The Social Background, Motives and Training of British Protestant Missionaries to India*, Appleford, 1984, pp. 65-72.
40. *MH*, Vol. LXXXVIII, January 1892, p.8.
41. IOR P/4247, F.Van Allen to Second-class Magistrate, Madura, 6/2/1892.
42. Ibid., Wynne to Government of Madras, 24/2/1892.
43. See also Kosambi's description, p.111.
44. WMMS, Lynch to Sec., 25/8/1820.
45. *MH*, Vol. LXIV, 1868, p. 408.
46. *CMG*, 1850/1, p. 18. See also *CMG*, 1845, pp. 123-5.
47. Ernest R. Hilgard and Josephine R. Hilgard, *Hypnosis in the Relief of Pain*, Los Angeles, 1975, esp. pp. 166-99.
48. *Medusa's Hair*, p. 136.
49. IOR P/4409 MJP, 21/12/1893, p.65.
50. See especially A.L. Basham, *The Wonder That Was India*, London, 1954, pp. 193, 197-8, 336-7; J. Hastings (ed.) *Encyclopedia of Religion and Ethics*, Vol.6, Edinburgh 1913, pp. 849-53; M. Monier Williams, p. 24; Dubois, pp. 70, 645-8; Elmore, pp. 43-4, 73-4; Oppert, p. 453.
51. H. Whitehead, pp.80-6.
52. Quoted in Rui Gomes Pereira, *Goa*, Vol. 1, *Hindu Temples and Deities*, Goa, 1978, p. 183.
53. For animal sacrifice in connection with the south Indian deities, see especially Oppert, pp. 459-63, 469,487, 496-8 and Elmore, Ch. V, and with respect to deities associated with hook-swinging in western India, see *Census of India*, 1911, Bombay, Part 1. Report, pp. 63-4; *Gazetteer of the Bombay Presidency*, Vol.XXII, Dharwar, pp. 807-12. See also *The Indian Antiquary*, Vol. 7, October 1878, p. 264 and Dubois, p. 638.
54. *Dnyanodaya*, 15/1/1845; *AJ*, Vol, VI, Sept. 1818, pp. 297-8; *CMG*, 1845, pp. 124-5, 1850-1, p. 15.
55. *HF*, Vol. 1, April 1862, pp. 135-7; See also Vol. 3, April 1864, pp. 140-3.
56. CMS CI 2/0222/11.
57. Sel. Mad., p. 15.
58. For various strategies employed in north India for achieving the same kind of results as hook-swinging (such as cure of barrenness or disease), see especially W. Crooke, *The Popular Religion and Folklore of Northern India* (1st edn 1893), Delhi, 1968.
59. *The Hindu*, 11/6/1894.
60. WMMS, Lynch to Sec., 20/8/1820.

61. *Medusa's Hair*, p. 149.
62. Ibid., p. 133.
63. *JAS*, No. 24, Dec. 1833, p. 610; *AJ*, Jan. 1828. p. 34; Ward, p. 23; IOR P/188/61, Commissioner of Cuttack, 21/6/1859.
64. Bom. JP, 31/7/1856.
65. *Dnyanodaya*, June, July 1843, 15/1/, 2/6/1845, 5/1/1846, 1/2/1848, 15/2/1850, 15/2/1854; J. Forbes *Oriental Memoirs. A Narrative of Seventeen Years Residence in India.* (2nd edn) 2 Vols., London, 1834, p. 115; More, pp. 411-2.
66. Sel. Mad., pp.1, 12, 14, 17-18; J.A. Dubois, p. 598; Thurston, *Ethnographic Notes*, pp. 490, 493; IOR P/3784, 27 Aug. 1890; WMMS Lynch to Sec. 25/8/1820; CMS CI 2/091/15, J.H. Elouis to Secs. 29/7/1838; IOR P/4409 MJP, 30 June 1893, p. 72; C.A. Elliott, *Report on the Land Revenue Settlement of the District of Hoshangabad, Central Provinces*, Allahabad 1867, p. 126.
67. Hoole, p. 357.
68. *Dnyanodaya*, 2/6/1845; Moor, p. 412.
69. WMMS, Lynch to Sec., 20/8/1820; IOR P/4409 MJP, p. 72.
70. IOR Bom. JP, 31/7/1856.
71. CI 2/0222/3, Sharkey's Journal, 19-20 Feb. 1848.
72. CI 2/0222/9, Sharkey's Journal, 15/2/1851. During his visit to a hook-swinging ceremony at Kollangoda in Travancore in the late 1890s, the Rev. Joshua Knowles noted that some of the men performed with children in their arms: 'The terror of the little infants and the feelings of the poor mother waiting below may be left to the imagination', he wrote. (*WWM*, Vol.III, April-Sept. 1899, pp. 589-90).
73. J. Pinkerton, pp. 360-1.
74. Sel. Mad., p. 14.
75. CI 2/022/3, Sharkey's Journal, 21/2/1848.
76. IOR P/4409 MJP, 30/6/1893, p. 84.
77. Ibid., p.59. On the reasons for the swinging ceremony in the Madura district, see also *MH*, Vol. 88, 1892, p. 8 and Elmore, pp. 32-3.
78. IOR P/4409 MJP, 30/6/1893, p. 70.
79. Ibid., p. 72.
80. Ibid., p. 72.
81. V. Ball, p. 232.
82. *Central Provinces District Gazetteers, Seoni District*, Vol. A, p. 49 and *Betul District*, Vol.A, pp. 56-77. One of the difficulties that could occur in cases such as these (where the swinging was done on behalf of the community) was in finding a sacrificial victim. If, as was sometimes the case in the Hosungabad district, a man who had vowed to swing could not be found, then 'someone else had to be hired for the purpose'. Further to the east, however, the problem, as in various parts of south India, was overcome because priests or village officials regarded the office as a privilege. C.A. Elliott, p. 126; Ball, p. 232.

83. IOR MPP, 17/3/1857, Pelly to Pycroft 7/2/1857.
84. IOR MPP, 21-30/4/1860, Fisher to Pycroft, 16/4/1860.
85. Thurston, *Ethnographic Notes*, p. 498.

CHAPTER III

Patrons and Profiteers

While our chief focus has been on the attitude and apparent motivation of men and women who swung, we have also noted in passing that there were others (quite apart from swingers) who were anxious to perpetuate the system. Some of these parties were prepared to pay, or even use force, in a desperate attempt to make sure the swinging continued. Who were these people and what reasons did they have for promoting hook-swinging exhibitions?

Before we explore these issues, something further might be said about the ritual itself, about its value as a public spectacle — a *tamasha*, which, while it might please the deity, could also be used to please the crowd.

The sights, the spectacle, the processions, the lampooning of public figures and the swinging were, in one sense, all aspects of entertainment at the *charak puja* in Bengal. Indeed, the popular amusement rationale for the swinging was much more important in the Lower Provinces (where much of it was done for hire) than in other parts of India.[1] Magistrates in the different districts of the Lower Provinces where the custom prevailed drew attention to its importance as a spectacle and form of amusement.[2] J.H. Young, Commissioner of the Burdwan Division, like several other officers, compared 'the exhibition' with fairs and festivals in the United Kingdom. He wrote:

> The spectators generally behave quite as well as an English crowd at a fair, and I think that they look upon the whole thing much in the same way as we do on Greenwich fair. It is a universal holiday. Plenty of people meet in their best clothes, and appear to enjoy themselves, and the swinging is the object of special admiration, just as the swallowing of swords or the eating of fire by a conjurer is the gaping wonder at Greenwich.[3]

This theatrical aspect of swinging, which was one of the reason for its viability and popularity in the Lower Provinces, was also a factor (though a less important one) in its continued attractiveness and practice elsewhere. For example, one magistrate, referring to the practice in Masulipatam district in Madras Presidency, noted that it formed 'part of the attractions and shows of the processions on such occasions',[4] and two Indian officials in Ahmednagar in Bombay Presidency remarked that, in their opinion, the performance of the ceremony exercised no religious influence upon the spectators, 'most of whom view it in the light of sport'.[5]

It was partly because hook-swinging was, among other things, an 'exhibition' and spectacle that it helped to draw the crowds at festivals and on other occasions. With the crowds came money and sometimes also the kind of fame and reputation which is a reward for those involved in the funding and management of popular forms of entertainment.

However, it was not only the wealthy patrons and managers who, though not themselves involved in swinging, helped to keep the custom alive. Some of its supporters were artisans and craftsmen, or even more lowly paid village workers who helped in staging exhibitions.

According to Rev. J.E. Sharkey, who penned one of the more detailed accounts of the financial interests various groups had in the practice, the festival he witnessed at Weyoor in Masulipatam district in 1851 was a profitable business, and not only for the *zamindar* who presided.

> The priests appropriate to themselves the rich and numerous offerings of ghee, oil, fruit and money, which are laid before the idol in fulfilment of vows, or as presents. The musicians and light bearers, the usual attendants on such occasions, receive a stated income for their services. The village peons, the carpenters for preparing and fixing the beam into the swinging machine, the shoemakers employed to raise and lower the beam, the village slave for twisting the cord to which the swinging hook is attached, the village accountants, generally Brahmins, the shroffs or bankers of the Vaisia caste and lastly, the first swinger that runs the hooks through the skin of his back are all suitably rewarded; the payment varying from 4 Annas to 5 Rupees according to a table of rates fixed, no one knows when.[6]

Carpenters, blacksmiths and other attendants, such as musicians and those who pulled the ropes, are also mentioned in other sources — very occasionally with some reference to the rates of pay.[7] Thus, the Deputy Magistrate of Ahmednagar, when referring in 1855 to numerous cases of females swinging in his district, stated that the woman was generally 'assisted by the carpenter or the blacksmith of the village who receives from eight to twenty annas as his fee'.[8] This was for carpenters the equivalent of at least one, perhaps several days' wages.[9]

Those who profited most financially or in other ways from such exhibitions were, however, neither the village officials nor the attendants, but the landlords (including *zamindars*) and the managers of temples, as well as *pujaris* such as the one mentioned in Sharkey's diary. In fact, these were the people who played a major role in keeping hook-swinging going and who found it very much in their interests to encourage and patronise exhibitions.

In Bombay Presidency and specially in the Tamil-speaking districts of Madras Presidency, where temples and shrines were numerous and played such an important part in the life of the people, the *pujaris* and managers of temples were conspicuous as patrons and advocates of the custom. For them the swinging, which was invariably performed in front of the deity, was beneficial in a material sense for at least two reasons: it not only attracted greater crowds and hence more people who would give offerings (perhaps including money) to the temple or shrine, but also provided them with an opportunity of imposing a fee on devotees wishing to perform the practice — the amount it was possible to charge depending on the popularity and importance of the site as a place where the ritual might be enacted.

Evidence of the role of mangers and *pujaris* in supporting the practice in Madras Presidency, and of the way in which they were able to profit from hook-swinging exhibitions, is clearly apparent in a wide range of sources. Recalling events connected with his early life in Chingleput district in the 1860s, P.C. Arunthacharlu, Collector of Bellary district, remarked that the hook-swinging festival at Periyapalayam (a village two miles from his house) was celebrated with 'great pomp' and 'attracted thousands of people from other parts of that district and of the neighbouring districts of North Arcot, South Arcot, Salem and Nellore, and contributed a large annual income to a manager of the Durga temple under whose auspices it was conducted'.[10] In June 1858 the Magistrate of the Kanara district, lamenting the fact that he was unable to report a decline in the practice in the territory under his jurisdiction, reported that at one of the places where hook-swinging occurred, 'the most influential man in the neighbourhood is interested in keeping up the festival, as the offerings, which are considerable in amount, find their way into his pocket as *Mooktessur* [attorney] of the village Temple, at which they are made'.[11] Furthermore, commenting on the issue in 1893 C.G. Todhunter, Sub-divisional Magistrate in Tanjore district, stated that the trustee of the temple in Negapatam, where hook-swinging was still performed, admitted that 'as far as the temple authorities were concerned, the performance was encouraged solely in order to increase the temple's popularity and with no religious object whatever'.[12] Evidence relating to swinging festivals in other parts of the south, including South Arcot,[13] Trichinopoly,[14] and Madura,[15] as well as the native states of Travancore and Cochin,[16] also suggest that the managers of temples and/or the *pujaris* made considerable profits from the fees, donations and offerings received as a direct or indirect result of the practice.

In Bombay Presidency the situation appears to have been much the same, *pujaris* and those associated with the management of temples augmenting their income from hook-swinging exhibitions. The Magistrate of Khandesh stated that *pujaris* there were in the habit of receiving small sums, varying from 6 pies to 8 annas for each individual who swung.[17] D. Davidson, Magistrate of Poona, also provides evidence of the income derived from the practice. He wrote that 'a person desirous to swing in compliance with a promise or vow to his idol for any object he wishes or has obtained, pays fee to the temple to which the swinging apparatus is attached'.[18] Hook-swinging appears to have been an even more profitable business at Yellamma's Hill where the *pujaris* and those involved in the temple's administration were locked in conflict over the issue as to who should have control over the temple's income. Referring to these disputes in 1856, H.W. Reeves, Revenue Commissioner, Southern Division, estimated that the temple received between 1,500 and 2,000 rupees annually, a proportion of which was derived from hook-swinging.[19]

While in southern and western India, it was the *pujaris* and managers of temples who, apart from the swingers themselves, stood out as the major exponents of a system, in Bengal it was the *zamindars* and wealthier *babus* who played a somewhat similar, though perhaps even more important role in keeping the practice going. In Madras Presidency, for example, it was not only the existence of *inams* and the support of wealthier individuals and groups (such as those associated with the more popular temples) who helped encourage and finance the practice, but also the income derived from the swingers which helped to offset the cost of staging exhibitions. However, in Lower Bengal, where individuals had to be hired or paid to swing to a much greater extent, the costs of staging such events were correspondingly higher and the practice was even more dependent on the attitude and patronage of the wealthier classes.

In Bengal, and as mentioned above, the most important patrons were landlords or wealthier urban-based *babus*, rather than people associated with the management or running of temples. Temples were fewer and temple culture was less important than in some parts of Bombay and Madras Presidencies. In Bengal swinging took place not only in front of temples but elsewhere in streets and squares and before the houses of wealthy patrons.[20] The latter included well-known members of the *bhadralok* class who, in Calcutta in particular, encouraged the custom partly for social reasons.

Calcutta was a comparatively new and developing society which included many people who still had roots in the countryside. In what had become a thriving inter-racial and culturally diverse metropolis, which also offered a range of non-traditional types of employment, the *bhadralok* in particular were exposed to a comparatively new and challenging environment where the rules relating to caste and social status were probably not as clear-cut as in towns and villages in the *mofussil.* The patronage of hook-swinging exhibitions was, therefore, important as a method of maintaining social prestige in a fairly new, volatile and competitive situation.[21] According to Marshman, editor of the *Friend of India*, who was writing in March 1819:

> Every swinging post belongs to some rich native. The notoriety of any post, and the honor which is reflected through it on him who owns it, are regulated by the number who swing, and by the novel circumstances with which the ceremony may be distinguished. The native to whom the post belongs, defrays the expenses of the devotees during the period of their engagement in this service. It is esteemed a mark of distinction for any native to possess a swinging post; it is called by his name in all the surrounding villages; and of the honor atached to this distinction, there are few

who are not desirous.[22]

For the wealthier higher status Hindus there were clear social, financial and economic advantages and gains to be had through

Figure 13. *Hook-swinging in Bengal:* from an engraving based on a drawing by an Indian artist and brought from India by the Rev. Daniel Corrie. The engraving was reproduced in CMS journals, including *Missionary Papers*, which was published for the use of the society's contributors. In describing the scene, the editor suggested that: 'as the Drawing from which the Plate was engraved was taken from a real scene of this kind, it is very likely that those better sort of people at the front of the picture are bargaining about the pay of the wretch who is swinging over their heads; for these tortures are sometimes suffered for richer persons, who pay the men for it, and think to get all the good by hiring another to swing for them'.

Source: Missionary Papers, No. XVI, Christmas 1819.

their continuing support of hook-swinging exhibitions. This does not mean, however, that they were unmoved or uninfluenced by religious considerations. The income derived from the practice helped maintain not only hook-swinging but also other rituals and activities associated with the temples and the deity. Some landlords and patrons were possibly also influenced by the age-old conviction that the establishment and endowment of religious festivals was one way of acquiring religious merit.[23] Moreover, it was not only a few low caste individuals who were convinced of the dire consequences of failing to perform the ritual. The peasant who, for example, complained in the 1890s that the stopping of hook-swinging had already affected the rainfall and caused epidemics and other disasters was speaking, not merely on behalf of the so-called depressed classes, but for the entire community, presumably including high caste Hindus. Lastly, the importance attached by the higher castes to the religious aspects of the ritual is reflected in the fact that they were not infrequently prepared to swing 'by proxy'. Thus, referring to hook-swinging 'in expiation of vows', the Magistrate of Masulipatam stated that 'if the parties are of the higher castes and can afford it, they usually swing by low caste proxies, to whom they pay a sum of from 1 to 4 Rupees'.[24] One carefully considered missionary account of the *charak puja* in Bengal claimed that Kayastas and 'other respectable sudras' often hired individuals to act on their behalf[25] (Figure13).

Unity and conflict

On some occasions, especially in central and southern India, hook-swinging served to unite the community. The village or groups of villages, including tribals or people of different castes, came together to witness the performance of a ritual which could have far-reaching consequences for the health or prosperity of all. As at Weyoor, the swinger was 'the victim' being offered up on behalf of all. The expenses were paid for out of a common kitty, and if the god or goddess was satisfied, then everyone would benefit.

While in cases such as these the practice was an expression of shared beliefs and of the solidarity of the group, in some other instances it was extremely divisive — reactions to it reflecting class and other disparities within society.

On some occasions the determination of the more powerful and dominant groups to maintain or promote hook-swinging exhibitions conflicted with the wishes and interests of lower caste and tribal peoples who were reluctant to perform the ritual. The prospect of the pain and risks involved, not to mention broken promises of land and money, sometimes outweighed any possible benefits individuals might gain from mounting the *charak* and swinging. Faced with this resistance, and the possible cancellation of the swinging display, some landlords and other interested and more powerful parties resorted to subtle forms of pressure, or even violence, in attempts to coerce recalcitrant though powerless people to perform.

The use of coercion was probably not uncommon in Bengal, where *zamindars* had extraordinary legal and quasi-legal powers of authority and control over their *ryots*.[26] Writing from Serampore and referring to the annual celebrations of the *charak puja* in 1813, William Carey wrote:

> Several Hindus employed in the printing office applied this year to Brother Ward for protection to escape being dragged into these pretendedly voluntary practices: this brought before us facts which we were not aware of. It seems that the landlords of the poor, and other men of property, insist upon certain of their tenants and dependants engaging in these practices, and that they expect and compel by actual force, multitudes every year to join the companies of *sunyasees* in parading the streets, piercing their sides, tongues, etc. To avoid this compulsion, many poor young men leave their houses and hide themselves, but they are sure of being beaten if caught, or having their huts pulled down.[27]

J.C. Marshman, one of the Serampore trio and editor of the *Friend of India*, also drew attention to the use of compulsion, as well as financial inducements, in swinging:

> In many cases rich natives compel those of the poorer sort to swing, especially where they possess any kind of authority over them... In country villages where the authority of the landlord is paramount, the poor inhabitants are completely under his influence, and various modes of petty oppression are put in practice against those who on these occasions refuse a compliance with his wishes. The barber is forbidden to shave them and their fellow-villagers to smoke, or even associate with them.[28]

That the use of coercion in cases involving swinging was not confined to Bengal is illustrated by an official report of an enquiry into the death of Pariah after a hook-swinging ceremony at Bheemanaikenpoliem, near Trichinopoly, in 1893. The report includes statements made before the town sub-magistrate of Trichinopoly by relatives of the deceased and by some of the swingers involved. From this evidence it is clear that the well-to-do Ambalagars, who derived profits for their temple from the ceremony, had not only encouraged the men to swing by false promises of land and money, but after the accident occurred, had also done 'their best' to prevent the parties from coming forward to give evidence.[29] In another case in Tanjore district in 1890, which was also the subject of an official enquiry, T.E. Thomas, Superintendent of Police, was of the opinion that the Pariahs would have preferred to give up the practice 'but were afraid to express such a wish for fear of the Kullars' who were unwilling to have it discontinued.[30]

Middling and higher class interests in perpetuating hook-swinging not only led to instances of coercion, injustice and violence, but also comprised one of the major obstacles to reform. As will become clearer in the next chapter, those who wished to suppress the practice, whether British officials, missionaries or Hindu reformers, could do little without first winning over those wealthier and influential groups and classes who continued to profit financially or gain in other ways from the custom.

Summing up: a non-Brahmanical ritual

An analysis of the evidence relating to the practice reveals a number of important characteristics — the explanation for many of which probably lies in the history and development of the custom prior to the nineteenth century.

All the indications are that the ritual was totally alien to the Brahmanic culture and that it had nothing to do with what might be described as the Aryan or Vedic traditions as they persisted into the nineteenth century. We have noted that while the rite was performed extensively in Lower Bengal, in the Deccan and in southern India it was largely unknown in the north and north-west of India — the original homeland of the Aryan culture. It is also apparent that the practice was neither mentioned nor sanctioned in the *Shastras*, or classical Hindu texts. The clearest statement to this effect was made by the 'learned pundits' of the Dharma Sabha established at Vizianagram in the Vizagapatam district of Madras Presidency. When consulted on the matter in the 1890s, they replied:

> Hook-swinging is not mentioned in the 'Dharma Shastras' or codes of 'Parasera', 'Jagnyavalkya', 'Nirnayasindhu' and others, either as a means to gain the blessings of heaven or as a preventive to such blessings, nor has it ever been adopted by the high-caste Hindus, who follow the various ways of religion according to the Vedic Form.[31]

In spite of every effort to defend the practice, conservative Bengali intellectuals and members of the Bengal Dharma Sabha could find no evidence that the specific practice was enjoined in the Hindu scriptures and these views were echoed by *pundits* and others elsewhere.[32]

One of the more striking aspects of the ritual is that there is no evidence, in the mass of material so far consulted, of a single Brahman ever having swung. The communities involved were either Sudras (those originally outside Aryan society) or more commonly untouchables or tribals. The extent of the practice among tribals in the nineteenth century becomes apparent not only in records relating to the three Presidencies, but also in material pertaining to central India. As we have seen, the custom was known and followed among all the major tribes spreading from east to west across the uplands of central India — among the Gonds of the Central Provinces, the Santals of the Central Provinces and Chota Nagpur, the Bhils of Bombay Presidency and the Orarons of Bihar and north Orissa.[33]

Lastly, an analysis of the deities concerned suggests that Siva alone, of all the gods and goddesses before whom hook-swinging took place, might be considered a classical Hindu deity. However, as is well known, there is strong evidence (for example in the seals unearthed in the Indus Valley) that Siva was originally a pre-Aryan deity. Furthermore, hook-swinging was linked in all the areas outside Bengali centres of influence more with ideas of blood sacrifice than personal austerities — blood sacrifice being a practice studiously avoided by Brahmans in the nineteenth century.

The argument that hook-swinging was essentially non-Brahmanical also helps to explain why it was less entrenched in Bengal than in Bombay and Madras Presidencies. In Bengal the influence and acceptance of the Brahmanic culture among the communities immediately below was perhaps greater than in the other regions where non-Brahman movements developed. For Bengalis, the concept of the Brahman was to some extent subsumed in the concept of *bhadralok* —'the respectable people' who included Kayasthas and Vaishas as well as Brahmans.[34] Being more influenced by Brahman attitudes and culture the higher non-brahman castes and classes were therefore less inclined to participate directly in hook-swinging rituals.

But if all the evidence suggest that the custom was a non-Brahman practice, does this necessarily mean it was of Dravidian origin — an argument that has been put forward by J.H. Powell in an article on the subject published in 1911?

The problem with this suggestion is that it seems to imply that hook-swinging was an ancient ritual. However, what is clearly apparent is that no-one (including the present writer) has been able to discover any evidence of the practice prior to the sixteenth century.[35] It appears to be mentioned neither in the more obvious inscriptions or in travellers' accounts before the arrival of the Portuguese, and the balance of scholarly opinion in the nineteenth century was that the ritual was of fairly recent origin. For example, in a petition to the Legislative Council of India against the practice signed by 34 Protestant missionaries residing in or near Calcutta, they pointed out that in the judgement of the better informed Hindus themselves the 'tortures' inflicted at the *charak puja* were comparatively modern.

Whatever be the case, it is clear that the practice originated some time during or prior to the early sixteenth century, probably among the lowest castes and tribes among whom the custom was especially well known and popular in the nineteenth century. In all probability, individuals and groups somewhat higher in status (perhaps impressed with the usefulness and apparent potency of hook-swinging as a tactic and ritual in controlling supernatural forces) gradually adopted the custom until, in some parts of the country, it was practised by almost all classes in the population except Brahmans. The process of sanskritisation, involving the adoption by lower castes of the practices and customs of those above them, is well known. But also important has been the opposite process whereby higher castes emulate the lower. This type of development, which may well explain the spread of hook-swinging among the higher status communities, has long been recognised by historians of ancient India, such as A.L.

Basham, Hart and others, as an important element in cultural and religious change.[36]

NOTES

1. Compare, for example, the comments of magistrates in Lower Bengal with those of officials from Bombay. (IOR P/188/61, 10/2/1860, Bom, JP, 31/7/1856).
2. IOR P/188/61. See magistrates of Patna, Rajshahye, Burdwan, Chittagong and Chota Nagpur.
3. IOR P/188/61, p. 37.
4. Sel. Mad., p. 14
5. Bom. JP, 31/7/1856. Comments by Krishnajee Wassoodew and Ramchunder.
6. CMS CI 2/0222/9, Sharkey's Journal, 15/2/1851.
7. *AJ*, Jan. 1828, p. 34; IOR Bom. JP, 17/9/1855, Richardson to Sudr Faijdaree Adawlut, 7/9/1855, IOR Bom. JP, 17/9/1855; LMS North India, Bengal, Box 5, 1837-8, Campbell to Ellis, 2/5/1837; Weitbrecht, p. 124.
8. IOR Bom. JP, 31/7/1856. See also the comments of the Duftedar (head Indian revenue officer of the collector's establishment) and the head accountant, enclosed with the magistrates' correspondence, and *Dnyanodaya*, 15/2/1856.
9. In 1833, when prices and wages were higher, carpenters in Ahmednagar received from 4 to 8 annas a day. *Gazetteer of the Bombay Presidency.* Vol. XVII, *Ahmednagar*, Bombay 1884, p. 322.
10. IOR P/4409 MJP, 21/12/1893, p. 61. See also IOR MPP 2/7/1867, Act Magistrate, Madras District to Govt. Fort St. George 9/7/1867. Writing in *Ethnographic Notes*, first published in 1907, Thurston remarked that 'the apparatus for hook-swinging still lies outside the Periyapalam temple near Madras', p. 489.
11. IOR MPP, 2/7/1858, W. Fisher to Chief Sec. of Govt. 5/6/1858.
12. IOR P/4409 MJP, 21/12/1893, p. 72. For Tanjore district, see also IOR P/3784 MJP, 27/8/1890, (Valambagudi).
13. IOR P/4409 MJP, 21/12/1893, pp. 55, 58.
14. IOR P/4621, 24/9/1894.
15. IOR P/4409 MJP, 21/12/1893, p. 59.
16. Knowles, p. 168; L.K. Anantha Krishna Iyer, p. 3.
17. IOR Bom. JP, 16/12/1856.
18. Ibid.
19. IOR Board's Collections, F/4/2691.
20. Alexander Duff, p. 269; CMS CI 1/1/M7, 1837-9, F. Wybrow to Sec. 4/5/1838; See, for example, comments by the Rev. T. Morgan, the Baptist pastor of Howrah and Salkiya that 'the richest babus had poles

erected in their gardens as usual'. (*Baptist Magazine*, Vol. XXXIII, p. 256.).

21. *FI* (monthly) Vol. II, No. 9, March 1819, p. 141.
22. See specially 'On the present celebration of the Hindoo Poojas', *FI* (monthly), Vol. III, No. 23, May 1820, pp. 125-139.
23. J. Duncan M. Derrect, *Religion, Law and the State in India*, New York, 1968, p. 484.
24. Sel. Mad., p. 14.
25. *CCO*, Vol. V, April 1836, pp, 195-6. See also *Dnyanodaya*, Vol. IV, 15/1/1845; C. Acland, *A Popular Account of the Manners and Customs of India*, London, 1847, p. 68; *The Hindu*, 3/9/1893.
26. See especially G.A. Oddie, *Social Protest in India. British Protestant Missionaries and Social Reforms*, Delhi 1979, pp. 110-28.
27. *Periodical Accounts of the BMS*, Vol. V, p. 521.
28. *FI*, Vol. II, No. 9, March 1819, p. 142. See also ibid., Vol. IV. No. XV, 1826, p. 581 and *FI*, 16/4/1835.
29. IOR P/4621 MJP, 27/9/1894.
30. IOR P/3784 MJP, 27/8/1890.
31. IOR P/4409 MJP, 30/6/1893, p. 78.
32. Infra, pp. 118-119.
33. For the Bhils and hook-swinging, see *Dnyanodaya*, Vol. 2, No. 6, June 1843, and for the custom among the Orarons see Clarence Maloney, *Peoples of South Asia*, New York, 1974, p. 444.
34. See especially S.N. Mukherjee, 'Class, Caste and Politics in Calcutta, 1815-38', in E. Leach and S.N. Mukherjee (eds), *Elites in South Asia*, Cambridge, 1970, pp. 33-78.
35. *CCO*, November 1858, p. 480. When consulted on the issue neither the late Professor A.L. Basham nor Professor Romila Thapar, both eminent historians of pre-modern India, could recollect any reference to the practice in ancient or medieval Indian inscriptions or texts.
36. Note for example, Basham's point that the legend of Visnu as a boar 'probably developed through a primitive non-Aryan cult of a sacred pig' in A.L. Basham, *The Wonder That was India*, London 1954, p. 302 and also the evidence of Tamil influence on the development of Sanskrit in B. Stein (ed.), *Essays on South India*, Honolulu, 1975, pp. 43-63. For a documented account of the same process of upward filtration operating in recent times see my discussion of Christian conversion among non-Brahmans in Andhra Pradesh, a movement which was very largely inspired by the prior conversion of untouchables: G.A Oddie (ed.), *Religion in South Asia*, 2nd revised and enlarged edition, Delhi 1991, pp. 110-13.

CHAPTER IV

Government Attempts at Suppression

Initial attempts to restrict the custom were made by police and municipal authorities in the larger Presidency towns such as Calcutta, Patna, Bombay, Poona and Madras during the first half of the nineteenth century.[1] Under mounting pressure from European residents, who for a variety of reasons regarded the practice with increasing aversion,[2] local governments introduced and gradually extended regulations preventing the performance of the ritual in major thoroughfares and in the neighbourhood of European residential areas.

Madras

The first attempt to curb the practice at the wider Presidency level occurred in Madras in 1854. In the course of its correspondence with the Madras Government in 1853, the Government of India included a copy of a despatch from the Court of Directors reporting on measures adopted in British Guiana of the suppression of hook-swinging among Indian emigrants there.[3]

Upon receipt of this information the Madras Government issued instructions calling on all district magistrates and the chief magistrate of Madras to report on the frequency of the observance of the festival in the Presidency and the means already adopted for discouraging it. Enquiries were made through subordinate European and Indian officials, including local police, during the last four months of 1853.[4] In an order passed on the magistrates' reports in February of the following year it was noted that the swinging festival appeared to be less frequently observed than formerly and that though the suppression of a practice so 'revolting' in its nature and so injurious in its effects on those who witnessed it, would be perfectly justifiable, the Government hoped that it might be greatly checked if not entirely abolished, by the influence of the magistrates, 'aided by the example and endeavours of the higher and more educated classes of the Native community'.[5]

It was suggested that the introduction of the practice in any place where it did not then obtain 'might' with propriety be prohibited, and that the ceremony 'should' also be prohibited in any village where the observance led to loss of life. However, in other circumstances (presumably in places where hook-swinging exhibitions were well established and did not involve loss of life), magistrates were encouraged merely to use their 'influence' and powers of persuasion.[6]

A great deal was therefore left to the 'discretion' of magistrates whom the Government felt sure (once the object of the measure was properly understood) would be willingly seconded 'by the influence of the great mass of the community, and, more particularly, of the wealthy and intelligent classes who do not seem, even now, to countenance or support the Swinging ceremony'.[7]

As we shall see, in its attempt to draw a distinction between exhibitions which 'might' be prohibited and those which should be allowed to proceed, the Government of Madras created a great deal of uncertainty and confusion in the minds of both magistrates and public alike. Indeed, the executive was not infrequently placed in the position of having to curb the enthusiasm of some of its own officers, countermanding their attempts at suppression and giving a general impression that it was not particularly serious about suppressing the practice.

Bombay

In the meantime, the question of hook-swinging was also raised in official circles in Bombay Presidency — not by the Government of India, but by one of the Presidency's own public servants, Arthur St. John Richardson, recently appointed Judge and Sessions Judge of Khandesh district in the northern part of the province.[8]

Most of the Judge's previous postings had been in the north-west, where the custom was unknown. However, the practice was common in Khandesh district and in April 1855 Richardson was dismayed to discover that his visit to the jail at Dhoolia coincided with the performance of what he described as a 'disgusting' hook-swinging exhibition nearby. In a letter addressed to the *sadr faujari adalat* (the

Company's Court)[9] in Bombay, he explained:

> Without any wish to intrude into such matters connected with Palace jurisdiction as appear to the Magistrate to be exclusively vested in his office, and without any intention of interfering with religious ceremonies in matters beyond my official control, I must confess that I was so shocked at the idea of so barbarous and cruel practice publicly exhibited in a town within the dominions of the British Govt. which had abolisehd self-immolation of widows, eradicated infanticide, and within the last ten years totally put down the inhumane rites of the Khonds, that I was under an impression that such a ceremony must be conducted without the knowledge of the Police authorities, and knowing that an exhibition of this nature would not be tolerated, for an instant, in the Island of Bombay or in the town of Poona, and being the only European Civil officer at Dhoolia, I sent a peon with my compliments to Mr Ram Naid, the Deputy Magistrate, to inform of this fact'.[10]

The judge, however soon learned from Ram Naid and also in correspondence with Mansfield (the magistrate and Naid's superior) that the local authorities were virtually powerless to intervene. Mansfield explained that though nobody deplored the 'cruel and barbarous' practice more than he did, there was nothing he could do under existing regulations to suppress the custom.

The judge therefore decided to take the matter further and raised the issue in a letter to the Bombay court in which he asked them:

> Whether the barbarous and disgusting ceremony of Swinging by the hook is one that should be publicly allowed in the towns of the British Government attended as it is by grevious bodily suffering to the victims and calculated to maime and destroy temporarily, sometimes permanently, the action of the limbs or whether it is of such a nature that being calculated to foster ferocious and fanatic feelings in the performers, as well as spectators, it is advisable to issue Notification condemning the practice, and recommending its discontinuance.[11]

In response the court asked the judge and magistrate for medical evidence. The magistrate, in reply, included a detailed letter from

Ram Naid, which strongly reinforced what both British officials had been saying about the necessity for legislation.

Ram Naid felt able to comment on the attitude of the educated classes and also report on conversations he had had with 'several persons' who had 'frequently undergone the penance themselves'. He stated that:

> The feelings of the more enlightened part of the native community are certainly shocked by so barbarous and cruel an exhibition of religious fervour; and the Shastras nowhere require or sanction such a penance, nor do I think its discontinuance would create any general discontent; but on the contrary, it would soon be looked upon as an addition to the blessing heaped on India since the commencement of British rule.

Referring to the debate about the possible physical and other effects of the ritual, he added:

> . . . Although neither death nor permanent bodily injury can be proved to have ever resulted from the penance of swinging by the hook, yet the impression which such an exhibition makes on the community, and the certain bodily pain and probably mental shock which it occasions to the person submitting to it, are such as to justify the interference of Legislature.

Mansfield's letter fully endorsed his subordinate's conclusions. He concurred with Naid in thinking that the discontinuance of the practice 'would not create any general discontent'. He emphasised that 'in the present state of law', nothing could be done, and he therefore suggested that the Legislative Council should be moved to introduce legislation suppressing the practice.

In laying the subject before the Government, the sadr court, looking for a solution to the problem similar to that proposed in Mansfield's letter, also recommended that the Legislative Council consider legislative action. In doing so, however, they intimated that there had been some disagreement among their members and that one of them had stressed the need for further information and had also raised the possibility of suppressing the practice by proclamation — a method of procedure based, not on special legislation, but on existing regulations — a solution which a majority of the court did not at that stage believe the Government could legally adopt.[12]

In his minute on the question in September 1855, Lord Elphinstone, the Govenor, recommended prudence:

> Though Mr Ram Naid's assurance that the swinging can be put down without creating dissatisfaction among the great bulk of the population is very gratifying, yet I conceive that we should not be justified in sending up a draft act without further enquiry both as to the extent of the practice in this Presidency, and as to the effect of putting it down by authority.[13]

Magistrates were consulted and in July 1856 the Government was able to summarise the tenor of their replies. These, it said, showed that 'the practice obtains extensively in all the zillahs excepting Ahmedabad, Kaira, Surat and Broach — That it is not generally regarded as part of the Hindoo religion — That its suppression would cause some dissatisfaction, but not to any serious extent — That fatal results or severe injury are not frequent'.[14]

Though the Governor-in-Council was of the opinion that the custom should be forbidden, the question remained as to whether it should be prohibited by legislative enactment or by proclamation — the latter being the way it had been suppressed among Indian immigrants in the colony of British Guiana. Elphinstone and his council were conscious of the fact that the sadr court's previous recommendation was not unanimous and that, since then, two new judges (W.B. Frere and R. Keays) had been appointed.[15] They therefore decided to ask the court to reconsider the question of how to suppress the practice. In its reply, the court reversed its earlier recommendation. They stated that the judges now present were 'unanimously of the opinion that no act of the Legislature is required for the purpose'. They declared that if the Government was determined to put down the custom 'they have, the Judges think, power to do so under Clause 1st — Section 19, Regulation 12 of 1827,[16] and the Judges would recommend that the Magistrates should by proclamation prohibit the exhibition at any particular Fair about to be held in the respective zillahs'.[17] The court's view that by proceeding in this way 'much less importance would be given to the subject', coincided with Elphinstone's determination to minimise all possible risks by adopting a low-key approach. The Governor was, in fact, apprehensive about 'the possible risk of disturbance', and in later correspondence with the Government of India explained that he thought that the suppression of the custom 'might affort a handle to designing and ill-affected persons just as the rumour about human sacrifices being required before the works on the Bhore Ghaut began might have led to something like a Santhal insurrection, and that Hook Swinging, however disgusting and deplorable it is, was not worth the risk'.[18]

The court's suggestion was seized upon as the method most likely to avoid disturbance. The idea of legislation was dropped and, as in Madras, the Governor-in-Council directed magistrates to adopt a cautious, piecemeal and selective method of suppressing the custom.

Magistrates were asked to ascertain whether there were any person in their zillah who were likely 'from mercenary motives' to encourage hook-swinging. If there was no reason to apprehend that the opposition of the above-mentioned parties received the support of the people, then magistrates were to immediately issue a proclamation prohibiting the practice at particular fairs in the areas under their jurisdiction. If, on the other hand, opposition was to be expected, then the local officers were to carefully consider the circumstances and factors involved before prohibiting the custom, and in some cases might decide that it would be better to tolerate the practice 'until the motives of humanity which call for its suppression, are understood and appreciated'.[19]

After receiving copies of the relevant papers on the Bombay Government's decision, including instructions to magistrates, which had been sent out in August 1856, the Government of India under Lord Canning expressed two main objections.[20] Firstly, the Governor-General in Council remarked somewhat sarcastically that he could not gather from the information before him 'whether the practice of swinging by the hook in the Bombay Presidency is or is not considered by the authorities at Bombay to be illegal'. Secondly, referring to 'the uncertain nature of the instructions' issued to the magistrates of the Presidency, he declared that 'no Government can rightly delegate to its subordinate officers a responsibility such as is left to those to whom the orders are addressed' and that it was in his opinion 'a very dangerous precedent under the same law to prohibit in one place an Act permitted in another'.[21] In his reply Elphinstone emphasised that discretionary powers were left to magistrates in order 'to avoid the possible risk of disturbance' and that he was happy to agree with his 'Honorable Colleagues' to direct the custom's 'absolute prohibition'. In conclusion, he stated that magistrates had now been instructed to issue a proclamation making the prohibition against hook-swinging 'absolute' in all the zillahs in the Presidency.[22]

Bengal

Like hook-swinging in Madras and Bombay, the issue was raised and debated in official circles in Bengal in the years leading up to the outbreak of the rebellion in 1857. However, no action was taken on the matter until 1860, largely because the Directors, apparently shaken by news of the Santal rebellion, intervened and postponed procedures which would have led to earlier attempts at suppression.

As in Bombay, initial enquiries were prompted by one of the Company's own servants. However, in this case the officer concerned, instead of raising the issue at a higher level, decided to deal with the question in his own way.

Francis Lestock Beaufort, who arrived in Bengal in 1837, was the author of a digest of criminal law procedure in Bengal which was published in 1850.[23] In the following year, as Magistrate of Jessore in East Bengal, he was accused by his superiors of mishandling a case. This may have been because they genuinely believed he was mistaken, or even because they were jealous of Beaufort's legal accomplishments.

According to his superiors, Beaufort 'took upon himself' to issue to the police of his district what was later described as an 'irregular' circular, directing them to prevent the swinging of devotees on *charaks* on the occasion of the *charak puja*. According to the official report of this incident, Beaufort 'construed the avowed intention of a Naib to resist this illegal injunction into a defence of his authority and sentenced him, contrary to the evidence, to 15 days imprisonment and labor, the latter commutable into a fine'. A petition against the sentence first drew the attention of the Deputy-Governor of Bengal to the circumstances, and a full explanation was called for. Although upon receipt of this information the Bengal Government passed 'a severe censure' on Beaufort's proceedings, he was later exonerated by the Court of Directors who regarded his explanation 'as entirely satisfactory'.[24]

The justice or otherwise of these proceedings is not the issue at stake. What is relevant is the fact that the incident reminded the

Directors of the problem of hook-swinging in different parts of India. In a despatch to the Bengal Government subsequent to the correspondence dealing with Beaufort's attempt to suppress the custom, they again referred to the 'practice of swinging in *churrucks*' and remarked:

> Should this practice be found to be attended with cruelty, and liable to be enforced without the free consent of parties submitting to it, we feel assured that you will not fail to consider and report what measures should be adopted with reference to it.[25]

Prompted by the Court of Directors, the Bengal Government immediately instituted enquiries though the Superintendent of Police, Lower Bengal. In June 1853 circular orders were sent to all magistrates and joint magistrates asking them to report especially 'all cases in which the practice of swinging at the Churruck Poojah is attended with cruelty or enforced without the free consent of the parties submitting to it'. The circular also asked for their opinion as to 'whether the Law as it stands is sufficient for preventing such cruelty or violent enforcement of the rite'.[26] However, before these enquiries were completed, the Directors, who were apparently disturbed by the outbreak and spread of the Santal rebellion,[27] developed second thoughts about the wisdom of outright suppression and suggested in 1856 that endeavours for the discontinuance of the practice should be based 'on the exertion of influence rather than upon any act of authority.[28]

In the following year, in February 1857, the Protestant missionaries in Bengal, dissatisfied with the Government's inaction, discussed the issue of hook-swinging at a monthly meeting of the Calcutta Missionary Conference — a well-organised and influential ecumenical association.[29] The 25 members present included representatives of the Church, Baptist, London and Presbyterian missionary societies and also W. Macleod Wylie, First Judge of the Court of Small Causes, Calcutta, a well-known advocate of social reform and Christian missions.[30] At this and the subsequent meeting in March 1857 a memorial to the Legislative Council respecting 'the tortures publicly inflicted and endured during the annual Churruck Poojah (especially the practice of swinging with hooks pierced through the back, and boring the tongue and other parts of the body)' was finalised and signed.[31] It was not, however, immediately presented to the Legislative Council because of the outbreak of the mutiny and civil rebellion, and was held over until October 1858 when it was finally presented and printed by order of the Legislative Council.[32]

In their petition, the missionaries stressed that the tortures that were practised during the festival tended to 'harden and corrupt the beholders'; and that, in the judgement of the better informed Hindus themselves, they were 'comparatively modern' and were 'neither warranted by the accredited standards of their religion, nor entitled to toleration on the ground of respect to popular usage'.[33] They argued that those who swung seldom endured the suffering 'with any hope of acquiring religious merit, but ordinarily from the simple desire of gain'. They held that hook-swinging had a 'brutalizing effect' on the spectators, was uncivilised and associated with violence, crime and cruelty. Referring to the need for more effective action, they also maintained that secular education would have little effect in encouraging the moral improvement of the people and that 'the Native community' though 'sensible of the real character of the scenes which distinguish the Churruck Poojah' lacked 'the moral fortitude' to suppress, or effectually to discourage the *charak* tortures. They therefore asked the Council to pass legislation to suppress throughout the East India Company's territories, 'all those public practices at the Churruck Poojah, whether nominally religious practices or not, which are in themselves cruel and inhuman'.

Upon receipt of the memorial, the Legislative Council resolved, perhaps not surprisingly in the light of the events of 1857-58, that any direct interference on the part of the Government was 'inadvisable'.[34] However, Lord Stanley, Secretary of State for India in the recently reorganised governing structure in London, disagreed. On reading the missionary memorial and the Council's response to it, he endorsed the missionary view that 'the progress of education' had not led, up until then, to the suppression of the *charak* cruelties. He pointed out that the Governments of Bombay and Madras had already acted to discourage hook-swinging, but that in Bengal where such practices were most extensive, 'the efforts made to discountenance them' had been attended 'with the least success'. He stressed that he had no intention of pressing for immediate legislative interference, but suggested that the Bengal Government could do more to secure the support of the landed classes and make known its views with regard to such exhibitions 'without causing alarm'.[35]

This despatch precipitated the Bengal Government's second and more extensive enquiry into the practice in Lower Bengal. As a result of that enquiry, and the Lieutenant-Governor's recommendations, magistrates were instructed to adopt two types of approach with respect to the rite.

1. Where the practice existed as a long-established custom, they were directed, by using their personal influence, and by obtaining the cooperation of *zamindars*, to induce the people voluntarily to abandon the practice.

2. On the other hand, where the *charak* swinging was not an established custom and more an occasional exhibition, magistrates were authorised to prohibit its celebration 'as a local measure of police for the preservation of order and decency'.[36]

These measures, which came into operation in 1859, were, according to the Government's own admission, 'only partially successful'.[37] In the next few years the Government was made increasingly aware of the Western-educated classes' desire for more effective suppression. Members of the British Indian Association (who had been divided on the issue) were consulted in October 1864. In replying to the Government's letter soliciting their views, they recommended the suppression of both 'the cruel practices of perforating the body commonly called *banphorah* and hook-swinging at the Churruck Poojah'.[38] A few months later, in February 1865, Raja Satya Sharan Ghosal, a member of the Bengal Legislative Council, moved for leave to introduce a bill to declare hook-swinging illegal. The motion was, however, withdrawn, in deference to the opinion of the President and a majority of the members present that the discontinuance of the practice might be brought about without recourse to special legislation.[39] In his comments, which like those of Digamber Mitter expressed basic agreement with the Raja's desire for reform, the Lieutenant-Governor pointed out that 'the matter had been for some time under the consideration of the Government, and it was his intention to issue orders in a short time, which he hoped would have the effect of discontinuing the objectionable practice of hook-swinging'.

In the following month, in March 1865, the Government finally took steps which they hoped would lead to the total suppression of the custom.[40] In a resolution dated the 15th of March 1865, they stated that the practice of hook-swinging and other self-torture, such as *banphora*, were 'cruel to those who suffer hurt from them, whether of their own will or otherwise, and revolting to humanity', and that they also presented 'a demoralizing public spectacle', which tended to keep alive among the people 'a feeling of indifference to the suffering of their fellow-creatures and to the value of human life'. The resolution referred to the Government's own efforts and those of 'the more enlightened, intelligent, and respected Hindus' to discountenance and discourage these customs. Finally, noting that these efforts had been only 'partially successful', they outlined new measures which the Government was now adopting, supported 'not only by a sense of what is due to the feelings of all classes of her Majesty's subjects, but by a decided expression of enlightened opinion on the part of the leading Members of the Hindu community.'

All magistrates were 'required' to direct people to abstain from 'hook-swinging, or other self-torture, in public, and from the abetment thereof', whenever they considered that such direction was necessary 'to prevent annoyance to persons lawfully employed, or danger to human life, health or safety'. Persons who disobeyed any such injunction were to be 'prosecuted and punished according to Law'. Finally, directions were given for notifying and gaining the further cooperation of landholders and other members of the public.

The Madras revivals

Even in Bombay and Bengal, where magistrates were eventually given definite authority to prevent hook-swinging *in all circumstances* in public places, there were still occasions when swinging continued to take place. This was no doubt partly because those involved were not sufficiently aware of the change in official policy and of the Government's determination of suppress the practice.[41]

The situation in Madras was, however, very different. There the Government tried to maintain the notion that the ritual could be suppressed in some circumstances and not in others. It was a policy which, as we have seen, left a great deal to the discretion of individual officers and which was also very difficult to interpret and administer in certain situations.

Spurred on by the Government's initial enquiries of 1853 and influenced by what one Bombay official described as 'the spirit of the age', some magistrates appear to have been either unable or unwilling to grasp the degree to which the Madras Government was reluctant to intervene. Some officers, like Henry Forbes of Tanjore district (who thought he had secured agreements with the managers of 72 temples to end the practice), were commended for using their influence and powers of persuasion.[42]

On the other hand, at least three magistrates were criticised for going too far. In 1854 the Magistrate of Coimbatore was informed that he had exceeded the intentions of Government by *entirely* prohibiting swinging festivals in his district.[43] Some years later a decision by J.D. Bourdillon, who countermanded an earlier order virtually prohibiting the celebration of all hook-swinging festivals in North Arcot, was upheld as being strictly in line with Government policy.[44] Lastly, in 1890 the Magistrate of Tanjore was asked to withdraw an order prohibiting hook-swinging festivals throughout the district on the grounds that government policy had hitherto been 'to discourage but not absolutely prohibit the custom'.[45]

Like the measures which were supposed to operate selectively in Bengal during the period from 1860 to 1865, this policy was only partially successful and was one of the principal factors which led to a revival of hook-swinging in some of the Tamil-speaking districts in the 1890s.

Judging from the reports of individual magistrates and also from the results of extensive enquiries in 1893, it appears quite likely that by that time hook-swinging had disappeared from most of Madras Presidency, including the Kannada-speaking district of South Kanara, the Telugu region and some, though not all, of the Tamil districts.[46]

In the latter region some district officers were obviously *unaware* that in some places, and in spite of all their efforts, the custom continued. For example, in August 1854 Henry Forbes boldly declared that 'the practice has been entirely abandoned throughout Tanjore, with the concurrence of every person heretofore connected with it'.[47] However, contrary to these claims, it appears that hook-swinging in Tanjore district had never completely died out. The Superintendent of Police, T.E. Thomas, writing to his superior in Madras, reported an incident of hook-swinging in June 1890 after the Mariamma car festival at Valambagudi village in the Vallam taluk. In the course of his enquiries he was told by the priest that swinging had been conducted at the same place 'uninterruptedly' for the past 30 years.[48]

Furthermore, there were other instances of swinging which magistrates knew about but which, because of Government policy, they felt powerless to prohibit. One of these festivals was in the village of Pariapolyam in Trivallore taluk near Madras where, in the late 1860s, it continued to attract large crowds and also a large amount of money into the coffers of the local temple. The acting magistrate who wanted to stop the festival in 1867 was told quite firmly that this would be exceeding the limits 'to which official interference had been restricted'.[49]

Apart from these festivals which, without the knowledge of local officials continued largely unaffected by Government policy, were others which came to be known as 'revivals'. These were celebrations which were reintroduced at certain locations after a period of years during which no swinging had taken place.

One of the first of these was a revival at Kambam in the Madura district — an event which was recorded by an American missionary in 1868.[50] Commenting on the revival of the ritual which had been 'discontinued for many years', he ended his account with a prediction, realised in the 1890s, that as the people came to understand that the Government would not interfere to prevent hook-swinging, 'it is likely to become a common occurrence'.

These revivals reflected the enduring and underlying needs of individuals who continued to regard the ritual not only as a method of making money or improving social and religious status, but of maintaining their own or the community's prosperity and welfare. The continuing interest in retaining the custom was reflected in petitions which were sometimes sent, asking magistrates for permission to revive the practice and also in the number of revivals which took place after the Valambagudi swinging festival in June 1890. These occurred in the Tanjore, Trichinopoly, Tinnevelli and Madura districts, all of them southern Tamil-speaking areas of the Madras Presidency, during the period from 1890 to 1894.[51]

Apart from the fact that the original financial, religious and social reasons for wanting to mount hook-swinging exhibitions were still largely present, Government inactivity gave an ever-increasing impression that swinging was, in fact, allowable and permitted by Government authority.[52]

Commenting on the publicity given to the Government's attitude towards the swinging at Valambagudi in 1890, C.W. Weir (subsequently Acting Magistrate at Ganjam) remarked that:

I was in Tanjore in 1890 when the case occurred in Valagambudi

> [sic], and I recollect that immediately afterwards when the people discovered they would not be interfered with, there were rumours that the exhibition was to be repeated at several other places in the district. Though this did not actually happen, imitators were speedily found in the adjoining districts.[53]

Once incidents such as these came to the notice of villagers and other interested people, with a clear message that the Government authorities were not prepared to interfere, then other exhibitions were organised and 'revived' in various parts of the country. These further displays (most of which were reported in English and Tamil language newspapers) again served to underline the point that those involved would go unpunished and that, no matter how much the police and magistrates might remonstrate, they could and would not stop the practice.

After witnessing the revival of hook-swinging at Sholavandan in the Madura district in 1891, the Rev. John Chandler, an American missionary, commented that ater 24 years of not having had the ceremony 'the people, having learned that the present powers that be would do no more than discourage it, have revived it again with great *éclat*'[54] (Figures 15,16 and 17). Furthermore, commenting on proposals for a repetition of the same festival at Sholavandan in 1894, the editor of the *Madura Mail* noted:

> For over thirty years, this festival has been given up. One of the four Kavalgars got information of a similar festival being indulged in with impunity in a village in the Trichinopoly district three years ago. Since then, those Kavalgars have revived this practice long since dead, owing to, we must say, the want of sufficient moral courage on the part of the authorities and owing to an absurd notion generally entertained by a weak executive — that it would be against the principles of religious neutrality.[55]

As is apparent from the tone of comment in the *Madura Mail,* the Government was coming under increasing pressure to suppress the practice altogether.

In 1891, there were at least two cases of revival in the Madura district and in 1892 many more cases generally — at least two in Madura, two or more in Tanjore and at least one in Trichinopoly. Early in 1893 there was every indication that the incidence of revivals was continuing to spread.

Many of these cases were reported in the Indian-controlled English language and Tamil press.[56] This included influential publications such as *The Hindu*, the *Madura Mail* and vernacular papers such as the *Satya Vartamani*, a Tamil bi-monthly, and the *Nagai Nilalochani*, a Tamil weekly published in Negapatam. All of these papers expressed their impatience with Government policy. For example, in June 1892 the *Satya Vartamani*, commenting on the revival of hook-swinging at Sholavandan (which was reported in the *Madura Mail*) remarked that 'it was at a loss to understand the motive that actuated the Government to allow the celebration of this festival, which has been considered penal for the last so many years, and that it is the bounden duty of the Government to frame such rigid regulations as will totally prevent the celebration of this festival, which is too often attended with loss of life'.[57] In May 1893 *The Hindu* which, like the *Madura Mail* and other papers, was critical of Government prevarication, stated that...

> ... it is evident that the Madras Government does not take the same view of this barbarous aboriginal superstition as some Hindu and Christian people do... We fear the Government's attitude is the result more of a passive disposition and of absence of earnestness and vigor than of a conviction that it is necessary to respect the religious scruples of any class of Her Majesty's subjects.[58]

The report of the swinging at Valambagudi in 1890 and subsequent revivals also gave rise to correspondence, including a series of despatches between the Secretary of State, Lord Cross, and the Governor of Madras.[59] In the first of these the Government of Madras was asked to comment on the *Madras Mail*'s allegation that the authorities took no steps to prevent the occurrence of the festival that was held at Sholavandan in October 1891.[60] In its reply the Government explained that its officers had indeed attempted to dissuade the parties involved from going ahead with the performance, but in view of Government policy, which was 'to discourage but not absolutely to prohibit these exhibitions', nothing further could be done to stop the practice.[61]

Pressure was, however, further increased by news of other revivals and, in an informal note to the Secretary of State in May 1892, the Governor, Lord Wenlock, made it quite clear that he wanted to do something but was uncertain about how to proceed:

> We have received notice of another swinging festival in the outskirts of Trichinopoly town — but we are powerless in the matter... There is no doubt the common people — intensely superstitious as they are — are much devoted to this peculiar form of religious service, but considering the age in which we live, and the period we have reached in the advancement of civilization in this country, I cannot help thinking this relic of barbarism might soon be prohibited without causing more than a transitory feeling of dissatisfaction. Perhaps it would be best to wait for an accident, and if any were to occur, sufficient excuse for Government prohibition would be forthcoming.[62]

Commenting on these remarks, the Secretary of State indicated that his Council was 'much exercised in the matter' and drew attention to the way in which the Bengal Government had suppressed the practice by applying regulations under the section corresponding to the 1882 section 144 of the Criminal Procedure Code.[63] And finally, in a formal despatch he raised the question 'whether the time has not arrived when, in the interests of civilization and common humanity, such degrading exhibitions should be prohibited'.[64]

In addition to consulting with the Home Government, the Madras authorities also corresponded with the Government of India.[65] The purpose of this was to obtain information about how the practice had been suppressed in Bengal, and, if the Bengal model of procedure was no longer applicable, to explore the possibility of India-wide legislation. In further correspondence with the Secretary of State and after receiving reports and comments from the Government of India, the Government of Madras declared it had received advice from its own Advocate General that the procedure adopted in Bengal 'is now illegal, and that section 144 of the present Criminal Procedure Code cannot be interpreted to authorise the prohibition of 'hook-swinging' or any other practices of a similar nature'.[66] Having stated their view that they saw no reason to differ from their Advocate General, they then went on to suggest that 'the only means of preventing the recurrence of such exhibitions would appear, therefore, to be by legislative enactment'.

After careful consideration the Government of India suggested this might take the form of '(1) declaring hook-swinging, when performed in a place to which the public have access, either on payment or without it, to be a public nuisance; and (2) appointing a penalty, which might be that mentioned in section 290 of the Indian Penal Code (fine up to Rs. 200), with an alternative of three months' imprisonment, for principals abettors in the offence'.[67] However, before the matter was carried any further, it was suggested that opinions on the subject might be obtained from the leaders of Hindu society in Madras Presidency and submitted for the information of the Governor-General in Council.

In an order referring to the Government of India's suggestions and asking magistrate and public associations for their response, the Madras Government indicated that it did not believe the Government of India's proposals went far enough. They declared that 'the Government doubts whether the legislation proposed by the Government of India is quite sufficient and is inclined to think that District Magistrates should have power to prohibit exhibitions of the kind in question and that disobedience to such orders should be made penal'.[68]

The views of the Mahajana Sabha (the Presidency's primary political association) and of a large number of public figures and local associations were solicited through the district magistrates. The results showed, in the words of the Government of Madras, that legislation 'would be viewed with approval by the great mass of the people and would cause but little discontent in any quarter'.[69] Reassured by these findings, but still doubtful of the effectiveness of the Government of India's proposals, the Madras Government implied that it had, at last, found a simple solution. In a letter to the Government of India, the Chief Secretary declared:

> It seems to His Excellency in Council to be advisable to prevent these exhibitions rather than to punish those participating in them afterwards and the mere declaration that hook-swinging in public is a public nuisance will not be sufficient of itself to enable the magistracy to issue prohibitive orders in respect of intended exhibitions. All that seems to this Government to be necessary is to insert in section 144 of the Code of Criminal Procedure a provision to the effect that prohibitive orders may be issued thereunder in respect to public performances of hook-swinging; any person disobeying such orders will then be liable to the

penalties prescribed in section 188 of the Indian Penal Code.[70]

While the Madras authorities continued to reflect on possible ways out of the impasse in 1892-93, public pressure continued to develop. It was not only the vocal Western-educated classes, including the contributors to the English language and Tamil vernacular press, who were increasingly critical of the Government's apparent unwillingness to act, but also the Madras Missionary Conference (an association similar to the one in Calcutta)[71] and like-minded friends of reform in Britian. W.S. Caine, MP, a well-known crusader and friend of missions, raised the issue of hook-swinging in the House of Commons in February 1893.[72] Referring to the hook-swinging festival 'which has recently been established at Sholavandan' (a report of which had appeared in the *Madura Mail*), he asked the Under Secretary of State for India what if any steps were being taken to suppress the practice. In reply, the latter reassured him that the recent revival had engaged the attention of the Secretary of State, and of the Governments of India and Madras, with whom the subject was 'now' under consideration.

Four months after these questions in the House, the Government of Madras sent its reply to the Government of India, enclosing information on Hindu opinion in the Presidency, and suggesting that the practice might be stopped without resorting to legislation. There were more report of 'revivals' and then finally, in August 1894, an opportunity the Governor had been waiting for (news of a fatality as a result of a swinging accident) arrived, giving the Government the pretext it needed for totally banning all further public exhibitions. The Superintendent of Police who investigated the circumstances surrounding the fatality at Bheemanaickenpoliem on the outskirts of Trichinopoly, and who interviewed participants in the swinging ceremony and their relatives, declared that there could be 'not the slightest doubt' that the man died from the effects of injuries caused by swinging.[73]

A report of the incident was thereupon sent to all district magistrates and the ceremony was prohibited by orders under section 144 of the Criminal Procedure Code.[74]

Conclusions

Though hook-swinging was strongly disliked by the European community, restricted by municipal regulations in the early nineteenth century, and also the subject of fierce controversy among the Western-educated classes in Bengal in the 1830s and 1840s, it was not until the early 1850s that serious attention was paid to the possibility of banning the practice at the Presidency level. While, as we shall see, Europeans generally regarded it as barbarous, cruel, and disgusting, as well as an annoyance in the proximity of European settlement, its suppression did not appear to be quite so urgent as certain other 'dreadful practices' such as *sati*, infanticide and human sacrifice. It may have involved accidents but, unlike the latter, its purpose was apparently not self-destruction or the killing of other human beings. Furthermore, it was always possible to argue that as a result of the growth of new Western-educated elites and the spread of enlightened ideas, the practice, like certain types of caste custom, would gradually disappear.

As has been noted, it was the Court of Directors in London and local administrators in Bengal and Bombay who first brought the issue into prominence in Government circles. This was, significantly, during Lord Dalhousie's administration, when the policy of social reform reflected what the Judge of Khandesh described as 'the spirit of the age' — when the Government had abolished *sati* and was then in the process of eradicating female infanticide in the North-West Provinces and the Punjab, and human sacrifice among the Khonds in the remote tracts of Orrisa and thereabouts.[75] Local officers were publicly applauded by Dalhousie for their efforts in putting down these practices, and some of them could perhaps have been forgiven for imagining that the Governor-General was also referring to attempts to suppress hook-swinging when he said that such efforts were 'eminently calculated to reflect honour on the British name'.[76] Indeed, that was probably what the Judge of Khandesh meant when he declared that he was shocked to discover such a 'barbarous and cruel practice' as hook-swinging still publicly exhibited in a town 'within the dominions of the British Govt...'

As in many other cases involving social reform, advisers in Britain and British administrators in India were nervous about 'the possible risk of disturbance'. A cautious, selective, step-by-step approach was adopted in all three Presidencies. Existing regulations (as opposed to fresh and possibly provocative legislation) were utilised so as to curb rather than totally prohibit the practice. In every case advice to magistrates was carefully framed so as to make exceptions to the rule and not upset those groups who, if sufficiently provoked, were most likely to be able to challenge British rule. The idea in Madras in 1854, in Bombay in 1856 (before the Government of India's intervention), and in Bengal in 1859, was to dissuade people from holding hook-swinging exhibitions in some cases while prohibiting it in others. In Bengal the Government was particularly worried about the attitude of the landed classes with a long-standing interest in swinging displays at the *charak puja* and, in those cases, the authorities promoted the idea of cooperation and agreement rather than outright prohibition. In Bombay the concern was with those who gained financially from the practice and, if magistrates expected resistance from these groups then, as we have seen, it was considered safer 'to tolerate' the custom. In Madras people with entrenched interests in hook-swinging were also taken into account — the Government trying to avoid the mistake of putting down the well-established popular exhibitions.

This concern with the attitude, especially of the dominant classes (the patrons and others who gained from the custom), was compounded in the case of Bombay by Elphinstone's fears of popular rebellion such as had occurred only shortly before, during the Santal insurrection in Bengal in 1855.

The initial tentative steps to suppress hook-swinging in all three Presidencies had either been discussed, were under way, or had been completed prior to the Mutiny and Civil Rebellion. The practice, as already noted, was totally prohibited in Bombay — one year before the uprising. The reform processes elsewhere, which were completed in Bengal in 1865 and in Madras in 1894, also had their origin in the period before the great upheaval. What is perhaps surprising is that these latter attempts at suppression continued and were fairly successfully implemented after 1857-58, when reforming zeal was no longer so apparent in Britain and perhaps even less so among British administrators in India fearful of a recurrence of rebellion.

However, what was crucial and the major factor which explains this continuing process of reform in both Bengal and Madras was the attitude, especially of the Western-educated classes, who even more than the British during that period set the pace and argued for complete suppression.

Even before 1857, authorities in Bengal and Madras drew attention to the growth of 'enlightened' Indian opinion favouring reform. After 1857 any misgivings and fears of rebellion were very largely, if not entirely, allayed by the attitude of the educated classes and other leaders of Hindu society. While in Bengal some of the more radical Bengali critics of the custom, like Raja Satya Sharan Ghosal and certain sections of the Bengali-controlled press, led the way, even the more conservative *zamindars* (at least those in the British Indian Association) expressed their willingness to go along with reform. In Madras the British authorities, somewhat hesitant to intervene with a total ban on public exhibitions, were not only pressured by the Indian-controlled English language and vernacular press but were left in absolutely no doubt as to the attitude of the 'leading members of Hindu society' as a result of the comprehensive and detailed survey of opinion conducted in 1893.

However, the crucial role played by the Western-educated Indian elites in the events leading up to total proscription in Bengal and Madras in the second half of the nineteenth century does not mean that other groups such as the public in Britain, the India Office, or British officials and European missionaries in India played no part in the developments which led to the general prohibition.

It was the Directors who delayed the progress of reform in Bengal in 1856, probably as a result of their fears connected with the Santal rebellion; but it was the India Office which again played a prominent role in promoting officials to do more in Bengal once the dust of the Santal rebellion had properly settled. Furthermore, British officials in India, under pressure from vocal sections of the Indian community in the 1860s and 1890s, knew that if they wished to totally prohibit the practice they could count on the support of their superiors in London. Though the initiative had been seized largely by Indians themselves, the British Government was quite ready to go along with the reform process, knowing that this would also appease friends of reform in Britain itself.

Finally, what of the role of Christian missionaries? How important were they in the process of reform? Because the missionary role was sometimes less direct than, for example, the influence of Directors or of Indian reformers, this does not necessarily make their contribution to the reform unimportant.

In the first place, their graphic reports and criticism of hook-swinging helped to keep the issue alive among their supporters and other members of the public in Britain. Missionary magazines published in Britain contained numerous accounts of the practice, sometimes with illustrations, such as Figures 4, 11, 13, and 14. Some of these appeared in more than one missionary publication. For example, the engraving from a drawing by an Indian artist (Figure 13) was used by the CMS to illustrate 'Hindu Superstitions and Cruelties', an article on hook-swinging published in the *Church Missionary Register* in 1819. The drawing was also reproduced in *Missionary Papers* in the same year to illustrate, among other things, the callousness of Hindus and the continuing need for Christians to volunteer for work among 'these millions of deluded people'. Figure 11 on hook-swinging in Belgaum appeared not only in the LMS *Missionary Magazine and Chronicle* published in 1839 but also in Rev. J. Campbell's book entitled *British India in Relation to the decline of Hinduism, and the Progress of Christianity* (London, 1839).

Apart from articles and illustrations in magazines, there were descriptions of the ritual (sometimes in highly emotive language) in a number of books. These included works by Ward, Hoole, Gogerly, Sutton, Mateer, Weitbrecht and others which continued to remind the British public of the need for reform.

The 'evil' of hook-swinging was also mentioned indirectly in a petition on Indian administration signed by representatives of leading missionary and other religious societies in Britain which was presented to and laid on the table of both Houses of Parliament in 1858.[77] Furthermore, it was W.S. Caine, a well-known supporter of missions, who drew the attention of the House of Commons to the revival of hook-swinging at Sholavandan in the 1890s.

It is impossible to know how far this type of propaganda and agitation in Britain had an effect on the attitude and views of the Directors, Secretaries of State and others responsible for the Government of India. What is abundantly clear, however, is that the Calcutta Missionary Conference's petition of 1858, drawing attention to 'the cruelties' practised at the *charak puja*, had a direct impact on Lord Stanley[78], who responded to it by suggesting that the Bengal Government consider further measures to put down the practice. The petition was, as we have argued, the origin of the Bengal Government's second round of enquiries, which resulted in the restrictions imposed in 1860.

Lastly, as will be argued in the following chapter, the missionary critique of hook-swinging (together with the views of some other Europeans) was to a large extent appropriated by the Western-educated reformers — the same concepts and ideas becoming part of the weaponry used by reformers in their debates with more conservative members of the new elite. If, therefore, Indian views and reactions were the crucial factor in the demise of hook-swinging in the second half of the nineteenth century, missionaries and others played a part in encouraging the movement and in helping to formulate arguments against the practice. This was the role that the missionaries tended to play increasingly as the rise of political feeling and the nationalist movement among the Western-educated elites made direct missionary intervention in social issues such as hook-swinging inadvisable.

NOTES

1. Infra. p. 110.
2. Infra. pp. 109-112.
3. Sel.Mad.
4. Ibid., pp.4, 12, 13, 17.
5. Sel. Mad., p.1.
6. Ibid., pp. 1-2.
7. Ibid., p.2.
8. The son of the Commercial Resident at Nagpore in western India, he was born in Trichinopoly in 1816. After receiving what was said to be 'the rudiments of a classical and commercial education', he was admitted to Haileybury and was appointed a Writer in the Company's service attached to the Tannah Collectorate in 1837. After further experience as an assistant to the Collector and Magistrate at Surat, Kaira and Broach, he proceeded on furlough in 1849, returning to Bombay Presidency in 1851. In 1852 he was appointed Oriental Translator, Deputy Secretary to Government with the Persian Department and Secretary to the Mint Committee at Bombay. In 1855, at the age of 39, and in the same year in which he raised the question of hook-swinging, he was appointed Judge and Sessions Judge at Khandesh. (J/1/94. Haileybury Nomination Certificates, 1834-7, No. 24; *Register of the East India Company's Bombay Civil Servants,* 1750-1858, pp. 330-1).
9. This was a Company Court, consisting of the junior member of the Governor's Council as chief judge and three puisne judges, which superintended at criminal and police matters in the districts outside the Island of Bombay. (*Cambridge History of India,* Vol. VI, p. 64.)
10. IOR P/406/43 Bom. JP, 19/9/1855.
11. Ibid.
12. Ibid.
13. Ibid.

14. IOR Bom. JP, 31/7/1856.
15. Ibid.
16. This clause stated: 'It shall be lawful for the Magistrate, when the public benefit and comfort is in question, to institute rules respecting *Dhurrumsalas* [rest-houses for wayfarers], liquor shops, public wells, town gates, and generally all places of public resort, regulating the hours at which they are to be open, the manner in which they are to be used, the equal and appropriate application of their accommodations, and such matters as conduce to maintaining orderly conduct among those who resort to them'. (IOR V/8/24, Bombay Regulations, 1827).
17. Ibid. 11/9/1856.
18. IOR Bom. JP, 31/12/1856.
19. IOR Bom. JP, 11/9/1856.
20. IOR Bom. JP, 31/12/1856.
21. Ibid.
22. Ibid.
23. Beaufort's father (Sir Francis Beaufort) was a man of some eminence. A retired captain of the Royal Navy, he had conducted a survey of the coast of Asia Minor from 1810 to 1812. He was one of the founders of the Royal Astronomical Society in 1820 and of the Royal Geographical Society in 1830 and was author of *Karamania or a brief description of the south coast of Asia Minor,* a travel book which became increasingly popular after its publication in 1817. (*Register of the East India Company's Bengal Civil Servants 1790-1842,* p. 24; IOR J/1/94, Haileybury Nomination certificates, 1834-37; F. Boase *Modern English Biography,* Vol. 1, Truro 1892.)
24. IOR Board's Collections (DN642) E/4/812 and 813.
25. IOR Board's Collections (DN 642) E/14/819.
26. West Bengal Archives, BJP 7/7/1853.
27. On the Santal rebellion, which was mentioned in the same despatch, see C.E. Buckland, *Bengal Under the Lieutenant-Governors,* 2 vols., Calcutta, 1901, Vol. 1, pp. 11-16.
28. IOR E/4/835 India and Bengal Despatches, 7/5/1856.
29. Calcutta Missionary Conference, Minutes, 3/2/1857.
30. He was the author of *Bengal as a Field of Mission*, London, 1854.
31. Calcutta Missionary Conference, Minutes, 3/3/1857.
32. Calcutta Missionary Conference, Minutes, 7/4/1857, 3/8, 5/10, 2/11/1858.
33. *CCO*, Nov. 1858, pp. 480-2.
34. IOR P/4409 MJP 30/6/1893, p.2.
35. IOR L/P+J/3/1207, Stanley to Govenor-General, 24/2/1859.
36. IOR P/188/61.
37. IOR P/188/70.
38. Ibid.

39. IOR V/9/1177. *Proceedings of the Council of the Lieutenant Governor of Bengal for the Purpose of Making Laws and Regulations from 1856 to 1867*, Vol. II, Calcutta 1868, 18/2/1865, Cols. 8-10.
40. IOR P/188/70.
41. It is significant, for example, that after a revival of the practice in Dacca in about 1872, the Bengal Government issued fresh instructions directing magistrates to republish every year the prohibition against hook-swinging, and other self-torture of the kind, in all places where the *charak* festival was celebrated. (IOR P/4409, p. 2; Buckland, pp. 438-9).
42. Sel. Mad., p. 18a.
43. IOR MRP, 24/2/1854.
44. IOR P/249/64 MPP, 20/10/1857.
45. IOR P/3784 MJP, 27/8/1890.
46. See especially IOR P/3784 MJP, 27/8/1890; P/4409 MJP, 21/12/1893.
47. Sel. Mad., p. 18a.
48. IOR P/3784 MJP, 27/8/1890.
49. IOR MPP, 20/7/1867. Note also the problems the magistrate was having in trying to suppress the practice in Kanara. (IOR MPP, 28-31/5/1859; 21-30/4/1860; 17/6/1862.)
50. *MH*, Vol. LXIV, 1868, pp. 408-9. For the magistrate's comments on this case, see IOR MPP, 24/6/1868.
51. See especially IOR P/4409 MJP, 21/2/1893, p. 95.
52. This feeling was probably reinforced by the Queen's Proclamation of 1858, which disclaimed any intention of interfering with 'the religious belief or worship of any of our subjects' and which appears to have been well known in south India. (For reference to the full text, see Michael Maclagan, *'Clemency' Canning. Charles John, 1st Earl Canning*, London, 1962, Appendix IV, and for comment on its effect in south India, see R.L. Hardgrave, *The Nadars of Tamilnad. The Political Culture of a Community in Change*, California, 1969, pp. 64-5).
53. IOR, P/4409 MJP, 21/12/1893, p. 91.
54. *MH*, Vol. LXXXVIII, 1892, p. 8. According to his wife it was Chandler who, after the incident of hook-swinging in 1868, secured the knives and hooks used in the swinging by one of the men and showed them to the Governor of Madras, Lord Napier, who visited Madura in the same year. As a result of Chandler's initiative and the Governor's intervention, the performance of the ritual in the district was suppressed for some time. (Elmore, p. 32).
55. *The Hindu*, 11/6/1894.
56. *The Hindu*, 19,30,/4/1893, 11/6/1894; *Indian Native Newspapers Reports*, Madras, fortnights ending 30/6/1892 and 20/9/1893.
57. *Indian Native Newspapers Reports*, Madras, fortnight ending 30/6/

1892.
58. *The Hindu*, editorial, 30/5/1893.
59. IOR P/44009 MJP, 30/6/1893.
60. IOR L/P & J/6/352, Despatch, 17/12/1891; *Madras Mail*, 23/10/1891; *Madras Weekly Mail*, 29/10/1891.
61. IOR P/4247, 17/5/1892.
62. IOR, 31/5/1892, MSS. Eur. E 243/47, Letters from Lord Wenlock, 7/1/1892 to 16/8/1892, Vol.II, Wenlock to Cross, 31/5/1892.
63. IOR, MSS Eur. D 592/7. Cross to Wenlock 29/6/1892. This gave magistrates power to prevent 'obstruction, annoyance or injury, or risk of obstruction, annoyance or injury, to any person lawfully employed, or danger to human life, health or safety, or a riot or affray' (V.V. Chitaley and K.N. Annaji Rao, *The Code of Criminal Procedure (V of 1898) with exhaustive analytical and critical commentaries*, 4th edn, Vol. I, Nagpur 1849, p. 721.
64. IOR L/PJ/6/322, Despatch, 14/7/1892.
65. IOR P/4409.
66. IOR L/PJ/6/322, Despatch, 27/10/1892.
67. IOR P/4409 MJP, 30/6/1893, p.3.
68. IOR P/4409 MJP, 30/6/1893, p.4.
69. IOR P/4409 MJP, 21/12/1893, p/ 97.
70. IOR P/4409 MJP, 21/12/1893, p. 97. For section 188 of the Indian Penal Code, see J.O'Kinealy, *The Indian Penal Code and Other Laws Relating to the Criminal Courts of India*, with *Notes*, 3rd edn. Calcutta, 1885, p. 126.
71. IOR P/4409 MJP, 21/12/1893 (Memorial) pp.95-6.
72. U.K., Parliamentary Debates, Commons, 6/2/1893, Col. 519.
73. IOR P/4621 MJP, 24/9/1894.
74. Ibid.
75. See especially M.N. Das, *Studies in the Economic and Social Development of Modern India: 1848-1856*, Calcutta, 1959, Chs IX and X.
76. Ibid. p. 342.
77. Commenting on the transfer of power from the Directors to 'the immediate Government of the Queen and her advisers', they took the opportunity of acknowledging, with gratitude, 'the abolition of the system of Suttee, and other foul and cruel rites', but they also went on to pray 'that the Government may be instructed to put down all practices abhorrent to humanity, and suppress all exhibitions, of every kind, dangerous and offensive to public morals'. (*CCO*, August 1858, pp. 342-4).
78. IOR L/P & J/3/1207.

CHAPTER V

The Western-educated Elites: Changing Attitudes Towards Suppression

There were at least three major reasons why British authorities were reluctant to intervene in socio-religious practices in India after the mutiny and civil rebellion of 1857-58. The drive and enthusiam for social reform in Britain and India itself were already beginning to decline prior to the events of 1857. The Queen's Proclamation of 1858, which enjoined 'all those who may be in authority under us' to abstain 'from all interference with the religious belief or worship of any of our subjects', underlined a new policy of religious neutrality and non-intervention, and thirdly, there was a very general fear (reflected in the Proclamation) that meddling in sensitive religious affairs would antagonise the people and provoke a repetition of the events of 1857. It is a measure of the importance and persuasiveness of Hindu attitudes and public pressure that, despite these factors, the British authorities finally felt able to completely prohibit the public performance of hook-swinging in Bengal in 1865 and Madras in 1894.

But the increasing strength of the Western-educated movement directed at banning the custom is also important as it raises questions about the relationship between these classes and various forms of popular religion. Their changing attitude towards the ritual was, in fact, part of a broader process whereby the elites were attempting develop their own identity more or less in line with European ideas and values, while at the same time they sought to retain their roots in certain selected aspects of their own cultural tradition. Hook-swinging, as we shall argue, became for them a symbol of some of the worst excesses they were determined to leave behind, and their attack on the practice, an expression of their solidarity, not only with each other, but also with the new forces they so much admired in cosmopolitan and Western culture.

The debate among the Western-educated classes over the issue, which arose in Bengal shortly after the suppression of *sati* in 1829, initially divided the community along much the same social lines as the *sati* debate. Those who advocated the suppression of *sati* were also inclined to advocate the suppression of hook-swinging, while those who defended *sati* (or opposed Government interference) were also inclined to reject any attempt to suppress hook-swinging exhibitions. In one sense, however, the hook-swinging controversy was different. It must be ascribed entirely to European influence, whereas the debate over *sati* had roots in conflicts and debates which had taken place in pre-colonial India.[1]

As is well known, the newly emerging educated elites were not only exposed to the whole gamut of Western ideas and values through education, but interacted with Europeans in trade and commerce, through the administration, and in the task of constructing a new social and economic order.[2] As Shils and others have argued, they were torn between tradition and modernity—rejecting many of the values of their parents' or grandparents' generations and influenced to varying degrees and increasingly by a more cosmopolitan and European view of the world.[3] Their very existence as a group was the result of the European trading and colonial system and, at least in the early nineteenth century, they tended to look to Europeans and European society for some sort of guidance or even as a model of what they themselves might become. Though some were critical of aspects of European rule, life-styles and customs, European thought and the attitudes and views of the official and non-official European communities were of considerable interest and importance for them.[4]

The debate over hook-swinging, which arose in Calcutta in the early 1830s, was prompted not only by the fact that Western-educated classes had been exposed to the basic ideas and values of Christianity and the enlightenment through the newly emerging system of Western education, but also by the fact that the European community in Calcutta had been expressing strongly held views and almost universally condemned the practice.

One type of European reaction to hook-swinging, not uncommon in the early nineteenth century, was to regard it as a public nuisance. These attitudes are clearly apparent in the Calcutta European press and are also reflected in municipal regulations in both Calcutta and

Madras. F r example, describing the *charak puja*, the Calcutta *Morning Post* of April 1813 claimed it was celebrated 'with all its wonted noise, shew and debauchery'.[5] A letter to the editor of the *Bengal Hukaru* in April 1823 also complained of the 'infernal din' which was not only 'much to the annoyance of all peaceable inhabitants', but prevented sleep at night.[6] Referring more especially to the swinging, the writer added that 'the horrid din and noise' occasioned by the *charaks* were enough 'to frighten any Horse, whether in Carriage, Buggy, or under the Saddle, and endanger the lives of many'. There were also complaints from other European residents of thoroughfares being blocked by the crowds who came to view the *charaks*, of roads being dug up in order to erect the swinging posts,[7] and of interruption to business.[8]

Complaints such as these had an effect on local municipal authorities. According to Bishop Heber's wife, writing in the 1820s 'trees [posts] for swinging' were not suffered to be placed near European residences in the town of Calcutta,[9] while in Madras there were similar attempts to restrict the places where swinging could be performed, partly on the ground that it was 'a nuisance and offensive to passengers on public thoroughfares, which are common to all' and 'a spectacle disgusting to a large portion of a numerous population composed of many creeds'.[10]

While Europeans continued, at least to some extent, to regard the practice as a source of annoyance, or personal inconvenience, these views and reactions were gradually overshadowed by deeper feelings of horror and moral indignation. The latter response tended to become predominant as Calcutta and other centres of European activity began to feel the effects of the Evangelical revival, and as European residents began to compare the 'evils' of Hinduism with what they regarded as a more humane and rational faith.[11] Among Europeans, the most outspoken opponents of hook-swinging and exponents of the idea that it was an outrage and offensive to all moral and human feeling, had long been the Baptist missionaries who settled at Serampore in 1793. Their attitudes and arguments are reflected in Carey's and Ward's writings and in the columns of the *Friend of India*, which had both Indian and European readers. The thrust of missionary arguments against the practice was that the *charak puja* had lost its original devotional basis, and that the swinging ceremony was not only not sanctioned by Hindu scriptures, but was also oppressive and contrary to the dictates of 'decency, humanity and reason'.[12] The inhumanity of the practice was, for the missionaries, reflected especially in its cruelty. It was 'a horrid work of torture'[13] and, in one instance reported in 1823, so 'horrible' that 'even the most barbarous savage' would have averted his eyes from 'this degradation of his species'.[14] Furthermore, as we have shown, the missionaries soon discovered that it involved a considerable degree of coercion — landlords in some cases forcing their tenants to swing against their will.[15] Hook-swinging was also 'irrational' — the swingers being poor 'deluded' creatures, the victims of a 'superstition'[16] which, unlike Evangelical Christianity, was based on false notions of God and of what He requires. This conviction, that the ritual was essentially the acting out of a delusion, is reflected in a variety of comments, including one entry in Ward's diary in 1800 in which he records the fact that, after the swinger was let down, Carey asked him why he was 'such a fool'.[17]

The concern with 'indecency', which was certainly there as a less prominent aspect of the missionary critique, was sometimes linked with the observation that only the most 'dissolute' took part in the swinging, while prostitutes and other 'depraved' people were also associated with other aspects of the *puja.*[18] The word 'indecency', however, has broader connotations, and probably also reflects a general sense of disgust with the entire proceedings.

Implicit in much of this criticism was the notion that the practice was essentially 'uncivilised'. The idea of rating peoples and cultures in the scale of civilisation became increasingly common in European thought towards the end of the eighteenth century, and is also reflected in James Mill's well-known work *The History of British India,* first published in 1818.[19] Hook-swinging was, in the opinion of the missionaries, 'barbarous' (and therefore uncivilised), outside the domain of 'rational' human beings and an appalling 'abomination' where, in this instance, 'man sinks even below the brute'.[20] According to Marshman (editor of the *Friend of India*), it was also an illustration of the way in which Hindu society had declined from what 'the natives term the purer ages of Hinduism'.[21]

There was very little in all this criticism that was distinctly or specifically Christian. It is true that the missionaries had their own idea of what constituted 'rationality' or 'superstition', but these could still be used by non-Christians even if they implied something different. Adjectives such as 'irrational' and 'superstitious', 'cruel', 'inhuman', 'indecent', 'barbarous', and 'uncivilised' were terms which were freely available as products of general European as well as of Christian thought. Even the ideas of 'light' and 'darkness', basic symbols in the Christian tradition, which were utilised by Carey in his discussion of the hook-swinging issue, were also part of the basic armoury of the European enlightenment.[22] It was, therefore, perfectly possible for Hindus, influenced by the same desire to suppress the custom, to use much the same language as Christian missionaries without being accused of having sold out or gone over to the Christian camp.[23] They could argue, quite justifiably, that they were influenced by ideas and arguments that had a universal validity over and above the ideas and values inherent in any one particular creed or religion.

The influence of the Baptist missionaries in Calcutta and its vicinity was reinforced in 1830 (one year prior to the outbreak of the Bengali debate on hook-swinging) by the arrival of the Scottish Presbyterian missionary, Alexander Duff, who established his well-known Anglo-vernacular college in Cornwallis Square, on land obtained for him by Rammohan Roy.[24] The missionary influence on the rising generation of young men through public lectures and education had some effect in stimulating reform, and these efforts were complemented by the influence of the Hindu College, which also presented a challenge to Hindu orthodoxy and had for some time been the centre of a radical movement inspired especially by the teachings of Henry Derozio and by ideas of the enlightenment.[25] Several owners or editors of Bengali papers that attacked hook-swinging had attended the Hindu College,[26] and the ideas of both Christianity and the enlightenment are clearly reflected in the pages of the burgeoning Bengali-controlled English language and vernacular press.

Figure 14. *Illegal swinging near Calcutta, April 1893* from a sketch by F.W. Bourdillion, CMS evangelist and artist, Calcutta.

The swinger was whirled around by two assistants who weighed down the other end of the bamboo, while in the crowd, were men 'dancing to the sound of *tom-toms* and of their own shouts'. The four men who swung were later charged, tried and sentenced to a fine of 5 rupees each (equivalent to a month's wages) or a week's imprisonment.

Source: The Church Missionary Gleaner, September 1893, p. 137.

Figure 15. *Adjusting the hooks, prior to the swinging at Sholavandan, near Madura, 21 October 1891.* The photo, and those reproduced in Figures 16 and 17 appear to have been taken by one of the American missionaries. Two of the photos (the above and Figure 17) were published in the *Missionary Herald* in January 1892. All these were subsequently enclosed in papers sent by the Governor of Madras, Lord Wenlock, to the Secretary of State.

Source: IOR L/PJ/6/322.

Figure 16. *The swinging at Sholavandan.* The photograph shows the car bearing the pole, a four-wheeled wooden structure crammed with spectators, and 'the victim' suspended more than 30 feet above the crowd. The crowd was officially estimated at about 5,000 people.

Source: IOR L/PJ/6/322.

Figure 17. *The swinging at Sholavandan.* The pole was decorated with coloured cloth and flowers. The man, a Kallan, was swung by hooks only. Note the canopy or sun-shield above and the safety rope by his left hand. After an hour and a quarter 'the victim' was lowered to the ground. When released, he was immediately examined by a mission doctor who declared that 'his voice was full and strong' and that 'his pulse was good'.

Source: IOR/L/PJ/6/322.

The initial shots in the debate appear to have been fired by the *Reformer* in 1831. The paper, which was launched by friends of Rammohan Roy, was owned and edited by Prasanna Kumar Tagore,[27] one of his closest disciples. It attacked hook-swinging and other 'brutalities' associated with the *charak puja*[28] in editorials throughout the 1830s. Using language strikingly similar to that of Christian missionaries, it described hook-swinging as 'cruel' and 'inhuman', 'a species of barbarous absurdity', and a 'superstition', in short, something which was 'revolting to reason and humanity'.[29] 'The heart weeps', thundered the editor on 16 April 1837, 'to think that there are creatures claiming kindred with rational men, who are capable of perverting so grossly all the better parts of their nature'.

While this language echoes that of the missionaries, other comments remind the reader of James Mill and the Utilitarians. Thus, according to the editor, the processions which took place during the *charak puja* had come down 'from times of semi-civilization, when a priest-ridden community was to be tortured, that the great power and influence of a crafty system might be more firmly impressed and rivetted'. Hook-swinging and other 'barbarities' associated with the celebrations were not only, according to the editor, 'revolting to reason and humanity' and an outcome of 'blind and cruel superstition', but also practices which should be suppressed for the sake of 'the greatest good for the greatest number'.

The *Reformer*'s call for government intervention 'to modify if not abolish these cruelties' was based on the widely-held view, reflected in the debate on *sati* and in Christian missionary thinking, that religious practices require scriptural justification, The editor, who emphasized that one had to draw a distinction between what was in the *sastras* and what 'the mob' believed, argued that abuses such as hook-swinging were 'unenjoined' by the revered text of the *Vedas* or the ancient tenets of the *Dharma sastras*, and that, as there was therefore no textual basis for hook-swinging and other forms of 'self-torture', the Government would be perfectly justified in suppressing the practice.

The *Reformer*'s campaign for the abolition of hook-swinging and other 'cruel' practices associated with the *charak puja* was reinforced by editorials in the weekly *Bengal Herald*,[30] which also represented the views and feelings of the reformist party.[31] The editor of the *Jnananveshan*, an organ of the radicals associated with the Hindu College,[32] also expressed a wish, in 1835 that something could be done about the 'evils' connected with the *charak puja*. However, he was critical of the *Reformer*'s remarks that government intervention could be based on the idea that these customs were not sanctioned in the Hindu scriptures. He could not see, he confessed, how far the Government would be right 'in putting down a practice which has been held sacred by a great portion of our countrymen from time immemorial' — even if there was not a basis for it in the scripture.[33] Furthermore, he was not sure that there were no passages authorising these rites. 'Let these questions be settled', he wrote, 'before any attempt is made to put down by force a practice, which, however horrid and cruel, is considered by a large mass of our countrymen as a means to propitiate the deity'.[34] But the *Bhaskar*, one of the more liberal of the Bengali language newspapers,[35] had no such doubts about the wisdom of government intervention. It endorsed the idea that a distinction could be made between those aspects of the *charak* sanctioned by the scriptures and those which were not. Writing in April 1844, the editor declared that:

> We have long requested the public generally to endeavour, by instruction, to persuade the charak sannyasis to restrict themselves to the performance of those rites only which are required by the shastras; and, on the other hand, we have attempted to induce the government to put a stop to the self-inflicted tortures of these ascetics, by actual prohibition of them.[36]

As might have been expected, the campaign for reform in the English language and vernacular press increased concern and stirred up opposition among the more orthodox and conservative Hindus. The Western-educated members of this group were represented in the Dharma Sabha, the primary original purpose of which had been to prevent government suppression of *sati*. Because they were concerned with defence of tradition, they retained closer links than reformers with the more ordinary vernacular-speaking Hindus who were less exposed to the new ideas and winds of change.

A brief insight into how at least one of the latter felt about what he thought were the motives to suppress not only hook-swinging but the entire *charak puja* is provided by a letter published in the *Darpan* in 1831. It was written by one of the *purohits* (priests) of Kalighat, the main centre and focal point of the Calcutta *charak puja* celebrations. He had heard that in the *Reformer* (which in 'our opinion' is 'the magazine that helps Hindu boys to become foreigners') some 'babu' had asked the authorities to ban the *charak puja*. He wanted to know how he and others, who lived by begging on such occasions, could survive if Hindus lost their religion and gave up such traditional customs. He objected to the high-handed procedures of anyone determined to forbid traditions or customs without adopting adequate methods of consultation, and without reaching agreement with 'the chief distinguished and aristocratic Hindus', or with people present at a public meeting. He argued that attempts to overthrow long-established customs showed disrespect for one's ancestors, as it implied that they were all 'fools'. Finally, reflecting still further the concerns of the ordinary traditionally-oriented Hindus, he wondered how he and others could continue to celebrate for their own pleasure or in fulfilment of vows if the wealthier *bhadralok* did not observe the occasion, 'plant the *charak*' and incur the costs.[37]

The *Chandrika*, the chief organ of the Dharma Sabha and a paper which also reflected views such as those of the priest at Kalighat, attacked the *Reformer*'s views in April 1833. Criticising the latter's contention that hook-swinging was not enjoined in the *shastras*, the editor quoted a passage which included the statement that 'whoever of the khettrees and inferior castes, through faith inflicts pain on his body, bathes at the three seasons of the day, at night eats light food, and in subjection of his senses, pleases Seeb [Siva] shall be as Seeb'.[38] The paper expressed satisfaction that 'the opponents of the Hindu religion' had failed in their attempts to get the Government to suppress the *banphora* and *charak*. It went on to say that this was hardly surprising as reformers were not favoured by the government which was satisfied if all subjects 'practise their own religion and live happily'. Finally, in lines reminiscent of the letter in the *Darpan*, and in which the editor expressed something of the conservatives' anger at what they felt was the reformers' cavalier dismissal of the majority view,[39] the paper suggested that, if reformers still wanted change, they should consult 'us' and not the government. Implicit in this remark was probably also the feeling (apparent in other debates on social reform) that if changes were to be introduced, then foreign governments were not the ones which should put the Hindu house in order.[40]

In spite of initial hostility among members of the Dharma Sabha and others to any move for the suppression of hook-swinging at the *charak puja*, there is clear evidence of a gradual shift in feeling — a trend towards the acceptance of some form of government intervention. In the first place it is important to note that as early as 1829 at least one of the more prominent members of the Dharma Sabha, Ramkamal Sen (1783-1844) was not uncritical of the *charak* festival. In 'A Short Account of the Charak Puja Ceremonies, and a Description of the Implements Used', a paper which he read before the Asiatic Society in May 1829, he complained that whether the ceremony was performed by a *muchi* (leather worker) or *chandala*, it was considered as Hinduism, and the whole body of the Hindus was charged with 'the absurdity of the act'.[41] In 1851 the *Sungbad Purnachandroday*, a Bengali daily edited by Uddoitochurn Auddy as one of the organs of the Dharma Sabha,[42] joined with other papers in urging reform. The editor's main argument was that while the *charak puja* was 'a part of Hinduism' which was commanded in scripture, there was no authority in the *sastras* for the sannyasis 'to pierce themselves as they do with iron spears, or run hooks into their backs, etc'.[43] The paper, which had long been involved in attempts to defend Hinduism from the assaults of Christian missionaries and others, declared that the continued adherence of lower class Hindus to these 'cruel' rites was doing much 'to lessen the glory of the faith they profess' and was giving just grounds 'to those who are hostile to Hinduism'. Among the important reasons for a change in the attitude of conservatives were, therefore, not only the recognition that certain specific practices including hook-swinging were not, after all, enjoined in Hindu scripture, but also the growing awareness that Hinduism was under sustained attack, and that the elimination of such practices would strengthen its ability to withstand internal and external pressures threatening disintegration.

The debate over the hook-swinging issue was not, however, purely ideological or tied up with arguments about the most effective way of defending Hinduism. As we have seen, it also involved questions relating to the landlord's status. How was it possible to end the practice without at the same time restricting one of the ways in which *zamindars* and others continued to display their powers of patronage, largesse and influence in the local society? There were signs from about the 1840s that the *zamindar*'s enthusiasm for hook-swinging exhibitions, like that of the members of the Dharma Sabha, was also beginning to wane. In 1841 it was reported in the *Calcutta Courier* that Raja Kalikrishna and his brothers, who were wealthy *zamindars* and well-known patrons of the *charak*, had 'discontinued' the performance of 'this unholy Poojah' and had not even erected the *charak* post in their private compound.[44] Although reports in subsequent years suggest that this was little more than a temporary change in practice (if not of heart) on the part of the Krishna brothers,[45] the editor of the *Prunachandroday* stated, in 1851, that 'the rich' (presumably including some *zamindars*) who used to encourage people to participate in the 'cruel' practices connected with the *charak puja*, had become 'adverse to such false pleasures' and 'do not help them as they used to'.[46]

Comments and editorials in the *Hindoo Patriot*, a paper which came increasingly to represent the views of the landed classes,[47] are also significant. Editorials in 1857 and 1858, when the paper was edited by Hurish Chunder Mookerjee, argued that the main problem associated with the 'abolition' of the *charak puja* was finding a substitute, some other form of pleasure or 'rational' amusement for the lower classes.[48] In March 1859, however, the paper went so far as to publish a letter to the editor from 'Reformer', which described hook-swinging as 'painfully' familiar and 'heartrending to every resident in Calcutta' and which urged the Governor-General, Canning, to act with the 'moral boldness' of Lord William Bentinck, in putting to an end what the writer described as 'this scene of ignominious barbarity riding rampant in this enlightened age'.[49] On the death of Hurish Chunder Mookerjee in June 1861, Kristodas Pal, Assistant Secretary to the British Indian Association, became editor of the paper.[50] From that time onwards it is quite clear that the *zamindars*, under increasing educated-Indian and European pressure, and represented through the *Hindoo Patriot* and by the British Indian Association, were more generally reconciled to the idea of ending hook-swinging exhibitions. In his first editorial on the issue in the *Hindoo-Patriot* in April 1864, Pal referred to the injustice of Europeans who totally disparaged 'the moral sense of the Hindoo community'. He noted that the educated classes were, in fact, 'unanimous' in their condemnation of what he described as the 'barbarisms' which characterised the *charak puja*. He opposed the idea of any general government interference in the festival, including interference with the harmless popular amusements of 'the mob'. However, he left no doubt in the mind of his readers about his own moral position, and of his conviction that some further government interference was required on the basis of 'humanity as well as of public decency'.[51]

As already noted, six months later, in October 1894, the Under Secretary to the Government of Bengal, which was already considering the possibility of outright suppression, wrote to the Secretary of the British Indian Association asking 'whether, in the opinion of the Association, the time had not come when the practice of hook-swinging may properly be prohibited by the Magistrates under the provisions of the Code of Criminal Procedure'.[52] The Association's committee (which included, as a vice-president, Narendra Krishna, one of the most notorious patrons of hook-swinging) took over three months to reply.[53] They admitted that the 'barbarous' practices of boring the body and hook-swinging at the *charak* festival were 'cruel and degrading', and that they were not sanctioned by the *Sastras*. Ignoring the role that some members had played (or continued to play) as patrons, they dwelt instead on the fact that the practices were 'not followed by the better instructed and higher orders of the community'. They emphasised that there was 'scarcely a single educated Native of Bengal who does not hate these revolting practices and anxiously wish for their cessation', and added that 'the influence of educated and enlightened *zamindars*, among whom the Committee are glad to count not a few Members of this Association', had already gone far 'towards the suppression of hook-swinging in their respective Estates'. Referring specifically to government proposals for further intervention, they stressed that government actions should not have 'even the remotest appearance to a violation of the policy of religious neutrality' — a point which they laboured, but which sat rather uneasily alongside their final recommendation in agreement with the idea of complete suppression.

The reasons for the *zamindars'* final decision to endorse government policy and to support the use of the Code of Criminal Procedure in banning the so-called 'barbarities' of the *charak puja* were no doubt complex and varied. One very important factor was government and public pressure. The position of Kali Krishna, who had had conferred upon him by Lord William Bentinck the hereditary title of Raja Bahadur[54] symbolises, perhaps in a somewhat extreme form, the degree to which *zamindars*, as a class, were dependent on the goodwill and patronage of the British. It was indeed difficult for them to bite the hand that fed them — to resist the pressure of those who were so important to them for their influence and well-being. The Government of Bengal, which, as we have seen, was already under pressure from Lord Stanley, the Secretary of State, had indicated its concern over hook-swinging exhibitions in official communications with *zamindars* at least as early as 1860.[55] Furthermore, even before this period, educated *zamindars* who continued to support the practice could hardly have been unaware of the increasing outcry in the public press, including both European and Indian comment. Though some European papers, such as the *Bengal Hukaru*,[56] argued that the government had no right to suppress practices such as hook-swinging if it could be shown that they were based on Hindu scripture, there can be no doubt that almost the entire European community, official and non-official alike, were revolted by the custom and hoped it would disappear.[57] Moreover, wealthy patrons of the practice, including *zamindars* such as Kali and Narendra Krishna, had ever since the 1830s been singled out and attacked in newspapers such as the *Reformer*, the *Friend of India* and the *Calcutta Christian Advocate*, as being among those largely responsible for encouraging hook-swinging and other 'barbarities'.[58]

In addition to these pressures, and possibly also as a recognition that the promotion of hook-swinging was no longer a source of quite the same degree of social prestige, were two other influential considerations. One of these was a growing conviction that the practice was not enjoined in the Hindu scriptures — a development which was likely to have a considerable effect especially on the more religiously conservative *zamindars*, such as Radhakanta Deb, Narendra Krishna and Rajkissin Sing, who were also members of the Dharma Sabha.[59] Secondly, there was also the recognition that the government was not, in fact, going to try to abolish all aspects of the *charak puja*. There had been some misunderstanding on this point as late as 1858, when the *Hindoo Patriot* felt compelled to defend the very existence of the festival against those whom it thought were advocating its entire suppression.[60] In their communication with the British Indian Association, however, the government assured the *zamindars* that it had no desire 'to interfere in any way with the religious observances of the Poojah, but simply to prevent hook-swinging and its attendant cruelties'.[61] As a result of these assurances, the *zamindars* could feel with some degree of confidence that, even if they were losing one of their traditional methods of displaying their importance and magnanimity, they could still continue to promote and encourage other popular aspects of the *puja*.

As we have noted, the reaction of the Western-educated classes to proposals for the complete suppression of the custom was also a key factor in determining the direction of government policy in Madras in the 1890s. In June 1893 suggestions for more effective measures against hook-swinging (and other exhibitions of self-torture) were referred to the Madras Mahajana Sabha (established in 1884) and to all district magistrates 'for their opinion as well as that of such local associations and individuals as the latter may think advisable to consult'.[62] Individuals consulted included Hindu government official and ex-officials, and a range of well-known or influential private citizens such as *pundits*, heads of *maths*, businessmen, municipal councillors, lawyers and teachers. The issue was also discussed at meetings of local municipal and district associations and by some Hindu religious associations, as well as by the more purely secular bodies such as municipal councils and people's associations.

As a result of these consultations, it became apparent that representatives of 'the educated section of the orthodox Hindu community' as well as those who were likely to reflect more 'advanced' or radical views, were almost unanimous in urging the government to take more decisive and effective action in eliminating what was widely regarded as a cruel and barbarous custom. Furthermore, the Hindu-controlled English language and vernacular press was, as we have seen, also outspoken in urging more effective government measures.

In at least one major respect, the situation in the Madras Presidency in the 1890s was different from circumstances in Bengal when the Western-educated Bengalis were debating the issue from about 1830 to 1864. While in Bengal some of the Western-educated *zamindars* continued to patronise hook-swinging exhibitions or had personal interest in the ritual's survival, most of their counterparts in Madras, as well as priests and trustees of temples, were already facing a situation where the practice was no longer as popular or even known among the various classes in the population. In spite of 'revivals', swinging took place or was seriously proposed in no more than four of the 21 districts comprising Madras Presidency.[63] It had never been practised in Malabar and appears to have completely died out in other parts of the Presidency, except in the southern Tamil districts of Tanjore, Trichinopoly and Madura. Western-educated Hindus, who in other circumstances or in an earlier period may have been patrons, had therefore less to lose and could afford to be more critical or outspoken in their attacks on the custom than the Bengali *zamindars* of an earlier period.

All the major criticisms of the practice made in Bengal reappeared in Madras in the 1890s. There were a few individual respondents who were not especially critical of the practice. One pensioned *sheristadar* (chief secretary to the district collector) in Cuddapah argued that 'as neither the people who perform or those who look on suffer, there is no reason why anyone should be horrified at the practice',[64] and a pensioned *tahsildar* (Indian collector of a subdivision) from the same locality held that the practice was, in a general sense, sanctioned by scripture, such self-sacrifice being similar to the ones narrated in the *Sastras.*[65] Notwithstanding these comments, the great majority of those whose views are known strongly condemned hook-swinging and held the opposite view: that it was not sanctioned or enjoined by Hindu scripture. This was not merely the view of most Indian officials and those who might have been expected to have more 'progressive' religious and social views, but was also the opinion of members of temple committees, *pundits* and other more conservative supporters of the Hindu religious establishment.[66] Asked for an expression of opinion, the head of the Lingayat *math* at Ujjini replied, for example, that these practices 'do not seem to be according to the shasters'.[67]

But what is also striking about Western-educated responses to hook-swinging in Madras Presidency during this period is not only the denial that the practice was sanctioned or enjoined by Hindu scripture, but an even more explicit rejection of the idea that it had anything to do with Hinduism. The growth of the nationalist and Hindu revival movements and the spread of theosophy in south India all helped to create a climate of opinion in which the educated classes came to fear and resent, even more deeply, Christian missionary criticism and assaults on Hinduism.[68] It was therefore felt to be extremely important (as some Bengali reformers had begun to realize) to dissociate popular practices such as hook-swinging from 'Hinduism', so as to demonstrate that Hindus were just as humane and concerned about popular 'abuses' as Christians. One Hindu official in Tinnevelly argued that hook-swinging had its origins in 'hatha yogum',[69] but most other commentators who addressed the issue denied that it had anything to do with the Hindu religion. Toke Jeyaram Nayudu, a retired Huzur *sheristadar* from Nellore, spelled out the assumption, explicit in a great deal of earlier comment, that as these rituals were 'not prescribed in any religious books', they were 'in no way' connected with the Hindu religion.[70] *The Hindu* newspaper referred to hook-swinging as 'an aboriginal' superstition and the *Madura Mail* described it as a 'bygone relic'.[71] According to the Raja of Venkatgiri, it was 'an act of demon worship',[72] while in the opinion of V. Anuntilarow, chairman of the Bimplipatam Municipal Council, the people's belief that the practice was 'a part of their religion' was a 'misconception'.[73]

The growth of the very clear trend among the Western-educated elite in both Bengal and Madras to condemn hook-swinging was probably reinforced by traditional caste and class prejudices against certain forms of popular practice. While, for example, Brahmans were among those who encouraged the practice, there is no evidence, as noted in previous discussion, that they themselves swung. A few of them paid others so they could swing 'by proxy', but engaging in the act of swinging was strictly taboo. Furthermore, critics of the practice in Bengal were not only Brahmans and other high caste Hindus but were also *bhadralok*, the respectable people, whom, as Mukherjee has pointed out, made a very clear distinction between themselves and 'the lower orders'.[74]

The editors of the *Reformer*, the *Purnachandroday* and the *Hindoo Patriot* in Bengal all made it perfectly clear that, in their view, the *charak puja* was a festival of 'the mob',[75] and the *Hindoo Patriot* at least initially rejected the idea of any government interference with *charak* celebrations on the ground that, if it was banned, the 'lower classes' would be deprived of one of their more important forms of recreation and amusement.[76] The sense that the festival was essentially for the benefit of the 'lower classes' and was also 'disgusting', was reinforced by frequent complaints that it was associated with prostitution, drunkenness and debauchery.[77] Some commentators in south India also felt hook-swinging to be an undignified and essentially lower class phenomenon. In the words of one Western-educated critic, it appeared to be 'an act of blind and superstitious devotion performed by the illiterate part of the population'.[78] In the words of another, it was 'merely an act of demon worship, undertaken by illiterate Sudra priests of village temples to induce the rude villagers to a faith in their gods merely to collect small fees', while according to Toke Jeyaram Nayudu, the higher castes, 'which form the sensible portion of the Hindu community', were the only ones who wished for legislation prohibiting these practices.[79]

Finally, the Western-educated classes' reaction to hook-swinging was also affected by questions of image and self-identity. A continuing acceptance of the practice seemed to contradict what they thought or were trying to project about themselves. The great majority still considered themselves 'Hindus', strongly rejecting the idea that they were somehow foreigners in their own land; but while retaining something of their roots and tradition, they also longed to be accepted as 'enlightened' and 'civilised' participants in the same cosmopolitan culture as British rulers. Their participation in the latter was, however, conditional on their disavowal of certain aspects of Hinduism, including customs such as hook-swinging.

In Madras many of them used the same epithets descriptive of the custom as Bengali and British opponents of the practice in the early nineteenth century. Hook-swinging was, in their view, superstitious,[80] cruel,[81] barbarous,[82] and inhuman.[83] It was not only 'offensive to all civilized feeling',[84] but totally unacceptable in an age of 'enlightenment'.[85] Hence, like upper classes in early modern Europe who were also influenced by cosmopolitan values and culture, they too tended to distance themselves from the unacceptable aspects of popular culture.[86] Their attacks on hook-swinging were certainly encouraged by a growing conviction that it had never been part of Hinduism; but their stance on the issue was also entirely consistent with the educated classes' view of themselves as copartners with the British and as torch-bearers of progress, civilisation and 'enlightenment'. The public debate provided them with another opportunity of declaring to themselves and to the world that authentic Hinduism was not reactionary, and that they themselves stood for the values and attitudes common to all enlightened and civilised peoples.

NOTES

1. A.S. Altekar, *The Position of Women in Hindu Civilization*, 3rd edn, Delhi, 1962, pp. 124-5.
2. There is voluminous literature on this topic. See especially S.N. Mukherjee, p. 33-78; A.F.S. Ahmed, *Social Ideas and Social Change in Bengal 1818-1835*, Leiden, 1965; B.B. Kling, *Partner in Empire. Dwarkanath Tagore and the age of Enterprise in Eastern India*, Berkeley, 1976.
3. E. Shils, *The Intellectual between Tradition and Modernity in the Indian Situation*, the Hague, 1961, especially Chapter V.
4. Ibid., p. 79.

5. *Morning Post*, 16/4/1813.
6. *Bengal Hukaru*, 15/4/1823.
7. *Indian Gazette*, 29/3/1833. See also comments in the same paper quoted in *Reformer*, 21/4/1833.
8. *Bengal Hukaru*, 29/4/1834.
9. R. Heber, *Narrative of a Journey through the Upper Provinces of India from Calcutta to Bombay, 1824-1825*, 3 vols., 3rd edn, London, 1828, Vol. I, p. 99.
10. Sel. Mad., p. 3.
11. See, for example, the description of the *charak puja* in the *Bengal Hukaru*, 15/4/1829.
12. *FI*, Monthly, II, 9/3/1819, p. 143.
13. W. Ward, *A View of the History*, p. 20.
14. *FI*, Monthly, II, 9/3/1819, p. 143.
15. Supra. pp. 76-7.
16. Extracts from Mr Carey's Diary, April 1794, *Periodical Accounts*, Vol. I, p. 174; W. Ward, *Farewell Letters*, 2/4/1821, p. 89.
17. W. Ward's Missionary Journal, 1799-1810, p. 78.
18. *FI*, Monthly, II, 9/3/1819, p. 141.
19. J. Mill, *The History of British India*, 5 vols., 3rd edn, London, 1826, Vol. II, Ch. 10.
20. *FI*, Monthly, II, 9/3/1819, p. 143.
21. *FI*, Monthly, III, 13/5/May 1820, p. 125.
22. On the use of these and other concepts such as 'ignorance' and 'superstition' in the enlightenment, see especially A. MacLachlan, 'The Myth of the French Revolution Revisited', in S.N. Mukherjee and J.O. Ward (eds.), *Revolution as History*, Sydney Studies in Society and Culture, Sydney, 1989, pp. 47-8.
23. For a similar argument about the way in which the Western-educated elites of western India were able to utilise missionary ideas without committing themselves to a specifically Christian position, see R. O'Hanlon, Ch. 3.
24. On missionary educational policy and Hindu reactions, see especially M.A. Laird, *Missionaries and Education in Bengal, 1793-1837*, Oxford, 1972, Ch. VII; M.M. Ali, *The Bengali Reaction to Christian Missionary Activities 1833-1857*, Chittagong, 1965, pp. 68-74.
25. See especially Ahmed, pp. 40-51; S.C. Sarkar, 'Der Ozio and Young Bengal', in A. Gupta (ed.), *Studies in the Bengal Renaissance*, Calcutta, 1958; B. Majumdar, *History of Indian Social and Political Ideas*, Calcutta, 1967, Ch. III.
26. Among these were Rasik Krishna Mallick, editor of *Jnanaveshan* and Kashiprasad Ghose, editor of the *Hindu Intelligencer* (Ahmed, pp. 49, 145; R.G. Sanyal, *Reminiscences and Anecdotes of Great Men of India*, Part II, Calcutta, 1983, p. 199.
27. Kling, pp. 18-19, 74; R.G. Sanyal, *Voluntary Associations and the*

Urban Public Life in Bengal (1815-1876). An Aspect of Social History, Calcutta, 1980, pp. 104-5.

28. Although hook-swinging was seen as main 'evil' associated with the *charak puja*, some critics were also, to a lesser extent, concerned with other forms of self-torture including *banphora*, or perforating the body. For a comprehensive list and description of the various methods of self-torture which were performed during the *charak puja*, see the *CCO*, Vol. VI, April 1837, pp. 182-3.
29. See, for this and the following paragraphs, *Reformer* editorials, 24/3, 7, 12/4/1833 and 16/4/1837, pp. 182-3.
30. See the article in the *Bengal Herald*, 16/4/1837, quoted in *Asiatic Journal*, new series 32, August 1837, p. 288.
31. Ahmed, pp. 70, 72.
32. Ibid., pp. 49, 71, 72, 97-8.
33. See extracts in *AJ*, new series, 18/10/1835, pp. 92-3, and further references to the paper's views in the *Reformer*, 7 and 21/4/1833, loc. cit.
34. Quoted in *AJ*, new series, Vol. 18, Oct. 1835, p. 93.
35. Ali, *Bengali Reaction*, p. 95; *CCA*, 24/4/1852.
36. Quoted in *CCA*, 4/5/1844.
37. Devleena Ghosh, translation of a letter dated 30/4/1831, in B.N. Banerjee (ed.), *Sambad Patre Sekaler Katha*, Calcutta, 1977, Vol. II.
38. Quoted in the *Reformer*, 21/4/1833.
39. In an editorial in 1857, referring to the Association of Friends for the Promotion of Social Improvement, the *Hindoo Patriot* argued that 'hardly one of the present reformers of Bengal has the sympathy of even a substantial fraction of the people of this country', 23/4/1857.
40. *Chandrika*, 20/4/1833 (trans. by Devleena Ghosh from the Bengali) in B.N. Banerjee, *Sambad Patre Sekaler Katha*, Vol. II.
41. *JAS*, 24/12/1833, pp. 609-13. See also *Government Gazette*, 14/5/1829.
42. *CCA*, 24/4/1852; Ali, p. 64.
43. 11/4/1851, quoted in the *CCA*, 19/4/1851, Vol. 13. p. 187.
44. *Calcutta Courier*, 9/4/1841, quoted in R.R. Choudhury, *Glimpses of Old Calcutta*, Bombay, 1978, p. 57. See also *CCO*, June 1841, p. 389.
45. *CCA*, 19/4/1845.
46. Quoted in the *CCA*, 19/4/1851.
47. Sanyal, *A General Biography*, pp. 51-86.
48. *HP*, 19/3/1857, 15/4/1858.
49. *HP*, 17/3/1859.
50. Sanyal, *A General Biography*, p. 82.
51. *HP*, 18/4/1864.
52. IOR P/188/70 BPP, March 1865, J.Geoghegan, Under-Secretary to the Government of Bengal to the Secretary of the British Indian Association, 31/10/1864.

53. IOR P/188/70 BPP, March 1865; British Indian Association, Calcutta Reports of the 14th Annual General Meeting, 14/2/1866.
54. *The Indian Press on the late Raja Kali Bahadur KGS,* Calcutta 1875.
55. IOR P/188/61; Buckland, Vol. 1, p. 177; *HP,* 18/4/1864.
56. Quoted in the *India Gazette,* 28/3/1833.
57. *CCO,* May 1833, p. 227.
58. *FI,* 16, 30/4/1835, 20/4/1837; *CCA,* 18/4/1840, 19/4/1845.
59. For membership of the Dharma Sabha see especially *FI,* 21/4/1836; *CCO,* January 1841, pp. 67-8.
60. *HP,* 19/3/1857 and 15/4/1858.
61. IOR P/188/70.
62. IOR P/4409, G.O., 30/6/1893.
63. IOR P/4409.
64. IOR P/4409, p. 64.
65. Ibid.
66. Ibid., pp. 54, 56-7, 61, 63, 75-6, 78-9, 80-1, 90-1.
67. Ibid. p. 63. See also *supra* p. 77.
68. R. Suntharalingam, *Politics and Nationalist Awakening in South India, 1852-1891,* Tucson, 1974, pp. 288-310; G.A. Oddie, 'Anti-Missionary Feeling and Hindu Revivalism in Madras: The Hindu Preaching and Tract Societies, c. 1886-1891', in F.W. Clothey (ed.) *Images of Man: Religion and Historical Process in South Asia,* Madras, 1982, pp. 217-43.
69. IOR P/4409, p. 94.
70. Ibid., p. 84.
71. Quoted in *The Hindu* 11/6/1894.
72. IOR P/4409, p. 84.
73. Ibid., pp. 77-8.
74. Leach and Mukherjee, pp. 52-4.
75. *Purnachandroday,* 11/4/1851, quoted in *CCA,* 19/4/1851; *Reformer,* 7/4/1833; *HP,* 19/3/1857, 15/4/1858, 18/4/1864.
76. *HP,* 17/3/1857, 15/4/1858, 20/3//1861.
77. See, for example, references in the *Reformer,* 24/3/, 17/4/1833, 16/4/1837.
78. IOR P/4409, p. 77.
79. Ibid, p. 84.
80. *The Hindu,* 30/5/1893; IOR P/4409, p. 77.
81. IOR P/4409 pp. 62, 75, 77, 81, 93-4.
82. Ibid. pp. 55, 62, 70, 75, 84, 93-4.
83. Ibid. pp. 57, 62, 84.
84. *The Hindu,* 30/5/1893.
85. IOR P/4409, pp. 76, 85, 89.
86. Peter Burke, *Popular Culture in Early Modern Europe,* London, 1978, pp. 270-87.

Conclusion

In the earlier part of the book we argued that whatever the origins of hook-swinging, there can be little doubt it was a non-Brahmanical practice which, in the nineteenth century, was almost entirely confined to areas outside of what was once the Aryan or Sanskritic heartland. There is no evidence in available data that Brahmans ever performed the ritual, and it does not appear to be mentioned in any of the better known and classical Hindu texts. It was most popular among the tribals and lower caste Hindus, though, in some parts of India, the ritual had gradually become accepted as being useful and efficacious by the middle and higher castes as well.

The practice was largely confined to followers of Siva, his wives or other *saktis* and was conspicuously absent among the devotees of Visnu and his benevolent *avatars*, such as Rama and Krishna. In Bengal and in areas where it was performed at the *charak puja*, it was most closely associated with ideas of propitiation through asceticism or bodily mortification, whereas in other parts of India it was more closely associated with ideas of appeasement through blood sacrifice.

While the rite was sometimes performed as a result of coercion by wealthier and more powerful parties, or for personal 'temporal' advantages, it was also acted out in fulfilment of religious vows which had been made during a personal or family crisis. As we have seen, it was also used as a strategy to influence tutelary deities on behalf of entire communities, the swinger who was sometimes paid being offered as the victim whose sacrifice would ensure the health and prosperity of all.

In Chapters IV and V our focus was on movements for the suppression of the custom in British India from the early 1830s until 1894. An account of attempts to modify or suppress the practice in the Princely States is a story which is yet to be told. Some attempts were made, for example, in Travancore, to improve the safety aspects of the ritual by insisting on the use of the waist-band.[1] For the most part, however, ideas of reform appear to have made little headway compared with developments in British India. Writing in a book published in 1896, J. S. Dennis complained that in several 'native' states hook-swinging was still in vogue.[2]

While it might be argued that the British administration did more to prohibit the practice than officials in the Princely States, it cannot be assumed that the measures adopted even in British India were entirely effective. Indeed, alongside Dennis' complaint about lack of reform and the continuation of the ritual in Princely States has to be placed his further remark that 'recent reports in many directions seem to indicate defiant attempts to revive the barbarous spectacle even in British India'.[3] As was the case with legislation banning *sati* in 1829, prohibition of the practice was no guarantee that it would completely disappear. Revivals, one of which is illustrated in Figure 14, were reported in the Lower Provinces after the introduction of prohibitory regulations in 1865,[4] and the continued performance of the ritual has been reported in other parts of India — in Bombay region since it was banned in 1856, and in what was or used to be Madras Presidency since the prohibition in 1894. A hook-swinging ceremony in Maharastra was observed and photographed by the historian D.D. Kosambi in 1966[5] (Figure 12). Further to the south-east, magistrates in Tanjore district were still passing orders under section 144 of the Criminal Procedure Code to prevent the performance of the ritual in the 1940s,[6] and, while in the same district some years ago, the author was given the impression that the rite is still surreptitiously performed in some localities.

The continuation of hook-swinging rituals, in spite of official prohibition, as well as the various attempts at substitution discussed below, highlight the fact that the practice evolved partly in response to deeply felt human needs. These included a yearning for some kind of control over one's life and destiny and the human needs for procreation, health and sustenance.

Frustrated by prohibition in one direction, devotees, village authorities and others searched for alternative methods of appeasing the deity. Those who in more normal circumstances would have vowed to undergo the ritual had to think of something else. In Chingleput district, they appear to have turned to fire-walking as a suitable substitute[7] and, in Poona district, to one of a number of other options. Referring to the situation at Jeguri, for example, one observer remarked that instead of hook-swinging, which was practised at all the fairs:

> . . . the usual vows are now to build steps on the ascents to the temple, to make cash gifts to the temple, to distribute cocoa kernel and tumeric in front of the temple, to kill and eat a sheep in honour of the god, to feed Brahmans, and to devote to the god male children or *vaghyas*, and female children or *murlis*.[8]

But if it was possible for individuals involved in swinging to find some other outlet, what of the more general communal needs? What would happen to the village if hook-swinging was no longer performed? How would the local *amma* react? Would there be drought, cattle plague or some other disaster? If hook-swinging was no longer allowed, then what was second best?

In some places men continued to swing but without hooks in the flesh, for example, in a basket or from a belt or *cummerbund*.[9] In many parts of south India where hook-swinging had always been associated with blood sacrifice, live animals such as sheep or goats were used as a substitute.[10] For example, Henry Whitehead, referring to a festival in honour of Ankalamma in Kurnool in about 1906 noted that 'on the fifth day of the festival...a large car is constructed, with an arrangement of poles projecting about 20 feet in the air. A sheep is then suspended from the pole by iron hooks fastened through the muscles of its back and a band round its middle, and swung round and round'.[11]

This type of swinging was not always accepted as completely satisfactory, or, to put it in the words of the Raja of Venkatagiri, it did not satisfy fully 'the blind faith of the illiterate votaries'.[12] But what else could be done? As the swinging of humans was no longer possible, the swinging of animals was felt to be some sort of substitute to at least moderate the deity's anger.

However, the problem was that in some circumstances, even this option was in abeyance, either because the people themselves recognised the cruelty of swinging live animals with hooks in their backs, or because the authorities banned even this form of propitiation.[13]

In some parts of India inanimate objects, either a vegetable (usually a pumpkin) or some type of representation of a man, were already being used as substitutes in the process.[14] For instance, referring to the demise of hook-swinging in Bellary in the 1870s, one

Indian official commented that 'instead of men being subject to this cruel practice, a large wooden doll representing a man is hung in his place and the car is drawn round Durgamma's temple every year'.[15] As pressure against the swinging of animals increased, the swinging of dolls and painted images became more popular.[16]

While hook-swinging expressed some kind of religious need, including the need to feel in control of future events, it was also a ritual which could be used or exploited by a variety of people for other purposes. As we have argued, some performers utilised the custom to improve their social status, or to obtain money or other material benefits. Patrons saw in it an opportunity to display their largesse, to improve their standing in the community or to raise money, either for themselves or for the temple. Hook-swinging also provided incomes for all kinds of village workers, such as carpenters and blacksmiths who, like the wealthier patrons, had a vested interest in perpetuating the system.

But the ritual was also important for its critics. It provided the Western-educated classes with another cause, with something else through the rejection of which they could demonstrate and affirm their new and enlightened identity. For the Christian missionaries it also provided ammunition. It was, as we have seen, used to demonstrate how far India was still sunk in cruelty and superstition and how desperately her 'deluded' inhabitants still needed the glorious light of the Christian gospel. Last, but not least, the hook-swinging issue provided exponents of the empire with yet another forum — a further occasion in which to spell out what they argued were the high and noble purposes of British rule.

The attitude of the most senior officials in key positions in British Indian administration was clearly condemnatory. Their view and those of most district officers tended to merge with the comments of Indian and missionary critics of the custom. Lord Stanley, Secretary of State in 1859, who read the Bengal missionary petition against hook-swinging and other displays of cruelty at the *charak puja*, referred to these observances as 'revolting' and as 'a cruel and demoralizing public spectacle'. If existing attempts at suppression failed, he warned, then the authorities would have to adopt more effective measures for putting an end to observances which were 'so flagrantly opposed to the dictates of common humanity'.[17] Lords Cross and Kimberley, both of them Secretaries of State in the early 1890s, described the practice as 'barbarous',[18] and Cross, referring to the situation in Madras, stated that, in his opinion, the time had arrived when 'in the interests of civilization and common humanity, such degrading exhibitions should be prohibited'.[19]

The language of the enlightenment, humanitarianism and Christian moral concern also peppered the writings of governors and their executive councils. The Governor of Bombay, Lord Elphinstone, and his council referred to the practice as 'barbarous' and declared that 'motives of humanity' called for its suppression.[20] John Peter Grant, Lieutenant-Governor of Bengal, using epithets such as 'disgusting' and 'shocking', declared that the real evil was 'moral',[21] while Wenlock, Governor of Madras in the 1890s, was even more comprehensive in his condemnation. In his view, hook-swinging was not only an illustration of 'superstition' (and therefore irrational) but was also 'barbarous, cruel and revolting to humanity'.[22]

Much the same views were expressed in reports of European district officers. These, together with the comments of the more highly placed officials, underscored some of the basic ideas which, it was implied, lay at the heart of the empire. Because of hook-swinging and other perceived 'evils' in the Indian society, British officials were able to remind themselves and each other that British rule represented forces which were the very opposite to those symbolised in such practices.

For them it was the antithesis of all that hook-swinging appeared to be. If, as some of them argued, hook-swinging was a survival of a dark and savage past, this reminded the reader that times were different, that there was 'progress' and that conditions were improving under British guidance. If the practice was condemned as 'demoralising', then this description was often used to imply that part of the British purpose was to protect or improve public morals. If it was complained of as 'absurd' or 'superstitious', this again reminded readers that one of the purposes of colonial rule was to encourage the growth of knowledge and enlightenment. The supposed cruelty of the practice was contrasted with the supposed humanity or humanitarian purpose of the British system. Lastly, when it was held that hook-swinging was 'barbarous' (the favourite epithet), then this usually implied that it was not only cruel, but contrary to the civilising standards and influence of British administration.

Participation in the campaign against the practice helped satisfy the need to feel caught up in some higher civilising purpose. If

British administration had doubts about the value of the British presence, their role in the movement against hook-swinging may have given them reassurance, or even encouraged the sense of self-satisfaction and superiority reflected in A.C. Lyall's remark that 'whatever may be the ultimate destiny of our Indian empire, we shall have conferred upon the Indians great and permanent benefits, and shall have left a good name for ourselves in history'.[23]

The prohibition of the practice, like the banning of *sati* and other 'evils', was subsequently used to justify and legitimise British rule. For example, in the chapter 'England's Work in India', in his book *The India of the Queen and Other Essays* (1903), W.W. Hunter wrote:

> The rising generation in India have been freed from superstitious terrors, they have been led to give up cruel practices, they have learned to detest and despise their forefathers' bloody rites. Widow burning, infanticide, hook-swinging, self-mutilation, and human sacrifice — these are a few familiar relics of the old bondage under which the Indian intellect cowered and the Indian heart bled. Great as has been the material progress of India during the past century, its emancipation from ignorance and priestcraft forms, to my mind, a far more splendid memorial of British rule. Truly the people that walked in darkness have seen a great light.[24]

Not only was British rule liberating from all that was dark and evil; it was, according to some apologists, the only guarantee that evils such as hook-swinging would not re-emerge in the future. In the words of Sir John Strachey, member of the Council of India, 'the more we learn about India the more we become alive to the fact that we are, to use Sir James Stephens' expression, the representatives of a belligerent civilization, which has to wage constant warfare against strange barbarisms, horrid customs, and cruel superstitions, ancient survivals, ready at any moment to start into activity'.[25] Should the day ever come when the British Government relaxed its 'watchfulness' then, in his opinion, there was 'hardly a province' in which 'horrid and cruel practices' would not instantly spring into vigorous life.[26]

As we have noted, Christian missionaries, top European administrators and many district officers, as well as members of the British public both in India and Britain, condemned hook-swinging in much the same language. Their attitude exemplifies what some scholars have recently come to describe as 'Orientalism' — in this case, a view of India which saw it as Europe's opposite.[27] Thus, for European critics, hook-swinging was a practice which illustrated the 'otherness' of Indian society. This society was, in their view, not only alien and inferior, but something of an abberation — the criteria for what was normal, natural and rational being reflected in European rather than in Oriental thought and practice.

Furthermore, this attitude was not strictly confined to Europeans, but was also influential among Indian critics of hook-swinging. While, on the one hand, they defended many aspects of their own civilisation, they tended to adopt a similar stance to most Europeans in their attitude towards hook-swinging. For them, it was also the 'other', the opposite of what they stood for — something essentially inferior and an aberration of what was normal and rational. In fact, the debates on hook-swinging show quite clearly that in certain circumstances the Western-educated classes viewed popular practices in much the same way as Europeans tended to view Indian society as a whole.

Indeed, their main complaint was not that Europeans were wrong about these popular practices, but that they tended to generalise and were over-zealous in applying the same negative concepts to Hinduism and civilised society.

Lastly, it is important to note that not all of those, even among the Orientalists who responded to Government enquiries or engaged in public debate, were prepared to attack the custom. As mentioned in Chapter IV, a writer in the Bengali vernacular paper, the *Darpan,* wondered how Hindus could fulfil their vows in the absence of the practice.[28] He and others interpreted the agitation as an attempt by a minority opposed to Hinduism to impose their views on the majority. There were others, European district officers as well as Hindus, who argued that the abuses associated with hook-swinging were greatly exaggerated and that it was a comparatively harmless custom.[29] One of the exponents of this view was the Commissioner of the Burdwan Division of Lower Bengal, who held that the cruelty of the practice was 'a good deal exaggerated', that there was nothing demoralising or indecent in it, that he did not believe the performers suffered much pain and that, for these reasons, he did not see why the Government should interfere.[30] Similar comments were made by other European district officers and a small number of Indian observers. One of the latter, an old Brahman pensioned *tahsildar* from Gooty in the Bellary district of Madras remarked, for example, that hook-swingers did not undergo any kind of suffering and that the practice could not be regarded as a form of self-torture.[31]

The debate over hook-swinging not only involved questions about the merits or demerits of the practice, but whether the British authorities should intervene.

For some, these issues were clearly linked — the decision to intervene depending on the extent of the so-called 'evil'. If, for example, it was found that a custom was comparatively harmless, then the argument might be that it should be ignored and would gradually pass away as a result of the gradual growth of enlightened public opinion. If on the other hand, it was found that the practice was essentially harmful then, in that case, it was sometimes argued that the Government was bound to intervene.

This approach, which was based on ideas about the extent of an evil was not, however, shared by all Western-educated Indian commentators. Some of them adopted a different position, rejecting totally the idea of government intervention in any circumstances on the ground that religious and social reform was a matter not for alien rulers, but for the people themselves. It was for Hindus and not the British colonial authorities to assess the extent of the problem and put their own house in order.

What is remarkable is that these various views reflecting either reservations or outright opposition to state intervention — arguments which were put forward by Western-educated Bengalis with reference to hook-swinging in the first half of the nineteenth century — found scarcely an echo in the Madras comment on hook-swinging in 1893. This was despite the growth of nationlist sentiment generally and despite the fact that the Age of Consent Bill controversy, in Madras, as well as in Bombay and Bengal, was raised and fought largely around the same question of Government interference in Hindu customs in 1891.

As Suntharalingam has shown, Western-educated Hindus in south India were sharply divided over the question of state intervention in the form of the Age of Consent Bill of 1891.[32] Yet two years later the same classes in the population were virtually unanimous in urging state intervention to prohibit hook-swinging rituals. *The Hindu* newspaper, which began by criticising Malabari's proposal for state intervention to raise the age of marriage, had no such doubt as to the wisdom of invoking state intervention in the case of hook-swinging in 1893. Nor was the opposition to the age of Consent Bill, which was expressed in resolutions passed at public meetings, paralleled by similar resolutions passed at meetings to oppose hook-swinging measures in 1893. On the contrary, public and ex-public servants, local public figures and members of a wide range of associations supported the idea of suppressing hook-swinging through some kind of state interference.

Almost certainly the main explanation for this difference lies in the character of the custom itself. What for many mattered more than the principle of Government intervention or neutrality were the merits or demerits of the practice involved. As far as they were concerned, the age of consent and hook-swinging issues were very different questions.

The raising of the age of consent was bound to affect Brahmans and higher caste households and was intervention in their domestic affairs. By the 1890s, by way of contrast, most Brahmans and higher caste Hindus, including the Western-educated elites, in Madras Presidency knew little of hook-swinging. For them it was an alien practice which even in its heyday was primarily a lower caste phenomenon. They had little, if any, vested interest left in the practice which, in many districts, had already disappeared. While they had little, if anything, to lose, they had something to gain from the suppression of a custom which tarnished the image of Hinduism and helped perpetuate European views of their culture and way of life as backward and barbaric.

NOTES

1. *The Chronicle*, Vol. XI. 1902, p. 165; Knowles, p. 590.
2. J.S. Dennis, *Christian Missions and Social Progress. A Sociological Study of Foreign Missions,* 3 vols., New York, 1896, Vol. I, p. 92.
3. Ibid., p. 92.
4. Buckland, pp. 438-9; *CMG*, September 1893, pp. 136-7.
5. D.D. Kosambi, pp. 109-112.
6. *The Hindu*, 3/4/1940, 8/5/1941, 3/4/1942.
7. IOR P/4409 MJP, 21/12/1893, p. 85.
8. *Gazetteers of the Bombay Presidency*, Vol. XVIII, Part III, *Poona*, p. 135. *Vaghyas* were male beggars and devotees of Khandoba, Lord of Jejuri, and *murlis* were their female counterparts who were wedded to the god and who, according to one source, were prostitutes. *IA*, Vol. 10, October 1881, pp. 286-7; *CCO*, Vol. VII, September 1838.

9. *BH*, 20/4/1865; IOR P/4409 MJP, 21/12/1893, p. 77; *Bengal District Gazetteers*, Hooghly, Calcutta, 1912, pp. 107-8; *Madras District Gazetteer*, Brackenbury, *Cuddapah*, p. 66.
10. Sel. Mad., p. 14; IOR P/4409 MJP, 21/12/1893, pp. 78, 84; Oppert, p. 477; Elmore, pp. 31-2, 75; *Madras District Gazetteer*, Brackenbury, Cuddapah, p. 65.
11. Whitehead, pp. 58-9.
12. IOR P/4409 MJP, 21/12/1893, p. 84.
13. *Madras District Gazetteers*, Brackenbury, Cuddapah, p. 65; Elmore, p. 32.
14. Sel. Mad., p. 14.
15. IOR P/4409 MJP, 21/12/1893, p. 62.
16. *Madras District Gazetteers*, Brackenbury, *Cuddapah*, p. 65; IOR P/4409 MJP, 21/12/1893, p. 78-9.
17. IOR L/P & J/3/1207, Despatch, 24/2/1859.
18. IOR MSS. Eur. E 243/47 and L/P&J/6/352.
19. IOR L/ P&J/6-322.
20. IOR Board's Collections F/4/2701 and Bom. JP, 11/9/1856.
21. IOR P/188/61, p.44
22. IOR MSS. Eur. E 243/47 and L/P & J/6/332.
23. Alfred Lyall, *The Rise of the British Dominion in India*, London, 1893, p. 281.
24. W.W. Hunter, *The India of the Queen and Other Essays*, London, 1903, p. 127.
25. J. Strachey, *India*, London, 1888, pp. 288-9.
26. Ibid., p. 353.
27. For a discussion on the Orientalist view as applied to India, see especially Ronald Inden, 'Orientalist Constructions of India', *Modern Asian Studies*, Vol. 20, No. 3, 1986, pp. 401-46.
28. Supra. p. 119.
29. IOR P/188/61, Commissioners of Burdwan, Dacca, Chota Nagpur and Chittagong; Bom. JP. 31/7/1856, Magistrate of Dharwar; IOR P/4409 MJP, pp. 14, 67, 68, 72.
30. IOR P/188/61, pp. 36-7.
31. IOR P/4409, MJP, 21/12/1893, pp. 60, 63.
32. R. Suntharalingam, pp. 311-23.

BIBLIOGRAPHY

I UNPUBLISHED SOURCES

India Office Library and Records
Board's Collections
Bengal Judicial Proceedings
Bengal Public Proceedings
Bombay Judicial Proceedings
Madras Judicial Proceedings
Madras Public Proceedings
Madras Revenue Proceedings

Note: This material includes replies of government officers and others to three important enquiries. See Bengal Public Proceedings, 10/2/1860 (P/186/61); Bombay Judicial Proceedings, 31/7/1856; Madras Judicial Proceedings, 21/12/1893, (P/4409)

School of Oriental and African Studies Archives, London
Methodist Missionary Society: incoming correspondence and reports
London Missionary Society: incoming correspondence and reports

University of Birmingham
Church Missionary Society: incoming correspondence and reports

II PUBLISHED SOURCES

A *Government Gazetteers*

Central Provinces District Gazetteers
Hosangabad District, Vol. A, Calcutta, 1908
Betul District, Vol. A, Allahabad, 1907
Seoni District, Vol. A, Allahabad, 1907

Gazetteers of the Bombay Presidency
Vol. XII, *Khandesh*, Bombay, 1880
Vol. XXI, *Belgaum*, Bombay, 1884
Vol. XXII *Dharwar*, Bombay, 1884
Vol. XVIII, Part III, *Poona*, Bombay, 1885
Vol. XVII, *Ahmadnagar*, Bombay, 1884

Madras District Gazetteers
C. Brackenbury, *Cuddapah*, Madras, 1915
J.D.B. Gribble, *Manual of the District of Cuddapah in the Presidency of Madras*, Madras, 1875
F.R. Hemingway, *Trichinopoly*, Madras, 1907

B *Reports, Papers, etc.*

Register of the East India Company's Bengal Civil Servants, 1790-1842
Register of the East India Company's Bombay Civil Servants, 1750-1858
Census of India, 1901, *Madras*, Vol. 15, Part 1
C.A. Elliott, *Report on the Land Revenue Settlement of the District of Hoshangabad, Central Provinces*, Allahabad, 1867
R.E. Enthoven, *Tribes and Castes of Bombay*, 3 vols., Bombay, 1920
J.Hastings (ed.), *Encyclopedia of Religion and Ethics*
L.K. Anantha Krishna Iyer, *The Cochin Tribes and Castes*, Vol. I, Madras, 1909
Proceedings of the Council of the Lieutenant Governor of Bengal for the purpose of making laws and regulations from 1856 to 1867, Vol. II, Calcutta, 1868
E. Thurston, *Castes and Tribes of Southern India*, Madras, 1909
Selections from the Records of Madras Government, No. VII, Reports on the Swinging Festivals and Ceremony of Walking through Fire, Madras, 1854 (Sel. Mad.)
U.K. Parliamentary Debates, House of Commons

C *Periodicals*

(i) General
Asiatic Journal

Anthropological Papers of the American Museum of Natural History
Folk-Lore
History of Religions
Indian Antiquary
Journal of Asian Studies
Journal of the Asiatic Society
Journal of the Royal Asiatic Society of Great Britain & Ireland
Journal of the Washington Academy of Science
Modern Asian Studies
Scientific American
The World Wide Magazine

(ii) Missionary
Baptist Magazine
Calcutta Christian Advocate
Calcutta Christian Observer
The Chronicle
The Church Missionary Gleaner
Dnyanodaya
Harvest Field
The Missionary Herald
The Missionary Magazine and Chronicle
Periodical Accounts of the B.M.S.
Wesleyan Missionary Notices

D *Newspapers*

Bengal Herald
Bengal Hukaru
Calcutta Courier
Friend of India
Hindoo Patriot
Indian Gazette
Indian Native Newspapers Reports, Madras 1892-3
Madras Mail
Madras Weekly Mail
Morning Post
The Hindu

E *Books and Articles*

C. Ackland, *A Popular Account of the Manners and Customs of India,* London, 1847

A.F.S. Ahmed, *Social Ideas and Social Change in Bengal 1818-1835,* Leiden, 1965

M.M. Ali, *The Bengali Reaction to Christian Missionary Activities, 1833-1857,* Chittagong, 1965

A.S. Altekar, *The Position of Women in Hindu Civilisation,* 3rd edn. Delhi, 1962

V. Ball, *Jungle Life in India; or Journeys and Journals of an Indian Geologist,* London, 1880 (reprinted, Delhi, 1985)

B.N. Banerjee, (ed.), *Sambad Patre Sekaler Katha,* 3rd edn., Calcutta, 1977

Duarte Barbosa, *A Description of the coasts of East Africa and Malabar in the beginning of the nineteenth century,* trans. by the Hon. H.E.J. Stanley, Hakluyt Society Vol. XXXV, London, 1866

A.L. Basham, *The Wonder That Was India,* London, 1954

F.Boase, *Modern English Biography,* Vol. 1, Truro, 1892

E. Boaz, *The Mission Pastor: Memorials of the Rev. Thomas Boaz, LLD. Twenty-Four Years Missionary in Calcutta,* by his widow, London, 1862

Thomas Bowrey, *A Geographical Account of Countries Round the Bay of Bengal 1669 to 1679* (Haklyut Society) No. XII, Cambridge, 1905

C.E. Buckland, *Bengal Under the Lieutenant-Governors,* 2 vols., Calcutta, 1901

•Peter Burke, *Popular Culture in Early Modern Europe,* London, 1978

George Catlin, *Letters and Notes on the North American Indians,* edited with an introduction by Michael Macdonald Mooney in 1 vol., New York, 1975

V.V. Chitaley and K.N. Annaji Rao, *The Code of Criminal Procedure (V of 1898) with exhaustive analytical and critical commentaries,* 4th edn., Vol. 1, Nagpur, 1949

R.R. Chaudhry, *Glimpses of Old Calcutta,* Bombay, 1978

F.W. Clothey (ed.), *Images of Man: Religion and Historical Process in South Asia,* Madras, 1982

W. Crooke (ed.), *Travels in India by Jean-Baptiste Tavernier* (1st

Indian edn.), 2 vols., Delhi, 1977
W. Crooke, *The Popular Religion and Folklore of Northern India*, (Ist edn 1893), Delhi, 1968
M.N. Das, *Studies in the Economic and Social Development of Modern India, 1848-1856*, Calcutta, 1959
J.S. Dennis, *Christian Missions and Social Progress. A Sociological Study of Foreign Missions*, 3 vols., New York, 1896-1906
J.Duncan M. Derrett, *Religion, Law and the State in India*, New York, 1968
J.A. Dubois, *Hindu Manners, Customs and Ceremonies*, trans. and edited by H.K. Beauchamp, 3rd edn., Oxford, 1897
A.Duff, *India and India Missions*, Edinburgh, 1840
J.Grant Duff, *A History of the Marathas*, Vol. 1, London, 1912
W.T. Elmore, *Dravidian Gods in Modern Hinduism*, Madras, 1925
E.E. Evans-Pritchard, *Theories of Primitive Religion*, Oxford (paper-back), 1965
J.C. Ewers, 'Self-Torture in the Blood Indian Sun Dance', *Journal of Washington Academy of Science*, Vol. 38, No. 5, 15 May 1948.
J. Forbes, *Oriental Memoirs. A Narrative of Seventeen Years Residence in India* (2nd edn.), 2 vols., London, 1834
A. Gupta (ed.) *Studies in the Bengal Renaissance*, Calcutta, 1958
Basil Hall, *Fragments of Voyages and Travels*, 3rd series, London, 1833
R.L. Hardgrave, *The Nadars of Tamilnad. The Political Culture of a Community in Change*, California, 1969
R. Heber, *Narrative of a Journey through the Upper Provinces of India from Calcutta to Bombay, 1824-1825*, 3 vols., 3rd edn.), London, 1828
Ernest R. Hilgard and Josephine R. Hilgard, *Hypnosis in the Relief of Pain*, Los Angeles, 1975
E. Hoole, *Madras and the South of India; or a Personal Narrative of a Mission to those Countries*, 2nd edn., London, 1844
W.W. Hunter, *The India of the Queen and Other Essays*, London, 1903
Ronald Inden, 'Orientalist Constructions of India', *Modern Asian Studies*, vol. 20, No. 3, 1986
The Indian Press and the Late Raja Kali Bahdur. KGS, Calcutta, 1875
J.C. Irwin, 'The Ancient Pillar-Cult of Prayaga (Allahabad): Its Pre-Ashokan Origins', *Journal of the Royal Asiatic Society*, No. 2, 1983

J.C. Irwin, 'The Sacred Anthill and the Cult of the Primordial Mound', *History of Religions*, vol. 21, 1982

B.B. Kling, *Partner in Empire. Dwarkanath Tagore and the Age of Enterprise in Eastern India*, Berkeley, 1976

J.Knowles, 'The Hook-Swinging Cremony as I saw It', *The World Wide Magazine*, Vol. III, April-Sept.1899

D.D. Kosambi, 'Living Prehistory in India', *Scientific American*, February 1967

M.A. Laird, *Missionaries and Education in Bengal, 1793-1837,* Oxford, 1972

E. Leach and S.N. Mukerjee (eds.), *Elites in South Asia,* Cambridge, 1970

Alfred Lyall, *The Rise of the British Dominion in India,* London, 1893

Michael Maclagan, *'Clemency' Canning. Charles John, 1st Earl Canning,* London, 1862

B. Majumdar, *History of Indian Social and Political Ideas,* Calcutta, 1967

Clarence Maloney, *Peoples of South Asia,* New York, 1974

P.J. Marshall (ed.), *The British Discovery of Hinduism in the Eighteenth Century,* Cambridge, 1970

S. Mateer, *The Land of Charity. A Descriptive Account Travancore and its People,* London, 1871

J. Mill, *The History of Brititsh India,* 5 vols., 3rd edn., London, 1826, Vol. 2

Edward Moor, *A Narrative of the Operations of Captain Little's Detachment*...London, 1794

S.N.Mukerjee and J.O.Ward (eds.), *Revolution as History,* Sydney Studies in Society and Culture, Sydney, 1989

G. Obeyesekere, 'The Firewalkers of Kataragama. The Rise of Bhakti Religiosity in Bhuddist Sri Lanka', *Journal of Asian Studies,* Vol. XXXVI, No. 3 May 1978

G.Obeyesekere, *Medusa's Hair. An Essay on Personal Symbols and Religious Experience,* Chicago and London, 1981

G.A.Oddie, *Hindu and Christian in South-East India: Aspects of Religious Continuity and Change, 1800-1900,* London, 1991

G.A. Oddie (ed.), *Religion in South Asia,* 2nd rev. edn., Delhi 1991

G.A Oddie, *Social Protest in India. British Protestant Missionaries and Social Reforms,* Delhi, 1979

Rosalind O'Hanlon, *Caste Conflict and Ideology. Mahatma Jotirao*

Phule and low caste protest in nineteenth century Western India, Cambridge, 1985

J.O'Kinealy, *The Indian Penal Code and Other Laws Relating to the Criminal Courts of India*, with notes, 3rd edn., Calcutta, 1885

G. Oppert, *On the Original Inhabitants of Bharatvarsa or India,* 1st edn., 1893), reprint, New Delhi, 1986

Rui Gomes Pereira, *Goa,* Vol. 1, *Hindu Temples and Deities,* Goa, 1978

B. Pfaffenberger,'The Kataragama Pilgrimage: Hindu-Bhuddist Interaction and Its Significance in Sri Lanka's Polyethnic Social System', *Journal of Asian Studies,* Vol. XXXVIII, No.2, February, 1979

M. Phillips, *The Evolution of Hindiuism,* Madras, 1903

S. Piggin, *The Making of Evangelical Missionaries, 1789-1858. The Social Background, Motives and Training of British Protestant Missionaries to India,* Appleford, 1984

J. Pinkerton (ed.), *A General Collection of the Best and Most Interesting Voyages and Travels in all Parts of the World,* London, 1811

J.H. Powell,'Hook-Swinging in India', *Folk-Lore,* Vol. XXV, June 1914

S. Srinivasa Raghavaiyangar, *Memorandum of the Progress of the Madras Presidency,* Madras, 1893

R.G. Sanyal, *A General Biography. The Indian Press on the late Raja Kali Bahadur KGS,* Calcutta, 1875

R.G. Sanyal, *Reminiscences and Anecdotes of Great Men of India,* Part II, Calcutta, 1983

R.G. Sanyal, *Voluntary Associations and the Urban Public Life in Bengal (1815-1876). An Aspect of Social History,* Calcutta, 1980

S. Settiar, *Inviting Death. Historical Experiments on Sepulchral Hill,* Dharwad, 1986

E. Shils, *The Intellectual Between Tradition and Modernity in the Indian Situation,* Hague, 1961

L. Spier,'The Sun Dance of the Plains Indians: Its Development and Diffusion', *Anthropological Papers of the American Museum of Natural History,* Vol. XVI, 1921

J. Strachey, *India,* London, 1888

B. Stein (ed.), *Essays on South India,* Honolulu, 1975

R. Suntharalingam, *Politics and Nationalist Awakening in South India 1852-1891,* Tucson, 1974

A. Sutton, *Orissa and its Evangelization*, Derby, 1850

E. Thurston, *Ethnographic Notes in Southern India*, Madras, 1906

Pietro Della Valle, *The Travels of Pietro Della Valle in India*, (Haklyut Society) Vol. II, London

W. Ward, *Farewell Letters*

William Ward, *A View of the History, Literature and Mythology of the Hindoos*, Vol. III, London, 1822

J.J. Weitbrecht, *Protestant Missions in Bengal*, 2nd edn., London, 1844

H. Whitehead, *The Village Gods of South India*, London, 1921

M. Monier Williams, *Religious Thought and Life in India* (1833), Delhi, 1974

P. Wirz, *Kataragama: The Holiest Place in Ceylon*, trans. from German by Doris Berta Pralle, Colombo, 1972

Clark Wissler, 'The Sun Dance of the Blackfoot Indians', *Anthropological Papers of the American Museum of Natural History*, Vol. XVI, Part III, 1918.

B. Ziegenbalg, *Genealogy of the South-Indian Gods*, trans. by G.J. Metzger, Madras, 1869

Select Documents

The Charak Puja and Hook-swinging in Lower Bengal

1. A Bengali scholar's account of the Charak Puja

A short Account of the Charak Puja Ceremonies, and a Description of the Implements used. **By Ram Comul Sen, *Native Secretary, Asiatic Society.***

[Read before the Asiatic Society, in 1829.]

In describing the instruments used in the *Charak Sanyasa* presented by me for the Museum of the Asiatic Society, a short notice of the origin and practice of the ceremony appears to be necessary to illustrate the subject.

The word *Charak* is derived from *Chakra* or *Charaka*, which means a circle, and is used to signify moving or swinging in a circular direction; *Charak Sanyasa* implies leaving off worldly business, living abstemiously, observing austerities, for the propitiation of *Siva*. It is a festival improperly termed by many *Charak Puja*, perhaps from the notion that every ceremony observed by the Hindus of Bengal, is a *puja* — or religious worship; and whether it be performed by a *muchi* or *chandala*, is considered as Hinduism, and the whole body of the Hindus are charged with the absurdity of the act.

There are two kinds of *Sanyasas*, called *Siva Sanyasa*, and *Dherma Sanyasa*; the first is celebrated in the month of *Chaitra*, and the second in *Baisakha*; the people who practise these *Sanyasas* are termed *Sanyasis*, and the priest who presides in the ceremony is called a *Gajaneya* brahman: the Charak festival is also called *Gajana*, (*Ga* or *Grama*, village; *jana*, people,) being observed by the villagers. There are several ranks amongst the *Sanyasis*, such as *Mula* or head; *Dhula*, or subordinate; *Sain*, or followers. The time occupied by the *Charak Sanyasa* is a whole month, and that of the *Dherma* is a fortnight; during this time the *Sanyasis* live abstemiously, and observe various ceremonies to be noticed below.

This act is performed by the Sudra class only, and generally by the lowest castes and most dissipated characters: some of them consider it as an act of piety and religion, in commemoration of the austerities performed by VANA RAJA, a king and Daitya, who by acts of self-torture and denial obtained the special favour of MAHA' DEVA; and who first introduced the festival, but the greatest number engage in it as a lucrative exhibition, or from a desire to acquire a character for courage in the opinion of their friends. In some cases, the rite is compulsory: the parents make a vow to SIVA, when involved in trouble and disasters, that their children shall perform *Sanyasas*, for a certain number of years, which the sons must fulfil.

The form and manner of *Sanyasas* varies: the original ceremonies consisted of,

1. *Phala Sanyasa*, playing with fruits.
2. *Phala Sanyasa,* do. flowers.
3. *Nila Sanyasa,* worshipping NILAVATI, a goddess.
4. *Jhula Sanyasa,* hanging, and
5. *Charak*, swinging. These have been multiplied, and additions have been introduced by the people according to their fancy.

The original rules have mostly fallen into disuse, and new ones have been substituted, as convenience required. The time of *Sanyasa* has been reduced from 30 days to 15, 8, 4, and 2, and in some cases only one day is taken. The ceremony which was called an act of piety, is converted into an occasion of dissipation, drinking, gambling, and acts of immorality.

The following are the ceremonies at present in practice:

Phala Bhanga and *Kanta Sanyasa*, or falling upon the branches of prickly plants, spread on the ground, collecting them, as well as fruits, and living solely upon fruits: the *Sanyasis* go in company, and climb upon date and cocoanut trees, and collect fruits; when they come back to the place of SIVA, with the fruits so collected, they throw and distribute the same; they also receive presents of fruits. Barren women resort to the place, on the occasion, and spread cloths, on which if by accident a fruit falls, they receive it with joy as an omen of their becoming pregnant through the favour of SIVA; at the same season, the *Mula Sanyasi* with his deputy goes into a forest, a burial place, or on the bank of river, &c. and there performs the worship of YAMA (king of death), and presents, as offerings to the evil spirits, boiled rice and roasted fish.

Pata Sanyasa. — Falling from a scaffold erected before SIVA, upon a row of *Bati* or knives. It is called *Hata Sanaysa* and *Ghati Sanyasa,* because the scaffold is erected in a market place, and on the bank of a river; afterwards when the *Sanyasis* return to the temple of SIVA, they lie on their backs, upon the bare ground in a row, close to each other, and the *Gajanaya* Brahman passes over them, treading upon their breasts.

Phula Sanyasa. — Collecting and playing with fuel; which they often procure by plundering gardens, and carrying off railings, loose doors, window frames, &c. They then make a large bonfire in the evening, and jump and walk over the flamc, and play with the burnt charcoal, throwing the same upon one another; this is also called *Aguna Sanyasa.*

Nila Sanyasa. — is the worship of NILAVA'TI, a wife of SIVA: the *Sanyasis* visit Kalighat or temples of SACTI and SIVA, where they pierce their sides, tongues, and the skins of their foreheads. This is called *Bana Phora,* and on the occasion they collect presents and gifts from the spectators, who far from encouraging these self-tortures, pay them something to get rid of the sight of their bleeding limbs.

Jhula Sanyasa. — is climbing upon a scaffold, hanging with the head downward, and making a fire below. The fire is fed with the powder of Indian pitch.

Charak. — Eating *Chehatu* or *bran,* and swinging on the *Charak Gach* or post, erected for the purpose. Among these *Sanyasis* there are several other ceremonies of note, some of which must be noticed here: *Khatuni,* shaking and turning the head, rolling about the shrine of SIVA, beating the forehead, sitting up all night, and singing *Tarja,* or songs addressed to SIVA; sometimes, but not always, in his praise. *Phula ka dana,* extracting or receiving the flowers laid upon the Linga, which they think fall down at their solicitation; and prayers to the god, who is pleased to throw them down as a sign of affirmation or negation to the question made to him by the *Mula Sanyasi,* or the priest for himself or on behalf of his friends. If the flower does not come down after a certain time, it is then supposed that the god is not propitiated, and the *Deyule,* (proprietor,) *Mandala,* (agent,) the *Mula,* (head,) and other *Sanyasis,* and sometimes the priest himself, are tied up by the hands, and suspended to the verandah, all round the shrine of SIVA, while the *Sanyasis* redouble their *Khatuni* before the idol, and the drummer beats his drum with all strength; the *Sanyasis* and others remain suspended from off the ground till the flowers fall. The flowers are at first laid upon one another, and then placed upon the top of the Linga, which is oiled, and is consequently slippery: water is thrown upon it by drops, which assists to wash off the flowers, and when it is obstinate, some person on the part of the priest, contrives to knock it off with a stick unperceived.

Description of the Instruments used in the Charak of which Specimens are deposited in the Museum and numbered accordingly.

The Vetrasana is an instrument made of ratan; No. 1: it means a seat of ratan, it is the staff of the *Sanyasi*, a number of ratan folded in the middle and tied up together, leaving a few inches open in the lower part, in an oval form, the upper part is kept loose. Its use is various — it is a sacred ensign of authority, which must be respected on particular occasions by the *Sanyasis*, who rattle it as their musical instrument, in their procession; it is made a broom for cleaning the place of SIVA, where the use of common broom is forbidden during the *Charak*. It serves as a weapon, with which they fight, or beat down the bundle of thorns used in the *Kanta Sanyasa* upon which they fall; they use it in playing with the burnt charcoal in *Phula Sanyasa*; it is used as ropes laid under the pot or bag No. 2, in the *Pat Sanyasa*. When any dispute or difference arises between the priest and *Sanyasis*, or when the latter in their procession meet with another party, they lay down the *Vetrasana* across the road and the entrance to the house of SIVA, and the party against whom it is laid down must instantly stop; it is a sacred bar which they must not pass over without violating the law of *Charak*, and committing a sin which would disqualify them from becoming *Sanyasis* again. They are finally allowed to pass only in compliance with certain conditions; and certain questions relative to SIVA, delivered in verses, called *Tarja*, must be likewise answered before the new comers are allowed to pass, and beat their drum, or do any business.

Sutasana, or a cord of twisted thread, No. 3; it is in two pieces, which they pass beneath the skin of the sides, arms and thighs; the ends are held by two *Sanyasis* or assistants, whilst the man dances and passes to and fro. This purpose is also answered by log-line, No. 4, ratan, No. 5, split bambu, No. 6.

Dasnakhi, (No. 7,) two pieces of iron rod, about 2 feet long: one end is pointed, which is passed into the sides, and the other is fork-shaped with prongs, each of which is called *nakha*, or nails, or finger-nail; the two pieces have often 10 nails, hence it is called *dasa-nakhi* or ten-fingered, but it has often three prongs: the upper ends are flat, and laid upon one another, which serves as a bed for fire, or a lamp, made of cotton dipped in ghee; which is lighted, and upon this the powder of Indian pitch is from time to time thrown, so as to make a blaze, while the *Sanyasi* dances as he goes.

Bati, or knife, No. 8. — Eight in number, fixed upon two pieces of boards, in a leaning posture, placed upon a bag, No. 2, stuffed with straw. This bag is held by four persons, aloft from the ground, and two *Sanyasis* join their *Betasana* No. 1, and lay the same across, to render to the bag additional strength, and the *Sanyasis* fall upon it from the scaffold, No. 9.

Visesaya, No. 10, or nails to the number of 120; one end is flat, the other is pointed and sharp, these are run into the skin of the forehead, upon both arms, and breast, in an ornamental form, close to each other, usually like the front or facing of a jacket. To the ends of the nails small beads or peas are attached or suspended like garlands hanging upon the forehead, and small pieces of talc are suspended by way of decoration.

Banas, Nos. 11, 12, 13, or arrows, iron rods of various sizes and thickness, used according to the strength and courage of the *Sanyasis*, whose tongues and sides are bored, and the rods are let in, which they often move about. When it is perforated, the tongue and the rod rest upon the lower jaw, or are held between his teeth; if it be heavy, another person holds the ends.

Kupali, No. 14, is an iron rod or nail: the lower end is pointed, and is passed through the skin of the forehead, the man holding it close to his nose, or a bandage is tied round the head, to prevent it from falling; a small lamp is attached to its top, which he burns on the day of Nila.

Charak kanta, No. 15, or swinging hooks. The *Charaki*, or one who swings, is often of the bearer caste, and other people, not *Sanyasis*, volunteer for this act, through the effect of liquor.

The skin of the back being drawn out, a perforation is made with a lancet, No. 16, on each side of the back-bone, and the hooks, No. 15, are let in; the twine attached to the hooks is tied to the rope, suspended to the *Charak Gacha*, No. 17. If the skin of the *Sanyasi* is thin, or he is weak, a bandage of cloth is tied round his chest, to prevent the hooks from giving way, as when they break the *Sanyasi* falls, and is generally killed; the standers by also are sometimes severely hurt.

No. 18, 19, 20 and 21, *Belkars,* or lancets of various sizes and thickness: with these the skin is bored. These are not kept by the *Sanyasis,* but procured from certain *kumars* (blacksmiths), who attend the place where the *Sanyasis* meet, and receive a certain fee, which varies from 2 annas to 2 rupees for each subject. The lancets are of various sizes, and a number is always brought by the operator.

Nagapasa, No. 22, two long pieces of iron, with a snake head, hooded top; two of these are run into the neck and back of the head, and brought down to the waist; each has two borings at least, one on the head skin and one on the back. The *Sanyasi* who can submit to this torture is considered a great hero, and when two similar ones are put in, he cannot turn or bend his body without breaking the skin through which they are bored.

There is also a head piece, No. 23, made of iron put upon the head; it has 3 to 5 pieces fixed to it like the hoods of serpents.

Charak Gach, No. 17, or a post, commonly of saul wood, for swinging: it is from 29 to 30 feet long, fixed into the ground, the upper part has a notch, or socket, called *Mocha,* B; in which a movable pivot is let in, called *Khakuyi.* On this, a cross piece made of bambus 5 to 10 in number is tied up together, and placed across the *Khakuyi*: to both ends of the cross thick ropes are suspended, one of which is tied to the hook, No. 15, and on which the *Charaki* swings.

Source: *Journal of the Asiatic Society,* No. 24, December 1833, pp. 609-13.

2. A priest of Kali on the evils of reform

The Charak Puja (festival)

30 April 1831 (18 Baisakh 1238)

To the respected publisher of *Darpan*

You are unbiased therefore, in the interest of ameliorating our losses, if you publish some matters impartially in your paper so that they come to the notice of the authorities, we will be forever grateful for your favour.

I am a Brahman who makes a living from begging. I live at Kalighat near the Mother (the goddess) and make a living by holding a bowl (i.e. begging). If Hindus lose their religion or give up their traditional customs then what will become of us. We eke out a living from what we receive on the morning of Ban-Pho(n)ra (piercing with arrows i.e. the custom of piercing various portions of the anatomy by means of arrows or hooks at the Charak Puja), the night of Syama Puja or the day of the Mahastami Puja and the like. We have now heard that in The Reformer, i.e. in our opinion the magazine that helps Hindu boy to become foreigners, last Tuesday some Babu has requested an order from the authorities to ban the Charak festival. It is essential that we reply to this, hence we say that regarding our religion, when anyone feels it incumbent on them to forbid traditions or customs that are in use at the present time, that person should put his opinions in writing and present them to the chief distinguished and aristocratic Hindus for their agreement. Or they should call a public meeting and only press for proscriptions on those matters on which everyone is in unanimous agreement. Matters on which there is dissension should remain unchanged. But what type of judgement allows someone to overule the customs of one's own country by appealing to the authorities but without any of the above actions. It is true that sannyas (the asceticism borne by those who wish to practice the rituals of charak puja) is taken up by the choto lok (non-aristocratic poor or lower classes) but who among them has a Siva temple or celebrates the festival. The fortunate Bhadralok (aristocratic, wealthy classes) celebrate the festival and incur the costs. The choto lok go there and take up sannyas for their own pleasure or because of a vow. So if these gentlemen do not celebrate the festival or plant the Charak tree (the tall pole from which worshippers of Siva swing on the day of Charak Puja) then where will the choto lok get a Charak tree to perform the Charak Puja. In this way, in the abovementioned meeting, if all the fortunate bhadralok decide not to observe the festival, then the taking of sannyas will disappear. It is unnecessary for the authorities to promulgate laws if you say that the gentlemen of the past were fools; they had no learning so they are not worthy of gaining assent from the new contemporary babus. But it is not right to violate or transgress all those opinions because that would reflect badly on the present babus to assume that their ancestors were all fools. Since these ancestors had not even heard of the methods by which the new babus obtained their learning and became so clever, it is improper to critize one's elders. You know that no festival of the Hindus is without enjoyment (pleasure, indulgence) and each person has his/her own way of expressing this delight. The choto lok experience pleasure by dancing on the road. Seeing this, the writer in *The Reformer* pokes fun at them. But there are some festivals where all the Bhadralok roam the streets dancing and singing and people of other communities poke fun and laugh at them. One or the other, everyone has a particular day and time for indulgence of pleasure and each one enjoys him/herself in his/her particular way. It is not seemly for any one person to criticize or censure another. What kind of judgement do the new (present) Babus have? We easily impute blame to others but do not admit blame ourselves.

— From a priest (purohit) of Kali

Source: B.N. Banerjee (ed.). *Sambad Patre Sekater Katha,* Vol. II, Calcutta 1997. Transl. Devleena Ghosh.

3. Protestant Missionary Memorial to the Legislative Council against hook-swinging and other forms of torture inflicted during the Charak Puja, 1858

To the Honorable the Legislative Council of India.

The Petition of the undersigned Protestant
Missionaries residing in or near Calcutta.

Respectfully Sheweth,

That your Petitioners have long had occasion to lament the existence of practices among portions of the Native Community, which tend to the increase of immorality and cruelty; and that your Petitioners believe that these practices may, without difficulty, be restrained by law.

2. That your Petitioners submit to your Honorable Council that the tortures publicly inflicted and endured during the annual Churruck Poojah (especially the practices of swinging with hooks pierced through the back, and boring the tongue and other parts of the body) manifestly tend to harden and corrupt the beholders; and that these practices, in the judgment of the better informed Hindus themselves, are comparatively modern, and are neither warranted by the accredited standards of their religion, nor entitled to toleration on the ground of respect to popular usage.

3. That while these practices are common in Bengal, and while in some other parts of the country they assume a peculiarly offensive character, (from the fact of women as well as men being there hurled through the air by the swing,) in the North-Western Provinces (the original cradle of Hinduism, and the primitive seat of its most ancient institutions) they are confined to the small Bengali communities; and your Petitioners apprehend, from this variety of custom, that local circumstances alone, and not any general traditions, have gradually led to these distressing and degrading exhibitions in particular parts of India.

4. That your Petitioners believe that in Bengal (whatever may have been the case in former times) the people who swing at the Churruck Poojah seldom at the present time endure the suffering with any hope of acquiring religious merit, but ordinarily from the simple desire of gain, and that they are in fact commonly paid for their service, and stupified with drugs for the occasion.

5. That the assemblage of multitudes to witness the swinging, the excitement which frequently prevails, and the wild demeanour of those who transfix their tongues or submit to similar tortures, attest the brutalizing effect of these spectacles, and exhibit lamentable evidence of a state of feeling most discouraging to all who desire to spread among the people the blessings of civilization, a sound morality, and the knowledge of religious truth.

6. That your Petitioners fear that these practices tend to foster dispositions most unfavourable to the public tranquillity; and they

believe that much of the violence and cruelty which, in the dacoities of Bengal, have long marked the criminal annals of the Presidency, may be traced to the sinister influences emanating from the popular public exhibitions of the Churruck Poojah.

7. That your Petitioners believe that the spread of mere secular education, unaccompanied by other measures tending to elevate the moral sense of the people and to enlighten their consciences, will avail comparatively little to their moral improvement. On the contrary, your Petitioners have good reason to fear that secular education by itself may tend to render them impatient of the restraints of authority, and more earnest and more successful in the gratification of their baser appetites and passions.

8. That your Petitioners believe that many in the Native community are sensible of the real character of the scenes which distinguish the Churruck Poojah, and lament their demoralizing effect on their children, their female relations, and society at large; but from the depraved popular taste for this species of excitement, they are unable to manifest the needful moral fortitude to suppress, or effectually to discourage them.

9. Your Petitioners therefore submit to your Honorable Council that a Legislative measure to suppress, throughout all the territories subject to the Honorable East India Company, all those public practices at the Churruck Poojah, whether nominally religious practices or not, which are in themselves cruel and inhuman, is necessary in the present state of native society; And your Petitioners do therefore pray your Honorable Council to pass such a measure prior to the recurrence of the Churruck Poojah in the present year.

And your Petitioners will ever pray,

ALEXANDER DUFF, D.D., LL.D. *Free Church of Scotland Missionary.*
A.F. LACROIX, *London Missionary Society.*
TIMOTHY SANDYS, *Church Missionary Society.*
W.S. MACKAY, D.D., *Free Church of Scotland.*
THOMAS BOAZ, LL.D., *London Missionary Society.*
J.H. PARKER, *London Missionary Society.*
C.B. LEWIS, *Baptist Missionary Society.*
J. LONG, *Church Missionary Society.*
CHARLES HENRY BLUMHARDT, *Church Missionary Society.*
J.G. LINCKE, C.M.S., *Missionary.*

JOHN ROBINSON, *Baptist Missionary.*
SAMUEL HASELL, *Church Missionary Society.*
J. WENGER, *Baptist Missionary.*
GEORGE LOVELY, *Junior Chaplain, Old Church.*
FREDERIC SCHURR, *Church Missionary.*
BERNARD GEIDT, *Church Missionary.*
ALBERT P. NEELE, *Church Missionary.*
JOHN TRAFFORD, *Baptist Missionary.*
JAMES VAUGHAN, *Church Missionary.*
ALEXANDER STERN, *Church Missionary.*
LAL BEHARI DE, *Free Church Missionary.*
RICHARD PEARSON GREAVES, *Church Missionary.*
GEORGE KERRY, *Baptist Mission.*
EDWARD STORROW, *London Missionary Society.*
THOMAS JONES, *Welsh Calvinistic Methodist Society.*
SAMUEL DYSON, *Church Missionary.*
JOSEPH MULLENS, *London Missionary Society.*
JAMES THOMAS, *Baptist Missionary*
A. LESLIE, *Baptist Missionary Society.*
WILLIAM WHITE, *Church of Scotland Mission.*
JAMES OGILVIE, M.A., *Church of Scotland Mission.*
C. BOMWETSCH, *Church Missionary Society.*
THOMAS SMITH, *Free Church of Scotland Mission.*
REV. J. BEAUMONT, *Free Church of Scotland Mission.*
Calcutta, March 3rd, 1857.

Source: *Calcutta Christian Observer*, November 1858, pp. 480-82.

4. Secretary of State's comments on the Missionary Memorial

[Although the Legislative Council rejected the missionaries' plea for measures to suppress hook-swinging and other cruelties at the charak puja. Lard Stanley, Secretary of State, agreed with them that some kind of Government action was necessary.]

Stanley to Governor-General, 24 February 1859

8. In presenting the petition for a legislative enactment to sup-

press cruel and inhuman pratices at the Churruck Poojah, the member for the Lower Provinces of Bengal referred to an opinion of the Court of Directors to the effect that endeavours for the suppression of the cruelties of the festival should be based on the exertion of influence rather than upon any Act of Authority. In accordance with this view H.M's Govt. would be disposed to leave the remedy, as suggested, by the Lieut. Governor of Bengal, to the progress of education and its legitimate effects, were any hope held out of the discontinuance within a reasonable time, of these public exhibitions of cruelty. Of this however, there seems to be but little prospect; so long as those who engage in them are left in ignorance of the light in which such exhibitions are viewed by the Govt.

9. In the Presidency of Bombay, the practice of Hook-swinging has been suppressed by order of the Govt. and (according to the reports of the District Magistrates) without any dissatisfaction on the part of the general population.

10. In the Madras Presidency, the sense of Govt. has been marked by the insertion, as opportunity occurred, in Sannuds for lands appropriated to the support of religious festivals, of a clause declaring that forfeiture will follow any repetition of the practice of Hook-Swinging, & in several parts of the Presidency the practice has entirely ceased.

11. It is in Bengal chiefly that the revolting ceremonies connected with the festival most extensively prevail, & the efforts made to discountenance them have been attended with the least success.

12. Although the suppression of a cruel & demoralising public spectacle is a fit subject for legislation, it is not the intention of H.M.'s Govt. in the foregoing remarks, to press upon you any immediate legislative interference in the matter. It appears to them however that the Lieut, Governor of Bengal might be instructed to take advantage of such opportunities as may occur, of discountenancing the practice as far as in his power. Possibly, a provision hostile to the cruelties of the Festival may be inserted in the leases of Govt. lands, or of lands under the management of Govt. officers; the sympathies of influential landed proprietors & other members of the Native Community may be enlisted in the same direction; & other means, such as will often be found in the course of official administration, may also be taken, of making known the views of the public authorities in regard to such exhibitions, without causing alarm as to the intentions of the Govt. or producing dissatisfaction in the minds of

the people. Should such measures fail to produce any perceptible diminution of the practice, it will then be necessary to consider whether the Govt. is not called upon to take more decided steps for putting an end to observances so flagrantly opposed to the dictates of common humanity.

I have the honor to be My Lord,

Your Lordship's most obedient
humble servant,
Sigd, Stanley.

Source: IOR L/P&J/3/1207. (Public and Judicial Department)

5. The British Indian Association on the Bengal Government's proposals to prohibit the practice

From Baboo Joteendro Mohun Tagore, Honorary Secretary, British Indian Association, to J. Geoghegan, Esq., Under-Secretary to the Government of Bengal, —(dated the 4th February 1865.)

Sir,

I have the honor, by direction of the Committee of the British Indian Association, to acknowledge the receipt of your letter of the 31st October last, calling the attention of the Association to the papers on the subject of swinging at the Churruck Poojah, published in the Supplement of the *Calcutta Gazette* of the 26th idem, and requesting the opinion of the Association, for the information of His Honor the Lieutenant-Governor, as to whether the time has not come when the practice of hook-swinging may properly be prohibited by the Magistrates under the provisions of the Code of Criminal Procedure as a practice dangerous to human life and safety, and as an annoyance to all educated and right-thinking persons.

There can be no doubt, the Committee admit, that the barbarous practices of boring the body and hook-swinging at the Churruck festival are alike cruel and degrading. They have no religious sanction, and their observance is principally confined to the lower orders of Hindoos. Long usage has, however, given these practices a religious character in the estimation of the masses, and they regard them with the same veneration as they do those ceremonies which have the authority of the Shasters for their basis.

The progress of education and enlightenment has, however,

considerably counteracted the evil. It may be said with truth that there is scarcely a single educated Native of Bengal who does not hate these revolting practices and anxiously wish for their cessation. The influence of educated and enlightened Zemindars, among whom the Committee are glad to count not a few Members of this Association, has already gone far towards the suppression of hook-swinging in their respective Estates, and as time will advance, and the blessings of education will be diffused, the demoralizing exhibitions noticed by the Lieutenant-Governor will doubtless cease to receive popular support.

The Committee are, however, ready to admit that, if the total abandonment of the custom were to depend on such a change of the moral feeling of the masses as to qualify them rightly to estimate its degrading character, the reform is not likely to be effected within such a reasonable period as the Government and the Members of the British Indian Association could wish. Under these circumstances, and bearing in mind that the practice of hook-swinging has been suppressed in the Bombay Presidency by order of Government, and in the Madras Presidency also by the agency of Government, though in a less peremptory manner, it has been mooted whether in Bengal the revolting ceremonies in connection with the Churruck festival should be left to die out by the gradual enlightenment of the masses, or legislative measures be adopted by the Government to bring about their immediate cessation.

Occupying the position which this Association does, the Committee are naturally anxious to see, as much for the sake of the credit of the Queen's Government as for the sake of the good will of the people towards it, that no alarm may be wantonly given as to the intentions of the Government towards their religion, nor any violation offered to their feelings, or even to their prejudices, calculated to produce dissatisfaction and discontent. The people of India, it is well known, are peculiarly sensitive in matters of religion, and it is therefore of paramount importance for the Government to avoid all semblance of interference with customs or usages which, whether directly sanctioned by religion or not, are still associated in their minds with religious awe and veneration, and cherished with undiminished respect. Hence it is that this Association, no less from a sense of loyalty to Her Gracious Majesty than from a sense of duty to their countrymen, venture occasionally to express their opinions respectfully, but unreservedly, regarding measures or proceedings of Government having even the remotest appearance to a violation of the policy of religious neutrality, and to contend for the preservation of time-honored customs, usages, or institutions which, however superstitious they may seem in the eyes of enlightened persons, are still entitled to respect when they are followed so reverently by millions of fellow-creatures and fellow-subjects. In fact it has been the cherished conviction of the Committee that social and religious changes must be effected by the natural progress of society; that intellectual and moral development is the only right road to that progress; and that the legal authority of the Government should be the last resource of the community wherewith to put down any social abuse or to promote any moral or religious reform.

But the barbarities of the Churruck Poojah do not fall within the scope of the foregoing observations. In the first place the custom is not, as the Committee have already observed, sanctioned by the Shasters; in the second place it is not followed by the better instructed and higher orders of the community; in the third place it may be abandoned without materially interfering with popular religion; in the fourth place the suppression of these cruel practices have been effected by many landholders in their respective Estates without producing dissatisfaction among the masses; and lastly, if these practices are now to be put down, as if proposed, with the authority of Government, it is not because that the Government wishes to suppress them arbitrarily, but because the Government has the consent and support of the upper and educated classes of the community, those on whom the ruler in every civilized country naturally relies for the eradication of any evils of long standing, or for the promotion of any measure of general usefulness affecting the well-being of the entire community.

The Committee would of course deprecate any interference with the religious observances connected with the Churruck, and they are glad to receive the assurance of the Lieutenant-Governor that His Honor entertains no such intention. Nor do the Committee see much objection in swinging in itself. If the mob in Bengal wish to amuse themselves by swinging from the Churruck tree without hooking the flesh, the Committee see no reason why they should be interfered with. In Madras, the Committee are informed, the people swing by sitting within a basket, and either this or any other contrivance may be employed by the swingers here for their own amusement. As a popular pastime simple swinging may, the Committee are of opinion, be fitly allowed to be continued without violence to the moral feelings of any educated or right-thinking persons.

This festival, His Honor the Lieutenant-Governor may not be unaware is made the occasion of a general *méla* in the villages, where thousands of people congregate, make purchases of edibles, play things, articles of dress, and interchange social reciprocities, and the méla, the Committee submit, deserves to be encouraged rather than otherwise. The continuance of the Poojah and simple swinging, without the attendant barbarities, will render the proposed interference of the Police innocuous.

The Committee should certainly prefer to see the suppression of the barbarities of the Churruck with the aid of the ordinary criminal law to the enactment of any special law on the subject. The action of the Magistrates and the Police in the usual course will not cause any needless alarm or suspicion in the popular mind, while it will not fail to be effectual, which, however, cannot be confidently said of any special legislation.

In conclusion the Committee deem it due to observe that, while they recommend the suppression of the cruel practices of perforating the body commonly called *banphorah* and hook-swinging at the Churruck Poojah, they humbly and respectfully hope that the interference of Government may not be extended beyond the prohibition of the barbarities under comment. Perhaps this object may be well attained by requiring the District Authorities to prevent simply the abovenamed practices without interfering with the Poojah and the amusements of the people.

Source: IOR P/188/70 (Bengal Public Proceedings, March 1865).

6. Hook-swinging among the Santals: Rajmahal Hills, Bihar, 1870

January 12th—Chudma to Paharpur (Rampur).—All the afternoon of to-day, after my return from work, parties of smiling but intoxicated Sontals were coming up to the tent as deputations on one pretext or another. Among other requests, they asked me to give them permission to perform the *Churuk Puja*, better known to English readers as the swinging festival, which has been forbidden in British India. They said that in consequence of the *Bhut*, or evil spirit, not being appeased, their women and children were dying from sickness, and their cattle were being killed by wild beasts. When I replied that I had no authority to give them such permission, they then became most urgent that I should send a petition to the Government (vaguely spoken of by them as Kampani Bhadur, *i.e.*, the Most Powerful Company) representing the hardships they suffered in consequence of the prohibition, and praying for its repeal. I did not attempt to argue with them, as I knew it would be useless. In their estimation the evidence afforded by the losses in their families and flocks would have been conclusive against anything which I might urge. Both in Manbhum and in the Daman-i-Koh I frequently saw the old timbers of the *Churuk* set up near villages, and I often observed in the small of the back of the men who preceded me to point out the road in my daily rambles the old scars left where the hooks used in the swinging festival had penetrated. These men were not unfrequently the *Chowkidars* and *Goraits*, or village watch, and I am inclined to believe that they must have had an *ex officio* claim to occupy the honourable position. Some of the scars looked so recent, and the men so young, that I suspect surreptitious *Churuks* have been erected in the remoter tracts since they were forbidden by the British government. As well as I can remember, in every case where I made enquiry I was told that the weight of the body was not supported by the hooks but by a cloth k*umarbund*, or waist-band.

I am well aware, however, that eye-witnesses have stated that the weight of the body was in some cases supported by the hooks which penetrated the interscapular muscles. Possibly these observers were not mistaken; but the men I alluded to above shewed no signs of permanent injury having been occasioned by their suspension. With regard to this, as also to some other Indian customs, highly-coloured narratives have, I fear, been drawn up for the especial benefit of the charitably-disposed among the British public.

In a small isolated scrap of French territory, it is said that the Zemindar derives a considerable revenue from the Churuk Puja and various other attractions forbidden in British territory, to which the people flock from all the surrounding districts, and are of course made to contribute their mites, which go to swell the Zemindar's annual receipts.

Source: V. Ball, *Jungle Life in India or the Journeys and Journals of an Indian Geologist* (1880). Reprinted as *Tribal and Peasant Life in Nineteenth Century India*, New Delhi 1985.

Hook-swinging in Bombay

7. A Brahman account, December 1844

[Editor's remarks and translation of a letter to the editor of *Dnyanodaya,* an Anglo-Marathi periodical published by the American Marathi mission based at Ahmadnagar.]

The following communication is from a learned Brahman who was present and saw what he describes. We ourselves witnessed the shocking spectacle which afforded painful evidence that this people are grossly ignorant of the character of God. Let no one suppose that God is an unmerciful and cruel being who can take delight in such scenes as this. The true God is compassionate and merciful, and it is his wish that all should love and obey him and be happy; not that they should inflict such tortures upon themselves. They who, forsaking him, worship such imaginary gods as Khundoba or Kanhoba, not only suffer evil in this life but their condition will be miserable in the world to come. This communication would have appeared in our last issue but for want of room.

To the Editor of the Dnyanodaya

Sir, Yesterday I witnessed a wonderful event from which intelligent persons will understand that there are no people so stupid as these whose conduct I am about to describe. The learned, even among the Hindoos, are not prepared for such a dreadful thing. But the customs and opinions of those who are opposed to learning are very extraordinary. Seeing their conduct I am much concerned, and am led to ask when will these people learn to direct their attention to better things.

In Kamattypoor the temple of Mahalukshmee and the temple of Khundoba (sometimes called Kanhoba) are near to each other. In this latter temple resides a certain *wunjaree,* who is a *waghya* or devotee of Kanhoba. For a long time he has been accustomed, as a substitute for persons who have made vows, to swing by hooks fastened into his back. For this he receives a compensation. He has now become old and his back is covered with the scars caused by the insertion of the hooks; he having swung nine different times. He boastingly said to me, "A sahib on one occasion came by as I was swinging. He was much astonished at what he saw, and caused me to go round the temple twenty-five times; and when I was taken down he gave me a *mohur* as a present."

This man, having become old, selected a strong, young disciple to follow in his steps, and placed him over the hook-swinging business. This devotee thinks that by the performance of hook-swinging the god is pleased. Therefore on the day after the night on which the god's marriage is celebrated, hook-swinging is performed. And lest the man elevated upon the pole, during the time of being drawn round the temple, should be seized and troubled by the evil spirits, therefore a living offering must be presented to *Poatraj* a certain Mahar connected with the temple, that he may devour it. This is for the purpose of propitiating the prince of the evil spirits. On the present occasion there was an abundant beating of tom toms, and a great crowd of spectators.

First I will speak of the sacrifice. The Mahar who acts as the god's substitute seized the offering (a young kid) having previous to the commencement of the ceremonies satisfied himself with spirits, and covered his body with yellow powder, and rubbed red powder upon his forehead. Then with his hair dishevelled and holding in his hand a large hempen rope, he began to dance around with great demonstrations of joy. Then the people thought "The god has entered into him". Afterwards the person who had made the vow having performed *pooja* to him, gave into his hands a young kid. Having received this he went dancing three times around the temple, at the same time wringing the neck of the kid. While passing around the fourth time he violently seized the neck of the offering with his teeth, and biting it and sucking the blood, he in this manner went three time more around the temple. Then the offerer thought, "The god has accepted the sacrifice. In like manner doubtless, the gods formerly destroyed the *Daityas*".

While I was noticing these things a certain Kamattee spoke reproachfully of what was passing, saying, "What a vain thing is this. Our god has required no such thing. These people are great deceivers".

How this devotee appeared with his body covered with blood can be known only to those who beheld him.

Afterwards the hook-swinging took place as follows. The chief *waghya* performed this cruel operation through his disciple as a substitute. Inserting the two hooks into his back and holding fast to them behind he first caused him to go three times round the temple. Afterwards by means of the hooks the man was suspended to the end of the transverse pole which rested upon the upright post that stood upon the *gadee* or wooden cart, and thus was drawn five different times around the temple. While being drawn around the temple in this manner, the man who swung held on to a rope by one hand, and with the other scattered tumeric powder upon the people below him. After this he was let down and with the hooks still in his back went on foot three times more around the temple. Then the people who had come to see the ceremony went to their homes. Thus the business of the *waghya* was fully accomplished.

On the same day three persons who had made vows for the purpose of obtaining children were to have swung in fulfilment of their vows. But as there were certain obstacles in the way, they, by the payment of money, obtained a reprieve for the present year.

From the above account it fully appears how foolish these people are. Are not those who take no such vows still blessed with offspring? This is a mere imposition. And those engaging in it are guilty of wickedness. Let the people open their eyes a little and consider what their state will be hereafter, and how happiness may be obtained.

Please, Mr Editor, do give this a place in your Dnyanodaya that those who do these things may be ashamed.

Your Friend, Observer 25th December 1844.

Source : *The Dnyanodaya*, Vol. IV, Bombay, 15 January 1845.

8. An English judge's reaction to an exhibition in Khandesh District

[The following letter of A.S. Richardson, Judge of Khandesh, to the Registrar of the Sudr Faujdaree Adawlat (Company's Court), 13 April 1855, was fundamental in initiating reform in the Bombay Presidency in 1855-56.]

While visiting the Jail at Dhoolia about 7 a.m. on Tuesday 3rd Instant, a cart drawn by oxen was driven towards the town, where in addition to the usual number of persons who attend the weekly market, a large concourse had assembled for the purpose of holding a fair which lasts at that full moon several days, and thus affording certain deluded persons an opportunity of exhibiting the disgusting ceremony for which that cart was prepared. The cart was furnished with an apparatus decorated with scarlet and white cloth, and consisting apparently of a large bar furnished with a large hook suspended at one end to be inserted into the dorsal muscles of the religious enthusiasts, and at the other end of the bar, which revolved on a pivot, there were ropes attached to enable the executioners to heave into the air and cause to revolve round the cart the person suspended by the hook. I was informed by a gentleman who passed thro' the fair that no less than four such carts were in attendance.

This barbarous ceremony is practised I am told by members of the Coolumbee and Mallee castes, generally by females, and the executioners are carpenters who make a kind of trade of affording aid, as of course do the owners of the said carts, and I may add that from information given me by the Medical Officer in charge of Dhoolia that very extensive injuries are inflected on those who thus make a public exhibition of their religious fervour, the result being often "lock jaw" or eventually death.

Without any wish to intrude into such matters connected with Police jurisdiction as appear to the Magistrate to be exclusively vested in his office, and without any intention of interfering with religious ceremonies in matters beyond my official control, I must confess that I was so shocked at the idea of so barbarous and cruel practice publicly exhibited in a town within the dominions of the British Govt. which had abolished the self immolation of widows, eradicated infanticide, and within the last ten years, totally put down the inhumane rites of the Khonds, that I was under an impression that such a ceremony must be conducted without the knowledge of the Police authorities, and knowing that an exhibition of this nature would not be tolerated, for an instant, in the Island of Bombay or in the town of Poona, and being the only European Civil Officer at Dhoolia, I sent a peon with my compliments to Mr Ram Naid, the Deputy Magistrate, to inform of this fact, and received, in reply, that officer's "Salam".

In proceeding to the Court later in the day, I questioned several peons as to the ceremony, and was informed by eye witnesses that many people chiefly women had submitted to the torture, and "much blood had been shed", and that the same ceremony would be performed in the evening; wherefore I wrote a private note to Mr Ram Naid on the subject, and on receiving his reply that he was aware of the fact, regretted that he "had no power to interfere, and that the exhibition would be repeated in the evening". I addressed him a letter No. 251 dated 3rd Instant recommending as I believe, I am authorized by clause 3rd of Section 17 of Regulation XIII of 1827 to do, to his attention, the provisions of Section 29, and Section 1 clause 7 of Regulation XIV of 1827 as applicable to the subject, under the hope that a remonstrance from him would prevent the repetition of such atrocious cruelty, which it was manifestly the intent of the Chief Actors to promote as well as for their own pecuniary advantage as to gratify the curiosity of the populace, but recollecting that until removed by the personal interference of the Magistrate, an extremely indecent figure was exhibited in the public road in Dhoolia for many days during the Hooly, under, I am informed, the expressed permission of the Deputy Magistrate — I knew a suggestion from him could stop this practice at once. The event shewed that I was not mistaken, for although Mr Ram Naid addressed me the letter No. 44 dated 3rd Instant, which I received on the 4th Instant, the exhibition was prohibited by the presence of two peons under the subterfuge that the Judge and his family were desirous of seeing the ceremony — this was the reason given by the populace to a gentleman who happened to pass along the high road on the evening of the 3rd Instant, and this fact will illustrate the facility with which the practice might be abolished.

Source: IOR P/406/43 (Bomay Judicial Proceedings, 19 Spetmeber 1855).

9. An Indian official's comment

[Ram Naid, Deputy Magistrate to Mansfield, Magistrate of Kandesh, reporting on whether he could ascertain that there had been any cases of death or instances of permanent injury to the person resulting from hook-swinging, wrote as follows:]

I have the honor to acknowledge the receipt of your letter No. 921 dated 29th May last, and in reply to report that there are no instances recorded of deaths or permanent injuries having resulted from the practice of hook-swinging in the town of Dhoolia.

I have also enquired of the oldest inhabitants of Dhoolia, and been informed that no such results have ever been known to have ensued from hook-swinging.

Several persons who have frequently undergone the penance themselves, assure me that they have never been persuaded or forced by others to swing — that they have always done so of their own accord, in fulfilment of some vow; and that except on the first occasion when they received a certain shock on the hook being first introduced into their back, they have always enjoyed the swing rather than suffered from it.

I have personally seen the operation in all its stages. The person is kept on low diet for a few days, and on the night before the swinging takes place, very little light food is given. The part of the back which is to receive the hook is continually rubbed with the hand by another person for several days previously. When the hook is introduced the person undoubtedly receives a severe shock, and shrinks from it, but the relatives and friends hold him or her up, and the vociferous shoutings of the people keep up a degree of excitement. Little or no blood flows at the time, but bleeding does take place after the hook has been removed; and a little red lead applied to the wound and low diet, heal it in the course of a few days; and mortification seldom takes place. It is supposed that the hook penetrates only the skin; but this supposition is not consonant to reason. It must penetrate the muscles or the skin alone could not bear the weight, especially whilst swinging. I have heard of the skin breaking and the swinger falling down on the ground and lockjaw setting in, on one or two occasions (not at Dhoolia but elsewhere) but death has never taken place as far as I can ascertain.

Whatever be the description given of hook-swinging by those whose reason is blinded by prejudice and bigotry, the feelings of the more enlightened part of the native community are certainly shocked by so barbarous and cruel an exhibition of religious fervour; and the Shastras no where require or sanction such a penance, nor do I think its discontinuance would create any general discontent; but on the contrary it would soon be looked upon as an addition to the blessing heaped on India since the commencement of British rule. I am therefore humbly of opinion that although neither death nor permanent bodily injury can be proved to have ever resulted from the penance of swinging by the hook, yet the impression which such an exhibition makes on the community, and the certain bodily pain and probably mental shock it occasions to the person submitting to it, are such as to justify the interference of legislature.

Source : IOR P/406/43 (Bombay Judicial Proceedings, 19 September 1855).

Hook-swinging in South India

10. Extracts from the Rev. J.E. Sharkey's journal of a visit to the festival at Weyoor, Masulipatam District

(a) February 1848

18th. This morning Mr Darling and I left Bunder [Masulipatam] for Weyoor a large village about 25 miles distant. We arrived at Weyoor at 10.0'c p m. Weyoor is remarkable for the annual bloody worship that takes place in its vicinity. The Brahmins and Comtis excepted, most of the other castes from the surrounding villages contribute by their presence and mite to the support and performance of an act of idolatry which without the offering of human blood is considered imperfect and ineffectual: The Zemindar of the District lends no inconsiderable aid towards the countenance of this horrid superstition. It was to witness this cruel and savage rite as well as to raise our voices against its barbarity & sinfulness that induced us to journey hither.

19th. The first thing that attracted our attention on approaching this heathen temple was a semi circular array of young females clad in wet clothes besmeared with tumeric and stretched at full length on the bare ground. They had their faces turned towards the earth and their hands with offerings of wild cucumber or sour oranges extended towards the temple. On enquiry we were informed that they were barren women imploring the aid of the goddess for power to conceive. We were further told that they remained in that posture until they were assured in a dream by the goddess that they would be blessed with children. Some of them receive no answer it would appear for two or three days. We were also given to understand that all those that had the promise of the goddess fulfilled to them brought their children to the temple — shaved their heads, tied the hair in a rag together with a copper coin all which they flung on the temple and then made a few offerings to the priest within...

This evening we went again to the temple. The prostrate forms still around the temple. The priests are the worshippers of Siva. The idol now being worshipped is, I was told, the wife of Siva who also has a temple in the village but removed from his wife's. The worshippers of the former do not approach the latter. There are thousands around the pagoda we visited <u>but not one professes to have come to have his sins pardoned & removed</u>. Many have come to vend their wares, about a hundred to petition the idol for children, about seventy to offer thank-offerings for mercies received such as restoration from some illness or success in any important undertaking, and about two thirds for *amusement* & for the uncontrolled commission of wickedness. With reference to the thank offerings, they consist of either presents of copper coin, sour oranges, wild cucumbers or of oil. This last is poured into a wide chatty containing a thick wick. The wick being lighted the chatty is then borne by the offerer on his head, sometimes for a quarter of a mile. . .

21st. We heard that the sanguinary rite which I have alluded to would be performed at noon, so we purposed to witness the horrid scene. . . The car on which the men were to swing had not arrived. A Pariah is always *made* to lead the swinging. This individual a boy of about 16 years old was prepared to submit to the painful process. He was under the influence of spirituous liquor of which a large quantity had been administered to him to deaden him to the pain of the approaching torture. His body was besmeared with tumeric and his person decked with jewels. By his side stood his nearest relatives and over his head was held a cloth in the shape of an umbrella. Around him were half a dozen of men mad with liquor dancing and yelling most fiercely to a deafening tune which they struck on drums borne and supported by their left arm. Around this infuriated circle was a dense mass of people all rushing to catch a glimpse of the swinger. Such was the scene witnessed by us on our arrival. I went up to the swinger and told him as well as his prompters the great sin they were about to commit, that instead of procuring for them the favor of God their conduct would bring down upon them the wrath of God — that they were just fitting themselves for hell. The machine for swinging this poor man was now advancing. It was a common cart consisting of two large wheels five feet in diameter, connected by a thick axeltree, in the centre of which was fixed a thick and well smoothened palmyra beam fifteen feet high; across this again was attached on a pivot a long heavy beam so as to be raised or lowered as was required. The transverse beam was raised as the cart was drawn towards the temple. It stopped within thirty yards of the temple. All the village officers attended by some of the peons of the Zemindar were seated on a raised ground about five yards from the cart. The man to swing went straight to the temple and prostrated himself before the idol. He then arose and walked round the temple and then approached the cart where in the presence and before the officials of the village he prostrated himself a second time. Again he arose and awaited the word of command which being given by the head man of the village he bent forward and offered his back to two of his own caste that attended him who began to rub it with sand and so deadened the parts. The horrid hooks in the custody of the village officers were handed to the executioner, if I may so call him, who forthwith ran them through the skin of the poor man's back, & then fastened by means of strong chords to one end of the beam, which was then raised amid the deafening shouts of the multitudes around. This done the machine was dragged to the Pagoda then around it then back to the place whence it set out and then toward the village. It was now stopped and was then run back to the starting place. The poor lad had no support whatever but hanged all the while for ten minutes on the hooks, and as the ground on which the cart was drawn was uneven the hooks every time that the machine shook widened the holes on the back. I was astonished that the muscles did not give way — as soon as the cart arrived his friends would not lower the beam until the head man of the village promised to remunerate him. The promise was given but the men would not be deceived by bare promises, they wanted to see the money first before they let down the boy. The Brahmins for they were the head-men, became quite enraged, the sight of blood quite sickened them, and they were anxious to liberate the bleeding boy. So one of them advanced with a cane and in a threatening attitude ordered the men to obey. This too proved ineffectual. One cried out that the money was coming, another that the cash keeper had not arrived, another that the cash *was* nearly ready — all was uproar and the poor boy still hanging quite worn out by pain. Till at last upon the most solemn assurance that the money would be given the beam was lowered and the boy set free.

It is customary I am told for the village treasury to pay 5 Rupees to any *Pariah* of the village that is willing to undergo this torture and the object of this was to ensure the favor of the goddess on behalf of the villagers. To proceed — the hooks were removed and the blood was rubbed [sic] to the cart. Now followed three more that went through the same painful operation but with this difference that each was raised and lowered & set free all in two seconds. These men paid into the treasury 2 Rupees each for permission to have the hooks run through, and permission was not given till a notary took down their names, the names of their villages & other particulars.

22nd. About twenty five men swung today each paying 2 Rupees. This horrid festival is a fruitful source of gain to the Zemindar and his policy is not to be despised. He pays 5 Rupees to the first swinger as if very sincere & devout in the matter, but gains in return a hundred Rupees besides the large sum of money paid by the people into the hands of the priest *at the Pagoda.* It is remarkable that the swingers when hoisted did not turn to the pagoda but towards the officials to whom they paid religious homage.

Source: C.M.S., CI2/0222/3.

(b) February 1851

In February 1848, I was present at an annual Hindu Festival, celebrated at Weyoor, a large village about twenty five miles distant from Masulipatam. On that occasion I penned a few remarks descriptive of the temple and worship as well as of the number and character of the assembled multitudes. But the account I then furnished was drawn from sources somewhat imperfect. In February this year, I revisited Weyoor and again witnessed the same festival. I took care to arrive early at the scene of action and to put forth every effort in gaining accurate information on several points which I was before unable to explain. My exertions met with ample success, and put within my reach materials sufficient for a successful exposure of one of those local links, which preserve this extensive district undivided in its idolatrous predilections. With one voice the thousands that constitute the lower orders invest Weyoor with all the importance of a holy resort, and place in it a goddess, whose exploits have procured for her titles and worship, which no one dares dispute or deny. In times of sickness or childbirth, in danger and distress, the goddess of

Weyoor is solemnly remembered and vowed to. Women desirous of children prostrate themselves before the idol and intreat for the precious boon. Many a miracle is thus said to have been wrought, and many a legend is told and prodigy related in honour of a block of wood shaped into the figure of a woman whose claims to divinity are as weak and dishonerable [sic] as the frauds by which they are supported. Nevertheless, that the goddess of Weyoor holds a prominent place in the religious affections of the people of this district, and forms no ordinary obstacle in the way of the gospel, is a fact worthy of our attention and of our most persevering efforts in refuting this doctrine of lies. I purpose to give one connected account of all the details as far as they are known to me of what transpires year after year at Weyoor, with the hope and prayer that it may lead all who read it, not only to mourn over the utter depravity of man, as seen in the cruel and grovelling rites which for ten days, thousands of immortal souls stand actively opposed to their Omnipotent Creator, but also to redouble their exertions of prayer, for God's pure word to go on and prosper in the regeneration of this thrice unhappy land.

I was in my tent encamped at a village north west of Weyoor, when the festival was about to commence. On the morning of the 15th February, after a short ride, I reached Weyoor. During that and several subsequent days, I received several versions or legends of the goddess, which was so soon to be worshipped. The history runs thus: It was, when the country was still under Mahomedan rule, that there lived at Weyoor, then a considerable town, a young woman of exquisite beauty of the shepherd tribe, whose name was Veerammah. Her parents married her to a wealthy man of the same tribe, whose name was Chintannah. But her personal charms, which were neither few or ordinary, soon attracted the attention of one of the village officers and awakened in him desires and plans of a seductive nature. Her virtue, however, proved unassailable. She treated his rich offers with contempt, and rejected his solicitations with horror and indignation. He was not discouraged. He regarded her resistance as simply an expression of her fears of her husband, whose destruction he proceeded to accomplish. Big with evil intent, and anxious for a speedy consummation of his evil purpose, he is said to have employed a certain spell of fatal power under which Veerammah's husband then absent from home, fell an unresisting innocent victim. The sad intelligence reached Weyoor. Veerammah received it with calmness, divined the author of Chintannah's death, and, with vows of speedy vengeance, resolved to immolate herself on the funeral pile and disappoint for ever the wicked design of the enemy of her happiness. But ere the doleful message could be told, Chintannah's lifeless form scarcely cold was hurried to the funeral pile and reduced to ashes, but his shoes and blanket went to her instead of his corpse and with these she now prepared to clasp the pile which a little before had erased the last trace of her husband's existence. But she was thwarted. The village authorities, secretly influenced by her husband's murderer, opposed her suicidal measures, and drove her to seek the aid of the Mahomedan Government. There happened at this time, to be at Weyoor a Mahomedan traveller of influence and power journeying to Masulipatam under some public disgrace. To him Veerammah applied for help, and strengthened and recommended her appeal, with a prediction of his speedy restoration to favor, as a reward for his cooperation. The Moslem at first treated the request with characteristic indifference; but secretly moved, it is said, by a supernatural impulse, laid aside his religious bigotry and, espousing her cause, vigorously supported it to the full extent of his power. Under his auspices, she prepared for the dread rite. With exulting defiance of her enemy's diabolical design, she ordered the pile to be made in a corner of his own yard. Richly decorated and attended with various kinds of music she proceeded to the house of her enemy and, there with a solemn pause she devoted [sic] him and all belonging to him to entire destruction, specifying, that on the ruins of his dwelling she would erect a swing and on it in her deified form sing her triumph over him and his abortive project. Thus disburdened of her indignation, she proceeded with a relieved heart to the pile and in a few minutes amid the noise of drums and shouts of spectators, Veerammah's spirit was reunited, we are told, and absorbed in the one universal essence. She was no sooner dead, than in a dream to the elders of her tribe, she represented herself — as an incarnation and signified a wish to have divine honours paid to her on the spot where her funeral pile was made. Her Islam benefactor, I was told, soon experienced a literal verification of her prediction and returning to Weyoor in the full enjoyment of public trust and favour, he was pleased to receive a deputation of the shepherd elders, whom he assisted in the erection of a temple in honour of Veerammah. The building was soon supplied with a wooden image, ornaments and cloths of considerable value, adorned the naked idol. The ceremony of consecration was over, and the image became a deity, and Veerammah became its name! Her husband Chintannah was not forgotten. His murder excited many a pity, and the enthusiasm of the people associated him with his divine wife to share with her the adoration of the bowing multitudes. Accordingly a molten image, with the name of Chintannah, was made and placed by the side of Veerammah; and both have ever since been the objects of general and enthusiastic worship. The temple erected over Veerammah's pile is an oblong building low and narrow with a flat brick roof. It is partitioned into two chambers the inner being two thirds smaller than the outer, and the whole building being scarcely twelve feet. In this inner apartment or adytum the images of Veerammah and Chintannah are worshipped: over the adytum rises a dome to the height of about fifteen feet, adorned with several brazen vessels, and facing the temple, is a smooth pole driven into the earth, with a dull light attached to the top of it. By the side of the temple is a large tank excavated by a harlot of the village in honor of the goddess, and about a hundred yards from it, are two stout logs of wood planted perpendicularly into the ground and at a considerable height attached to a traverse beam, from the centre of which suspend two strong leathern cords, constituting the swing, of which Veerammah had already given notice...

The priests of Veerammah are of the shepherd tribe, and the office, a lucrative one, is confined to the descendants of those elders who originated the worship of the goddess. To them is committed the care of the idols and their expensive ornaments. In a separate house adjoining their own, and not in the temple which from its isolated and remote situation from the town is exposed to the inroads of robbers — the charge is inviolably preserved, while one of the men the oldest generally, ministers daily before the idols, with incense and offerings of rice and occasionally with the blood of goats and fowls... The priests do not confine themselves to their religious office, but being shepherds, tend sheep, cultivate the ground and freely engage in every secular calling. The festival presented the following scene. Within the adytum were the idols, one of them well polished with Tamarind, and the other richly painted; and both clad and adorned in costly array. Around them were several small earthern vessels filled with oil feeding as many lights, one of which after the festival is over, is preserved and never extinguished. In front of the idols was a quantity of tumeric and saffron, a pinch of each, one of the priests served to every woman that presented herself with offerings before the idols. The Tumeric thus received was rubbed on the forehead and the saffron on the face. At the door of the temple and in a sort of amphitheatre fenced with a low mud wall, were the musicians, consisting of drummers and trumpeters, rending the air with shrill discordant, deafening sounds. Around the adytum outside, stretched at full length, were a number of young females, in wet clothes, covered with tumeric, with their faces turned towards the earth and their hands extended, in supplication to the goddess within. Around them were their nearest relatives and spectators not a few. The prostrate forms kept their position for hours together, until assured, I was told, by the implored goddess of a speedy conception. No direct promise, however, is given by the idol, but what is reckoned equivalent to it, a promise of either a cucumber, an orange, or some such article! Thus gifted the girl arises from her sleep, and accompanied by a female relative, and attended by a religious beggar ringing a bell she rounds the temple and then entering it, presents her offering of fruit, and prostrating herself, worships the dead idol. She then rises and departs, rejoicing at the prospect of becoming a mother soon. The prostrations this year were few, so few as to arrest the attention of many; and they have attempted to account for it by the growing poverty of the people in general, who could not come to the festival without the command of money. But I trust many were not present from other and better motives. From the village in which I was encamped not one attended save one old woman and her son. One woman in particular had repeatedly prostrated herself before the goddess; and though often sent away, as she declared, with a favourable answer, she still continues childless, and such is the infatuation of her family, that her husband, a weaver, was actually engaged weaving a cloth for her to be tied and worn *after* it had been presented to the goddess on this occasion!

The very soul of the festival is the civil power which maintains it, and, under its fostering care, priestcraft is not slow in exerting its baneful sway. The festival was ever a fruitful source of revenue to the Government; but ever since the partial disconnection of our government with abominable idol-worship of this country, the Zemindar of Noogaveed in whose territory the temple stands, bestows all the care of a patron in the celebration of the festival in honor of Veerammah. One of the Zemindar's chief revenue officers attended by a suitable number of assistants and peons is present on the occasion to give weight to the proceedings and even to defray a portion of the expenses. But the real object of the public countenance and support is to secure as had already been hinted, the revenue arising out of the festival. The sum realised this year was Rs.62-12-6 and the outlay did not exceed Rs. 42-11-9 so that a clear balance though small of 20,0,9 remained for the Zemindar. Thus superstition is made to subserve the interests of covetousness, the bond is strengthened to render the victim more submissive, and the cause of idolatry favoured for the sake of the mammon of unrighteousness. But the festival is profitable to many more, besides the Zemindar. The priests appropriate to themselves the rich and numerous offerings of ghee, oil, fruit and money, which are laid before the idol in fulfilment of vows, or as presents. The musicians and light bearers, the usual attendants on such occasions, receive a stated income for their services. The village peons, the carpenters for preparing and fixing the beam into the swinging machine, the shoemakers employed to raise and lower the beam, the village slave for twisting the cord to which the swinging hook is attached, the village accountants, generally Brahmins, the shroffs or bankers of the Vaisia caste and lastly the first swinger that runs the hooks through the skin of his back are all suitably rewarded; the payments varying from 4 Annas to 5 Rupees according to a table of rates fixed, no one knows when. The festival likewise furnishes an ample opportunity for the profitable sale of bamboo boxes, canes and sieves, and a variety of wares brought from the neighbouring towns, and sold under little tents pitched in two long rows, with sufficient space between to form a broad street, which, is so thronged at times, as to render a passage without force a matter of considerable difficulty. Jugglers, story tellers and beggars look to the festival as one of the chief means of their livelihood, while for those who pick and steal, the occasion is a most favourable one. Thus the festival whatever its religious pretensions, is unquestionably a source of amusement to all; of profit, to not a few; an aid to revelry, and an opportunity for crime.

In regard to the swinging I have not much to add to what has already appeared. The swingers this year were thirty three in number, most of whom were women! and some of the rest girls!! All with the exception of three were taxed by the Zemindar at 2 Rupees each. One of the swingers became so terrified at the sight of the machine, that he refused to hook himself; and declared his refusal with a flood of tears; his wife, however, stepped forward and boldly gave her back to the executioner and was presently aloft, to the surprise of the gazing crowd. A young girl too screamed and shouted and craved deliverance from the horrid rite, but no substitute being found, the hooks were forcibly driven into her skin, and unmindful of her shrieks, the beam was raised, with the writhing girl attached to it. Several women bearing in their cloths their new born infants, endured the torture with manly courage. I have thus endeavoured to put together the fresh matter I had gathered regarding this festival which I have already said possesses a strong hold on the minds and hearts of the people of this district. It remains now to mention some of my engagements at Weyoor during my stay there. On the 15th February, the day of my arrival I went direct to the temple and there heard some very silly stories told by a Pariah, in a kind of chant accompanied by a drum, which he struck at intervals with the palm of his right hand producing abrupt hollow sounds. I however said nothing that day, but on the following one I preached Christ to a large multitude, the Lord granting me much boldness. Several advanced to discuss but went away without a word of answer. Some of them pointed exultingly to the prostrations, but they were compelled to admit that they consisted entirely of young females, who were still too young to be *mothers*, who in due time would in all probability be so without the interposition of their goddess, and that it would serve their cause better, if the prostrations consisted of barren females of *advanced* ages, whose fruitfulness after so remarkable a solicitation could not but gain for the idol a large measure of credit. My opponents then mentioned the swingers, how that the hooking was to them painless, and how the flesh and skin on the back did not give way though violently pierced and torn. That it gave no pain I said was an assertion I replied [sic]; that under the influence of spirituous liquors and the excitement of the occasion it may seem so; but why an idol that had the power of rendering the operation painless, could not at the same time heal the wound, instead of leaving the individual to several days of suffering and to all the inconveniences and losses of confinement to a bed of sickness, which to a poor labourer dependant for his daily subsistence on the labour of that day was a very grievous trial they could not explain. They then pointed to the crowd, as if numbers constituted the excellency of the festival, but I very minutely explained how some had come for amusement, others to buy and sell, others again to drink and rob, and others to beg. I told them what the Zemindar derived, what the priests within received, and how all were concerned to uphold a festival which ministered to the pleasure of some, or the pecuniary profit of others.

Source: C.M.S., CI2/0222/9.

11. Continuance of the practice in Tanjore District

GOVERNMENT OF MADRAS
JUDICIAL DEPARTMENT

Read — the following paper:

From Colonel C.A. PÓRTEOUS, Acting Inspector-General of Police, to the Chief Secretary to Government, dated Rénigunta, 12th August 1890, No. 4598.

The Superintendent of Police, Tanjore district, having mentioned in his weekly report that a case of swinging (Chedel kuttu) had taken place, during the festival, in honor of goddess Mariamman, at Valambagudi, in the Vallam taluk of his district, I called for a special report on the subject, copy of which I have the honor now to submit for the information of Government.

The practice of swinging having been prohibited many years ago, it is difficult to understand how it has continued in the Tanjore district to this day.

Enclosure

From T.E. THOMAS, Esq., Superintendent of Police, Tanjore, to the Inspector-General of Police, Madras, dated Koradacheri, 2nd August 1890, No. 738.

I have the honor to report, for your information, that on 10th June 1890, after the Car festival of the Mariamman goddess at Valambagudi village, in the Vallam firkah, Tanjore Taluk of this district, was celebrated, a Swinging "festival . . . took place". This is a vow performed by a Pariah to propitiate the deity known there as the"Muthu Mariamman", and this year the duty devolved on Para

Vythi of Palyaputty, a strongly-made man aged 35 years. Two iron hooks were passed through the skin of the back in opposite directions, below the shoulder blades, and on both sides of the spine, and tied to the end of a long beam which rested on its centre on a granite pillar about 12 or 13 feet high; a rope was attached to the other end of the beam, and a man lowered it, and thus elevates the end to which Vythi was hooked and then pulled it round six times. The Inspector described it "as if the man were floating in the air, at a height of 50 feet", but from the length of the beam and height of the pillar, I should say it could not be more than 20 or 25 feet. After the sixth round the man was lowered, and the hooks were removed, and his wounds were dressed, and he was given some arrack, and conducted to a place near the temple of the deity, and allowed to rest; after which he appeared all right, and moved about. Only the Pariahs of Palyaputty are allowed to perform this vow; the temple is common to 18 villages, and its affairs are managed by a Brahmin, Swamy Iyen, who is the temple priest or "goorucal". Both the priest and the Pariahs profit to a certain extent by the alms that are given by the people that witness the ceremony. It has been going on uninterruptedly for the past 30 years, as the priest told me. The Inspector mentioned in his diary that the Pariahs would really like the thing stopped, but are afraid to express such a wish, for fear of the Kullars; but from what I learned from a Pariah who had been swung some few years back, I should say they are not willing to have it discontinued. In 1888 the villagers were split into two factions, and one of them put in an application to the Division Magistrate and District Magistrate praying for an injunction to discontinue the practice. The prayer was not granted and serious breach of the peace was apprehended, but averted by the presence of the Inspector and Sub-Magistrate. Since I mentioned the circumstance of this Swinging festival in my weekly report, the District Magistrate has issued the following order under date the 10th July, 1890, No. 1132, on the arzee No. 85, dated 2nd July 1890, reporting on the Swinging festival at Valambagudi:

"It appears that in 1888 Mr. Gibson, on a petition made, passed orders directing the Sub-Magistrate of Vallam to see that the celebration of a certain Swinging festival is not revived if the petitioner's statements were true. The undersigned regards this order as prohibiting such festivals and now also distinctly prohibits them everywhere: the Sub-Magistrate will see that this order is communicated to all concerned."

Source: IOR P/3784 (Madras Judicial Proceedings, 27 August 1890).

12. The Revival at Sholavandan, Madura District, 21 October 1891: A mission doctor's account

From F. Van Allen, Esq., M.D., to the Second-class Magistrate, Madura Taluk, dated Madura, 6th February 1892.

With reference to your letter of 30th January 1892 asking for particulars of the circumstances attending the swinging festival which occurred at Sholavandan, India, in October last, I have the honour to say that I attended the said festival, saw the man who was swung twice before the swinging and once afterwards. I saw him first at a distance of about fifteen yards, this time about two hours before the occurrence, the second time close at hand when I observed him carefully for about two minutes, this time about five minutes before he was swung. During the time he was hanging aloft I was watching him nearly all the time. On his completing the circuit and being lowered to the ground I examined him carefully as soon as he was released from the pole.

I may state that Sholavandan is a village of some 1,500 souls located twelve miles north of Madura. Much publicity had been given to the hook-swinging and the village was filled with a large crowd of 10,000 to 12,000 people. So far as I could see, the people were well behaved, their only emotions being curiosity and subdued excitement. The temple stands in the centre of the town, near this stood the car bearing the pole on which the victim was to swing. This car was made of timbers, was about fifteen feet square and was supported by four wheels. Projecting from the centre of the car was a large timber, the top of which rose up about twenty feet high from the ground. The top of this timber acted as a pivot for a pole about sixty feet long. This pole was spliced in the middle and where spliced rested on the point of the timber. [See Figure 5].

The distance from the end of the pole where he swung to the ground was thirty-eight feet.

Promptly at 3 o'clock the man who had been chosen to be swung was seen coming down a side street on a run accompanied by a shouting and excited crowd. I was standing near the front of the temple and as the man came near me I saw that the hooks had already been inserted. This had been done probably in a house some distance away, though it had been advertised to be done publicly at the temple. They were two iron hooks inserted into the skin and subcutaneous tissues, one on each side the backbone and brought together back to back. [See Figure 9]. Some blood was running down his back.

I could not learn just how the hooks had been inserted but had heard before that a curved gouge was to be plunged into the tissues, cutting down in and then up and out, and in the path thus formed the hooks were to be passed. It is probable that this was the procedure judging from the fact that a curved gouge was shown together with the hooks and ropes afterwards. It is said that the parts were made somewhat insensible by slapping and pounding before the hooks were put in. As to this I cannot say. As the man came up to the front of the temple he was seen to be a splendid specimen of brute strength, though not of large frame. He was of medium or under size, stockily built and muscles markedly firm. His attendants were fanning him and urging to a dancing motion. The man was evidently under strong excitement but was self-controlled.

He was then hurried away to the car which stood a few yards away. I proceeded to the car at once and watched them tie the ropes which were attached to the hooks. When all was made secure, traction was made on the further end of the pole and he was raised into the air. When he first left the ground he winced decidedly and the skin and muscular tissues were drawn up from the surface of his back about three inches. He had no other support than the hooks in his back. As he went higher into the air I could not see plainly the expression of his face, but as well as I could make out, it took on a dogged or determined look. On his ancles were bangles and in his hand he carried a silk cloth. His body was naked except a cloth about his hips and a turban on his head. He kept beating his ancles together with a steady cling-cling and kept waiving the cloth in his hand. These motions were probably to show that he had not fainted, but as a physician, I must say that I fully expected that he might faint at any time. There can be no doubt that he had strong stimulants.

The car was drawn through four streets forming a square, about one mile in distance and after one hour and fifteen minutes it returned to its starting place. During the time of the ordeal the victim was encouraged by the shouts of the people.

When he was lowered to the ground again I examined him in less than a minute after the ropes were untied. His face wore a somewhat exhausted look but his voice was full and strong, he answered questions promptly, his pulse was good. The hooks were still left in his back, in fact were not taken out for several hours. The hooks, which at first had fitted snugly in the hold in the holes in the skin and deep tissue, had now worn their way about one-third out.

The man was able to walk around the town that afternoon and night and collect money from the people for his performance. It is certain that he took large quantities of arrack afterwards, for he did so openly.

As a physician I am much surprised that the ill effects on the man were so small. No ordinary man could pass through such an ordeal without serious danger to his life.

Source: IOR P/4247 (included in the Despatch of the Government of Madras to the Secretary of State 17/5/1892).

13. The Hindu newspaper's criticism of the Madras Government's apparent inertia

Hook Swinging

For some time past instances of the horrid practice of hook-swinging have now and again come to public notice in different parts of the Presidency. The latest instance, which was reported in our columns, took place in the Tanjore District, and it is evident that the Madras Government does not take the same view of this barbarous aboriginal superstition as some Hindu and Christian people do. It does credit to the native Press that it showed no sumpathy with the superstition, and without entering into defence or apology condemned it in unqualified terms. The comments of the newspapers drew the attention of Mr W.S. Caine, that vigilant and untiring critic of all Anglo-Indian back-sliding, who interrogated the Under-Secretary in the House of Commons in February last. Mr Caine's query was sent to the Madras Government from the India Office, and we understand that correspondence passed between Ootacamund and London and that the local Government did not by any means pledge itself to suppress hook-swinging, however cruel and offensive to all civilized feeling it might appear. The *Madura Mail* referring to an instance of this practice which took place last year had started that Surgeon-Major Reeves examined the person who was about to undergo the ordeal, implying thereby a charge against Government that it countenanced the practice. The examination it is true, was conducted at the request of the District Magistrate who had received information that the person chosen for swinging was under the age of eighteen and sickly. Had this information been correct, the District Magistrate would have had power to prohibit the performance of the ordeal, but so says the Madras despatch, as a fact it was incorrect, which to ascertain a medical examination was necessary. So far, neither the District Magistrate, nor the Government to which the action taken by him in the case was duly reported, is to blame. But we should like to know more about the attitude of the Government against this ordeal as a whole, whether underwent by a person sickly and below 18 years of age or by one healthy and of advanced years. We certainly think that the British authorities in such matters can act with greater confidence in the strength and righteousness of their conviction, and without taking an absurdly exaggerated and often erroneous view of the obligation of neutrality in so-called religious matters, can suppress the play of instincts which have survived old barbarous times. The Government can easily satisfy itself that hook-swinging is no more sanctioned by the religion of the classes which supply heroes on these occasions than small-pox or cholera which is said to seize its victims under the direction of a special deity. We fear the Government's attitude is the result more of a passive disposition and of absence of earnestness and vigor than of a conviction that it is necessary to respect the religious scruples of any class of Her Majesty's subjects.

Source: *The Hindu*, 30 May 1893.

14. Vizagapatam pundits on the lack of a scriptural basis for the practice

From the Manager, Vizanagrum Samastanam, to the Collector of Vizagapatam, dated 6th August 1893, No. 207.

In reply to your letter, No. 2162, dated 21st July last, covering a copy of G.O., No. 1331, of the 30th June 1893, I have the honor to inform you that I have consulted learned pandits of Dharma Sabha, established in this town by his late Highness, and they replied me that "Hook-swinging" is not mentioned in the "Dharma Sastras" or codes of "Parasera," "Jagnyavalkya," "Nirnayasindhu" and others, either as a means to gain the blessings of heaven or as a preventive to such blessings, nor has it ever been adopted by the high-caste Hindus, who follow the various ways of religion according to the Vedic form.

Then as to the question why such a dangerous step was often taken up by Sudras at the annual or occasional festivities of the village goddesses, it can only be said that, even among the high or the low classes of Hindus, there are some that think that what is more difficult or dangerous to practise is more conducive of prosperity and divine favour or spiritual good and the hook-swinging seems to have had its origin by one of such thinkers ages ago.

The Government Order stated above is herewith returned.

(Signed) V.V. KOTHUNDA RAMEM,
Manager.

Source: IOR P/4409 (Madras Judicial Proceedings, 21 December 1893).

15. Enquiry into the death of a hook-swinger at Bheemanaickenpoliem, Trichinopoly District, 1893

GOVERNMENT OF MADRAS
JUDICIAL DEPARTMENT

Read the following paper:

From Colonel C.A. PORTEOUS, Inspector-General of Police, to the Chief Secretary to Government, Ootacamund, dated Madras, 8th September 1894, No. 5252.

With reference to G.O., No. 1624, dated 28th June 1894, Judicial Department, I have the honour to state that the Superintendent of Police, Trichinopoly, reports that he has not the slightest doubt that the man Para Pandaram, who was swung at the Bheemanaickenpoliem feast in 1893, died from the effects of injuries caused thereby.

The Superintendent's letter (in original), with its enclosures, is herewith forwarded for the information of Government.

Enclosures

From F.T. BAGSHAWE, Esq., Superintendent of Police, Trichinopoly District, to the Inspector-General of Police, Madras (through the

Deputy Inspector-General, Southern Range, Coimbatore), dated Trichinopoly, 30th August 1894, No. 1447.

With reference to your instructions (Vide your No. 3889, dated 7th July 1894, and reminder, No. 4956, dated 27th August 1894.) received with a copy of G.O., No. 1624, Judicial, dated 28th June 1894, I have the honour to report—

I have not the smallest doubt that the man Para Pandaram, who was swung at the Bheemanaickenpoliem feast in 1893, died from the effects of injuries caused by the swinging, though at this distance of time it is difficult to get any absolute proof; and further the well-to-do ambalagars of Bheemanaickenpoliem, who like the festival and derive profit for their temple therefrom, do their best to prevent parties from coming forward to give evidence.

I beg to attach translations of statements taken by the Town Sub-Magistrate of Trichinopoly from neighbours of the deceased Pandaram; also statements taken by the Town Inspector of Police, Trichinopoly, from the widow of Para Pandaram and one Muthukaruppan.

According to the Municipal Register of deaths, the man Para Pandaram, who was also known as Andy, died of fever on 27th August 1893, *i.e.*, within three months of being swung.

The opinion of a local physician, Doctor F.G. Oliver, who witnessed the swinging in 1892, was obtained by me, which was that the operation is attended with much danger to life as the hooks are passed through the muscles of the back so near to the lungs as to cause probable injury to them. The deceased is said to have died of fever. This is a very broad definition in common use by natives as a cause of death. It is certain that the wounds caused by the hook-swinging were not healed, but suppurating at the time of the man's death, and that he had convulsions and was suffering from fever before it took place.

The general belief in the neighbourhood is that the man Para Pandaram met his death as a victim to this barbarous hook-swinging.

I do not think at this distance of time that it would be advisable to have recourse to a criminal prosecution of the Bheemanaickenpoliem Poojari, the prime-mover in the hook swinging, nor would it probably end in a conviction. Paragraph 18 of G.O., No. 1418, dated 27th August 1890, is relevant to the abovementioned hook-swinging.

There has been some unavoidable delay in submitting this report as the widow of Para Pandaram, Vulliammai, could not be found for a long time to get her evidence, and the statements taken by the Town Sub-Magistrate were not at first forthcoming.

Sworn deposition of Para Sappani before the Town Sub-Magistrate

Last year I, Pandaram, Perinattan, Poovan and Mari were swung. Pandaram died. He died after three months of the swinging. He died from fever. Fever was brought on by injuries. He died of the consequent convulsions. All the village people instigated me and I was swung. As they promised a grant of three cawnies of land we consented. None paid me anything for swinging. Kullan's wife has the hereditary right. I was swung as her adopted son. When Pandaram died there were injuries on both of his sides.

Sworn deposition of Para Andy

I was swung 40 or 50 years ago. There is intense pain caused by the swinging. One should take strong meals for it, or else he will be attacked with sickness. Pandaram was ill-fed. Fever was brought on and he died. There were four wounds on Pandaram unhealed.

Sworn deposition of Para Periannan

It was on the third year I was swung. There were four others who were swung with me. All the mirasidars of Abishekapuram instigated us to undergo swinging. For it, we were promised a grant of three cawnies of land. We were also promised payment of As. 4 or As 8 or Re. 1 from each house according to their situations. Neither were we granted lands nor were we paid anything. Rungan of Devadanam and Sembattiyan were also swung with us. We were not swung last year. As swinging should take place by turns we were not swung. Last year Sappani (1), Perunadan (2), Pandaram (3) of Abishekapuram, Poovan (4) and Mari (5) of Devadanam were swung. All the five who were swung on the previous year are still living. Persons swung cannot take up work or anything for one and-a-half months owing to the pain out of the injuries received. Out of the five swung last year, Pandaram died. He died for want of good nourishment. Persons swung should take strong meals. He died of fever. When Pandaram died, one of the wounds healed and the other did not heal. In this year the turn of hook-swinging falls on one of the male members of my family. The parties proposing to celebrate the feast did not ask either me or any one of my family to undergo swinging. Either myself or any one of my family is not willing to be swung. Even though they offer grant of lands or good nourishment, I am not willing to be swung this year. On the third year the Tahsildar did not take from me any deposition. Pandaram died three months after the swinging. None treated him. I don't remember the particular month he died. There is a faction between myself and the poojaries. I am not serving the poojaries now. The wives of the four supported them during the illness caused by the swinging and they regained their health.

Statement of Valliammai, widow of late Pandaram *alias* Andy of Bheemanaickenpoliem, who died from the effects of hook-swinging.

Pandaram *alias* Andy is my husband. He died 11 months ago. He swung himself last year at the Bheemanaickenpoliem Mariamman feast at the instigation of the poojari and others. There were serious injuries in his back owing to the swinging. He was sick at home for two months unable to pursue his usual avocations. One of the injuries in the back never healed. The others were gradually healing. The leaves of Neem tree well ground were applied to the injuries. At last he died on account of the three days' strong fever and consequent fits. No one assisted him for his subsistence during his illness. Neither the poojari nor the village people. No one treated him. He was in his early age when he died. He was about 30. I being an ignorant woman did not complain to anybody. I complained to the Village Magistrate, but he was deaf to my cries. When my husband died, I went away to my mother's house at Kannikudy from which place only I was brought here by the police.

Statement of Muthukaruppan of Bheemanaickenpoliem.

Pandaram, who died 10 or 11 months ago, is my nephew. My aunt and his grandmother are sisters. Poojaries and others instigated him to undergo the hook-swinging on promise of payment of money and grant of inam lands. He underwent the operation. One of the injuries on his back never healed, he died two or three months since. I was with him when he died. One of the wounds brought on fever and he died at once. There was no room for proper treatment. Sub-

Magistrate has enquired me previously.

Order — dated 24th September 1894, No. 2314, Judicial.

The Inspector-General's letter will be communicated to all District Magistrates for information. There seems no doubt that the man Para Pandaram died from the effects of hook-swinging, and the ceremony can and should, therefore, be prohibited by orders under section 144, Criminal Procedure Code, in future.

(True Extract.)

J.F. PRICE,
Chief Secretary

To the Inspector-General of Police.
To all District Magistrates.
To the Commissioner of Police, Madras.
Copy to the Chief Presidency Magistrate.
Copy to the Government Solicitor, with reference to the Advocate-General's opinion, dated 25th July 1892.

Source: IOR P/4621 (Madras Judicial Proceedings, 24 September 1894).

Index